GOD'S HIDDEN
TREASURE

GOD'S HIDDEN TREASURE

Batya Shemesh

To order additional copies of this book, contact:
Xlibris
1-888-795-4274
www.Xlibris.com
Orders@Xlibris.com
724102

TABLE OF CONTENTS

INTRODUCTION

While driving down the highway from Jerusalem to the Dead Sea with my husband and children, we noticed a small road sign that read, "The Secret of Qumran." We stopped there to find a beautiful tourist site containing a small museum with a splendid audiovisual exhibition. The Qumran village displayed stone tables, benches and ritual baths created by the Essenes who resided there 2100 years ago.

The Essenes were a Jewish sect that lived in Qumran starting in the beginning of the first century BCE. The Essenes fled to live in the desert near the Dead Sea, away from the wars and famine in Jerusalem. Fearing that the Bible would be lost in the chaos of war, they felt obligated to preserve the precious works on parchment. With great expertise and precision, they saved their writings in special clay canisters and hid them in the local caves. The dry desert conditions kept them intact for almost two thousand years. They were discovered by an Arab Bedouin in 1946 and were named the Dead Sea Scrolls.

The finding of the Dead Sea Scrolls marked a great discovery in archeology. The entire content of the Bible scrolls was revealed to be almost identical to our own Hebrew Bible. All of the books of the Old Testament were found with the exception of the book of Esther. In the chapter entitled "The Scroll of Esther," I will expose astonishing facts about this part of history that help explain why this precious book was not included in the Essene works.

The Dead Sea scrolls provided proof beyond a shadow of a doubt that the Bible that the Jews have been reading and studying for the past two thousand years is authentic. It's quite amazing that with all the troubles and tribulations the Jews suffered through the millennia, there has been virtually no changes in the words of the Bible. There are some very minute changes in spelling in a small number of places but any slight differences never change the meaning in any way.

Now that we have proof that the Bible didn't change for two thousand years, it is my goal to try to prove that the Bible didn't change for thirty-five hundred years, since it was given to the Israelites by Moses.

In *God's Hidden Treasure* I will reveal the true story of the whereabouts of the Torah, the first Five Books of the Bible, from the death of Moses until the end of the Second Temple Period.

The cover of this book presents a picture of a replica of the Holy Temple in Jerusalem and the wall around it. God's Hidden Treasure is the Torah hidden in the Holy Temple awaiting for the day that it will be loved and cherished in a society that would be fully literate in its holy language.

We are living in an era where God is allowing archeologists and historians to discover the truths of the Bible. *The Exodus Case*, by Dr. Lennart Muller is an account of the most modern proof of the accuracy of the Bible. As I am writing, a new set of books and DVDs came out to prove the validity of most of the events of the Bible. *Exodus, Myth or Mystery*, by David Rohl, was recently published, along with a DVD of his lectures and a documentary film called *Patterns of Evidence, Exodus.* These publications mark a new era in the world of religion—there is a growing proof of the Bible's authenticity.

Most of the stories in the Bible are true, but some of the narratives are parables that can teach us lessons about life. Their significance is not reduced because they are allegories. Actually, their importance is augmented. Some stories have both an actual basis in historical truth and they metaphorically contain deeper meanings. This book will give new interpretations and new meaning to ancient Bible stories.

Bring a Background to the Foreground

A basic background in Jewish history is helpful in order to fully understand this book. The internet has all kinds of multimedia and easy-to-read accounts of Jewish history, and much of it is surprisingly accurate. There are many DVDs and books on the subject to see and read. I recently saw the DVD *The Jewish People: A Story of Survival,* by PBS and I was very impressed. *The Kingdom of David: The Saga of the Israelites,* by PBS, is an excellent introduction to Judaism and to this book. *The Mystery of the Jews* is a free movie online. It is available on jewishhistory.org. Stan Mack wrote a hysterical comic book about Jewish history named *The Story of the Jews: A 4,000-Year Adventure.* It is a pleasure to read for yourself and to share with your children.

Synagogues

Israeli archeologists have found remnants of synagogues in Israel from the first century BCE until the seventh century CE. The original purpose of the synagogue in Jewish villages was to have a place to store a handwritten Torah scroll to share with the whole community.

Today a Torah scroll, which by tradition continues to be handwritten, costs over $40,000, a prohibited cost for personal use. For two thousand years, the synagogue was the place to house these dear and treasured writings so Jewish villagers could sit and study it. Today, almost every synagogue across the world has a few handwritten Torah scrolls to be read aloud to its congregants.

The oldest archeological synagogue sites that were found date back to the first century BCE. This book will illustrate how the beginning of the widespread availability of a written Torah scroll to all the towns of Israel began.

Who is a Jew?

In this book, I sometimes call the children of Abraham Israelites, and other times as Jews. Originally, *Jews* referred to the people of Judea. When King Solomon died, the land was divided into two kingdoms: the kingdom of Judah and the kingdom of Israel. The story of Purim written in the Scroll of Esther is the first time that the Bible calls the people of Judah "Jews". In referring to people and events that happened before the period of Purim, I use the name Israelites, Children of Israel, or Nation of Israel. The Romans also referred to the land of Israel as Judea up until the Bar Kokhba revolt in 135 CE. Then they renamed the land of Israel to be Syria Palaestina and Jerusalem became Aelia Capitolina. In modern times, we call our nation Jewish, considering the Judean past. I use this name Jewish for our nationality when referring to modern times denoting anyone who is a descendant of the historical nation of Israel or a convert that observes the Torah of Moses.

God's Hidden Treasure will also reveal surprising facts about the whereabouts of the Ten Lost Tribes with evidence from the Bible. This is a spectacular discovery, which was never revealed before.

God's Name

We are observant Jews and while we at times call our Creator God, we prefer to label Him "Hashem," which means "The Name." This is the name that we use in daily conversation. Hashem revealed to me that this is His favorite appellation because we call out to the Almighty as Hashem when we are tired, hungry, angry, or happy and grateful. The word Adonai, which is used in prayer and Torah reading, means "my Lord." The name "Hashem" is what we use in every day speech, when communicating with our friends and family. The common use of the name of Hashem by the God-fearing children of Israel gives this term its holiness and beloved characteristic.

This book is written for the purpose of giving answers to anyone who seeks the truth no matter what their background. Therefore, I tried very hard not to use Hebrew words. However, there are some words that are a part of our daily language and using an English word in its place would take away from its meaning. For example, the word, *Torah* means the Five Books of Moses, or what is formally called the Pentateuch. The word *mitzvah* means an obligation that the Torah demands from us, whether it's a prohibition, a positive command, or simply a good deed. The plural of *mitzvah* is *mitzvot* or *mitzvoth*. I translated or defined other Hebrew words when I use them for the first time. There is also a glossary at the end of the book with more explanations for this word and for the other Hebrew terms mentioned in the book.

Translations

When translating the Bible, I started out by using the NIV translation, but sometimes I corrected it to be more accurate. In any translation, the hidden meaning or double entendre can be lost. I tried my best to translate and explain the words of the Hebrew text accurately in verses where the NIV translation is not perfect.

How Do I Know?

The ideas that I explain here are not at all popular, some are completely unknown. How did I figure out these amazing findings?

The discoveries that I will relate to you in this book are some of the many explanations that I received from God since He spoke to me the first time in 1988.

Hashem never stopped speaking to me since that day. He was with me through many hard times, giving advice for myself and to others. I have seen thousands of patients and helped them with their physical and emotional health, usually through natural herbs and supplements. Some of my clients began to catch on and understood that I have a secret, but to most of them I was simply a wise woman. While working hard to heal the inhabitants of the Holy City, I took advantage of my relationship with God. I had so many questions. One of the biggest question I had was, "How is it possible that we have the identical Torah that was given to Moses?" I was an Orthodox Jewess who based the majority of her religion on the Bible and on the oral tradition. I also wondered, *Where does this Oral Law come from? How can it be an addition to the Torah? What does God really want us to observe?"*

We lived in a world where Torah is our life. Since I was six years old, we studied Bible in Hebrew a few hours every day in the original text. We observed Torah law because it was God's law. I was constantly concerned that what I believed and lived for was the truth. Of all my books, this is the one I cherish the most. It is in this book that I will reveal secret and unrevealed answers to questions that bothered me my whole life. My husband, David, wrote me a cute poem about this book:

The Hidden Treasure

The meaning of what's in the Bible,
Is so very much concealed.
For thousands of years, people theorize,
While His secrets have been sealed.
People argue over what God meant,
Interpretations have been repealed.
Until we come to the present time,
When understanding is more ideal.
Computers advance our knowledge,
New wisdom in every field.
A simple woman graced by God,
Makes all the wise men yield.
For through her Hashem decided,
To have His Hidden Treasures revealed.

God's Hidden Treasure will show how the Torah was written with the intention of saving it for the future. The Israelites of thirty-five hundred years ago were too drenched in pagan cultures to even learn how to read and write, let alone understand and follow what Hashem meant in His Torah. The Torah was given on Mount Sinai and subsequently hidden, waiting for a future generation that would be smart enough to learn it in depth, appreciate its everlasting wisdom, and observe every detail of Torah law and pass it on to future generations.

Chapter 1
God Is My Shepherd

Psalm 23: "God is my shepherd." He's been my shepherd for twenty-eight years. That's a long time for Him to be so patient with me until I finally tell the world about my relationship with Him. Of all my books, this is the one I cherish the most. It's the book that has information that I have kept secret. I have been afraid to tell a soul these secrets so no one leaks them before I explain them properly. This book is my hidden treasure. There are lots of secrets in this book; the first is the secret of my life story. I wrote about my first encounter with God in the book *Who Is God?* In the following pages, I will tell the story from a different perspective, revealing more about who I am and where I came from. As much as my father and school-teachers taught me, my real teacher is my Father in heaven. Since September 1988, God has been my teacher and my guide.

My Father, My Teacher

I grew up in New York as a religious Jewess. Our lives were segregated from the Christians and all other people from different religions. We lived in a Jewish orthodox neighborhood and attended a private Jewish school. Every morning we began to pray, singing in unison with our classmates. It was an all-girls school. After a half hour of prayer, we began to learn. We always started with Bible studies. Some teachers spoke in Hebrew, some in Yiddish and some in English. After a half hour of Torah, we had recess and went back to class to learn the writings of prophets and other Bible studies. The morning classes concluded with a lesson in Jewish Law or Hebrew grammar. In the afternoon after lunch, we learned English, math, science, and history. Great rapport existed among the students. We had marvelous fun at recesses playing ball and jumping rope, just like other schoolchildren living in the 1970s.

Every Sabbath my father would convene with us at the table and teach us Torah, tell us stories and lead in the singing of songs in honor of *Shabbat* (the Sabbath). We sat at the table with him for two hours every Friday night and another two hours on Saturday afternoon.

The strongest message that my father gave me is the one I retold at his funeral. These were his words, "It says in the Torah to love your God with all your heart and all your soul; it doesn't say to love your parents. You must respect your parents, but I am human and will disappoint you. Don't love me; love God. If you love God, He will always be there for you."

This message accompanied me my whole life. Of course I did love my father, and it took me a whole year to recuperate from his death. However, his legacy lives on. He encouraged me to love God and to question Him; quite a combination. He didn't believe in blind faith. He believed in the existence of God because it is the truth. He would ask me to prove to him why it is good to be a religious Jew. The tutelage he provided me plus the education of the schools to which he sent me set the stage for who I am today.

Both of my parents were very Zionistic, they supported the development of a Jewish homeland in Israel and always aspired to live in the Holy Land and speak Hebrew. In 1977 my family emigrated to Israel. At the time, it was a very poor country, but we loved it. We were happy to eat the simple foods and live in a small apartment. We felt so elated to be in the Promised Land that physical possessions were not important. My father found a job as a geriatric social worker, and he was really the happiest he had ever been. My sister and I attended a religious high school, and we cherished it. I particularly enjoyed visiting the open market to buy fruits and vegetables. I had always loved to cook.

When I reached the age of eighteen, it was time to look for a match. Just like in the movie *Fiddler on the Roof*, we had matchmakers. In the past generations Jewish religious women married men who were chosen for them. In modern times, many orthodox Jewish families allow their children to get to know their perspective match and decide whether to choose him or her. The matchmaker or friend suggests a date and the couple goes out on a formal date or dates for a couple of hours in order to decide if they are fit to be life partners.

In September of 1977, I saw a man on an arranged date and we returned late at night. My father was furious. "You go out nine hours with a man! That's it; you can meet one more time and you must decide if you're getting married or not!" Under pressure to make a speedy decision on the most important choice in life, I chose to accept marriage with this man and the wedding followed three months later.

I was well trained by mother to be a good housewife, but unlike my friends and classmates, I didn't conceive immediately. I really wanted to have children and would get very upset every month that I did not conceive. My husband suggested that I return to school to free my mind from worry. I attended a teachers' seminary and I took a major in Bible and the Hebrew language.

While still in school, I underwent fertility treatments and eventually gave birth to my first son, Jonathan, a couple of months after my graduation. I couldn't believe that I actually had my own child. I nursed my baby and constantly attended to him with loving care. I didn't have the heart to leave him with a babysitter ever.

I relished being a stay-at-home mom. Three years later I had another baby, a beautiful girl named Gila, which means Joy. She was definitely the joy and delight of my life.

My husband was a businessman and became entangled with all kinds of questionable associates. These entrepreneurs pretended that they wanted to help Jacob build an enterprise selling religious books. He had dealings with more than one man that tricked him. These swindlers put us deeply into debt to the point where I was worried that we wouldn't have food to eat. It was scary.

With no money or income, Jacob wanted to sell our apartment. I was a co-owner, so I had to consent in order to complete the sale. The apartment was only worth $40,000, so it was hardly a lifesaver. This price might seem ridiculously low to you. It was a nice two-bedroom apartment in Jerusalem that my family helped us buy before the sudden increase in the price of housing in 1989.

I was very afraid of starvation. We were living in a poor country where people were even worse off than us. There were no food stamps or other state benefits. I cried to Hashem every day that we could have food to eat. I felt that I had no right to beg for food if I owned my own apartment. I thought that I must sell now and trust Hashem that tomorrow will bring a better fortune. We decided to sell our residence and moved to a rental apartment in a better vicinity.

The new neighborhood in Jerusalem was made up of at least fifty percent American Orthodox Jews, just like me. I quickly found nice people with whom to chat. A library of English books and audiotapes was located right down the block. Every day I took little Gila for a walk to the library. I brushed up on my English, as I had not read a book in my mother tongue since tenth grade. More important than just brushing up on my English was what I absorbed from the beautiful wisdom that these books and tapes had to offer.

The library's books and tapes contained tremendous insight. The rabbis on the tapes spoke of faith, peace in the home, and about science verses religion. I was so excited to learn that I listened every night while cleaning the kitchen, and every day I took a walk to the library with my little daughter, my second child, in a baby carriage and exchanged materials.

The tape I remember the most, discussed evolution. It explained how the possibility that a pea protein molecule just happened to develop and appear was so minute, estimated at one in a couple of hundred million, that it was virtually impossible to have occurred through evolution. The possibility that a blood cell could evolve on its own was hundreds of times more impossible.

This consideration woke up my soul. One morning I went out with my baby Gila for our daily walk and I felt that I had changed. The thought that went through my head was, "The difference between who I am now and who I was a few months ago is as great as the difference between a religious Jew and a nonbeliever."

The Power of Prayer

A speech by Rabbi Avigdor Miller about prayer from which I learned was also on one of the audiotapes that I borrowed. He delivered a strong message that sometimes we pray for things that we can't obtain because they are not part of the eternal plan—for example, a new job, a house or a child. However, if we pray for spiritual development, a good attitude, or even good conduct, there is no reason Hashem wouldn't bestow that to us.

I was so desperate for Hashem to answer my prayers that I said, "Okay, if I can pray for something that I will surely receive, that's what I want to do." I decided to start to pray for my spiritual development and closeness to Hashem. Every day I read from the prayer book and prayed with all my heart that I would be able to feel love and devotion to God.

It took years for me to figure out that this rabbi taught one of the biggest secrets of success in life. We are only human. We can live the illusion that we on our own are good-natured, well-rounded, talented, and successful but these are actually all gifts from God. If you are doing well, then thank Him. If you are having trouble with your mood, your patience, or even completing your daily activities, you must ask Hashem for help.

If He gives you help on seemingly minor details, success is on its way. If Hashem grants you a good mood and good rapport with people, all you have to do is the physical actions to complete tasks. One time when I had serious problems in life, I turned to Hashem crying, "What should we do?" He answered, "Don't worry, just do what you have to do." Hashem wants us to go through the bureaucracy of solving problems, whether at the hospital, the bank or even the IRS. Just do it without the pain of anxiety and worry.

We are called upon to pray to have the strength and patience to have a good disposition, happiness in our hearts and to get along with our friends and family. Most of all, we must pray that every day should be a day to help our soul become more aware of Hashem's presence and love so we can grow emotionally and spiritually.

Psalm 119, the longest psalm in the Book of Psalms, teaches us to pray to Hashem to have the ability to learn His laws and succeed in observing every directive. This shows that we must pray for the ability to do what's right instead of blaming ourselves or others for making mistakes. Simply beseech to Hashem for assistance. If you don't know what to say to Hashem, just read Psalms. Any chapter in the book of Psalms can be your prayer for success and salvation from your troubles. Just choose the chapter that best describes your personal situation and aspirations. Chances are that the first chapter that your book of Psalms opens to will be the one that has a message for you.

Marital Tension

At the time I was borrowing these tapes, I was not happy in my life or my marriage. I loved my children, but my husband was a tyrant and showed little love or concern for me. When he criticized me, I simply cringed and didn't answer. When contemplating about my situation, I thought that I was not capable of supporting myself and my children. Furthermore, in our circles divorce was a possibility that was reserved for only very extreme cases.

When my son Jonathan was six years old, Jacob, my ex-husband discarded his bed even though it was in good condition. Jacob didn't like that Jonathan's bed was a hand-me-down from my grandmother. After that, Jonathan slept on a mattress on the floor. I cried to Hashem to give me a bed for my son. We were still very poor. We sold our apartment because of debts so we had nothing. I felt insecure and poverty-stricken. I said to Hashem: "I see that you don't want to give Jacob money. If you don't want to give him, give money to me directly!" I spoke to Hashem all day from my heart about my feelings of anguish and poured out to Him my requests for help.

We moved to a new neighborhood and Rachel, one of my neighbors, recognized me as my father's daughter. She came to my apartment to visit and asserted that I should reconcile with my father as I hadn't seen him for five years. I had disclosed to Jacob how strict my father was in his upbringing and how he used to hit me and my siblings when we were children. Jacob feared that my father would be aggressive towards Jonathan so after he was born he decided to cut off our relationship entirely.

During this five-year hiatus of no contact, my father cried day and night that he yearned to see me again. Over this period I had asked permission from my rabbi to meet my father without my husband's knowledge. The rabbi did not consent. He merely told me to try to convince my husband to allow me to see my father without the children. My husband still refused, and I obeyed the rabbi's ruling. That is why I kept dismissing Rachel until my father finally wrote me a letter:

> To my eldest daughter,
> Ever since you have severed contact with me I have been crying. I have no appetite nor will to do anything. All day I have been crying about the mistakes I have made in the past and about the pain I have in my heart because I can't see you. If I don't see you soon my blood will be on your hands.
> Your loving father,
> Mordechai

I was very moved by my father's words. I concluded that in no way was I going to be a murderer by refusing to meet with my father. I subsequently discounted the lack of approval and consent from the rabbi and my husband.

Taking the initiative, I decided to clandestinely encounter my father and mother in a nearby park. I wrote them short letter informing where and when to meet me. I took my little daughter Gila in the baby carriage while my son was at kindergarten. I shook with fear. I was terrified that my husband would catch me. I was also petrified to face my father.

This was a huge breakthrough for me. I decided that I didn't care what the rabbi said. I refused to be the cause of my father's early demise. I gathered courage and conviction to conquer my own fears and I followed through with my plans to visit my father. While I trembled the whole way to the park, I shuddered even more from shock when I saw him. Daddy had lost about forty pounds and his beard had turned white. My mother did not appear to have aged as my father had. They were very nice and pleasant. I showed them the kinesiology that I was learning. Kinesiology is a scientific study of human body movement and a form of alternative medicine. An American neighbor of mine began teaching kinesiology to me as a gesture of gratefulness for my willingness to help her by translating a few sessions from English to Hebrew for an Israeli patient.

The next week I convened with my parents again, at the same time and same place. On this occasion my father's mother Yocheved accompanied them. My grandmother was a psychic. When she was three years old she dreamed that an angel came down like a flame and told her that Arab zealots were planning a riot in their town. She told the dream to her father, who was the rabbi of the town, and he believed her dream. He instructed everybody to abandon their town and head for relatives in other locals. The Arab zealots indeed arrived as my grandmother dreamed and destroyed property but following my great grandfather's order, no one remained. All escaped injury or worse. In her merit, my grandmother's entire hometown population in Turkey was saved.

Grandmother Yocheved continued to offer free psychic advice to people her whole life without ever considering herself special. At this point in time, my grandmother had cancer. She said she didn't want to use her psychic powers anymore; she wanted to bestow them on me. She blessed and assured me that I would become a healer and help a lot of people. As soon as she said this, I started to have unusual feelings and visual experiences. As we were walking together toward my apartment, I continued to see all kinds of visions. When I arrived home, I began hearing sounds. Among all the different voices came a voice that said, "I am Hashem."

I replied, "What? It can't be!"

He said, "Yes, yes, it's Me!"

"How is that possible?" I asked.

Hashem responded, "It's really Me. I've been watching you all the time. I remember how good you were as a little girl. You helped your parents endlessly with all your strength and prayed to Me with all your heart." The voice felt close to me. Hashem spoke as if we were good friends. I realized that nothing I ever did went unnoticed by the Almighty.

I stopped and thought to myself, "What can I demand of God to prove that He is God? If I ask Him to do a miracle, maybe He won't want to do so. If I ask Him to tell me the future, I won't know if it's true until the future arrives." I quickly thought to seek proof by asking Hashem questions. I understood from years of Bible study that God loves to teach. I said to Him, "I am going to test You. I am going to ask You a question, and You'll tell me where the answer is in the Bible, in what book and on what page." I asked many questions, and the pages that Hashem had me open were amazingly accurate.

Rumor soon spread that I could diagnose and heal. This was 1988 in Israel and it was a phenomenon. People arrived from all over town to see what I could do. Whenever I touched anyone, I would instantly know what their emotional and physical problems were and what they should do to better or resolve their conditions. I was quite in shock from seeing all kinds of psychic visions. I started becoming very confused. I was hearing voices from all over. I couldn't concentrate on prayer. I wasn't sure what was happening to me.

I asked rabbis and friends who introduced me to other psychics in order to help me understand from where these voices emanated. Many psychics shared their experiences, which were not all similar, even though they were very impressive and powerful. Strangely enough, it didn't even cross my mind to think that maybe I was going crazy. I received so many different opinions as to what was occurring to me that I became even more confused. Hashem continued to send me all kinds of voices to further add to my bewilderment.

I kept attempting to pray, but I couldn't focus because I was distracted by so many voices. I continued to ask myself, "What is the source of these voices?" If they were from heaven, they had to be from God. There was no other explanation. I made a strong decision that since I believed in only one God, there couldn't be another supernatural power that is talking to me except for God. I decided to demand God to stop driving me crazy. I said, "I know it's You; stop it!! You're not going to be able to trick me. Take all the other voices away!" I persisted to scream these words to Hashem all day long. Within two weeks, everything stopped except one voice that was calm and clear. I felt that this was the same God that knew me since I was an embryo in my mother's womb.

I learned something very important from this episode. Every paranormal experience that people have comes from Hashem. If someone feels like Buddha or Jesus is speaking to him, it is all just Hashem masquerading to be what people expect Him to be. Even if you dream of a deceased person addressing you, it is Hashem speaking as though the dead could communicate. No person alive or dead has the power to enter your mind and talk to you. God is the only superpower who can do so.

After this experience ended, I settled down and was able to chat with Hashem as a friend, asking Him questions and understanding the divine answers. People heard that I was successful in my work as a healer and they continued to come to me from all over the country. Sometimes people would ask me how I knew things. I would ask Hashem what to say to them. To some, He said to say that an angel was informing me, but many times God told me to tell the truth.

I was afraid to converse with people because I was used to being shy, so in the first months Hashem dictated everything that he wanted me to say, word for word. After so many years of loneliness I felt comforted to have guests in my home.

Hashem blessed me with an extremely powerful urge to get more customers. I spoke to many people at length on the phone to convince them to come. When they arrived, I had them lie down and I touched their foreheads with the palm of my hand. Hashem told me what their problems were and how to solve them. Sometimes I would receive answers that weren't correct! Today I know that this happened with those that Hashem didn't want me to help or have contact. It was and still is His way of choosing my patients. The more someone received accurate diagnosis and correct advice, the more he or she returned and developed an increasingly stronger relationship with me. Some patients have stayed in contact with me for over twenty years.

Hashem taught me that vitamins and supplements are good for people. Even though I knew a lot about them, I thought that a person should be able to advance his health only from good food. Hashem told me that these people were too sick to become healed by diet alone. He told me what supplements to give them in order to improve their health as quickly as possible.

At this time, I also made an effort to learn more about natural medicine from books, from other natural health practitioners, and eventually from proper classes. When I was fourteen years old, my parents introduced eating wholesome foods at home and taking vitamins. They purchased all kinds of health books and magazines. I have felt a real fervor to learn about health and healing since then.

While advancing in my ability to help others emotionally and physically, I became pretty overwhelmed with the clairvoyance that enveloped me. I asked Hashem to tell me what was happening to me. He had me open Maimonides' book *The Guide to the Perplexed*. I read that if someone has a goal to be a messenger of God for any specific purpose, he is driven to learn and work for that goal with no apparent explanation. This is very important for parents to know. If your child has a certain fervor, love, or ambition, always encourage him or her to fulfil their dreams. Don't force your child to change to the goal that you set out for him or her, no matter how crazy or useless you think his or her goal is.

If someone has a chance to speak to God or to address someone who receives messages from God, the first thing many people may ask is what the future holds. Not me. I didn't even think of it. I knew that by Jewish law, I was not allowed to tell people the future, so I shunned anyone that tried to ask about it. I even sent people home if they came just in order to know the future.

Once, a couple that was coming to me for health asked me to help them decide whether a prospective man would be an appropriate match for their daughter. I quickly said, "No, I'm sorry, I can only answer questions about health." That night I woke up at two o'clock in the morning. I saw the following quote from the Scroll of Esther written on my wall in blue Hebrew letters with silver borders.

> Esther 4:14
> *"If you will be silent at this time, relief and salvation will come to the Jews from another place, but you and your father's house will be lost."*

I was very scared. I felt that Hashem was mad at me. In the morning, He told me that He wanted me to answer people's questions even if they weren't asking about health. Hashem said to me that my friends need help and I should pray for them. He explained to me that I shouldn't tell people about their destiny because the future because is actually in their hands and they could always change it for the better. However, when others need help to make a decision, or to know the true character of a person before marrying, I should try to be of assistance.

One evening a young woman named Judith came to me. She was nineteen years old and experiencing a hard time because of a breakup with a young man. I impressed upon her to speak to God. Even though she was brought up in an orthodox Zionistic family, she never realized that God cares about her and is watching over her. She asked me questions and Hashem provided her the answers through me almost like a medium. She was so excited about this new idea that one can converse with God that she started calling me every day. We would learn Torah together over the phone. She was totally lifted from her depression and immersed in godliness. I myself acquired a lot of knowledge and learning from Hashem as I was speaking to her. I became very happy and even elated. I felt so lucky that Hashem chose me to be His friend. For me it was more than the thrill of winning a lottery ticket. It was more akin to what Columbus probably felt when he discovered America. He always believed it was there but when he came to know it for a fact, he was elated.

I never doubted that Hashem really existed, but now I knew who He was and that He had been observing me my whole life. He especially mentioned how he enjoyed watching me help my mother when was a teenager. We weren't strangers. I felt the closeness of Hashem like nothing I ever felt before. I realized that He knew me before I even knew myself.

Over the next few months I asked Hashem questions about life and about anything else of which I was curious. It wasn't a test anymore; I really wanted to know.

Of course, I asked about the Holocaust. In my first book, *Who is God?* I devoted a whole chapter called *Why a Holocaust?* to answer this terrifying question. The chapter reveals many historical explanations that describe the situation that the world was up against at that point in history, as well as spiritual reasons for such a major catastrophe to occur.

There was one question to which I didn't get a clear answer. I asked "What happened to the Ten Lost Tribes? Why did you cause them to be lost?"

I didn't realize then, but I hit on a Pandora's box. I wasn't ready for the answer. Only, twenty-five years later, did Hashem disclose the secret to me. In this book, in the chapter entitled "The Scroll of Esther," you will learn some amazing facts and findings that will be convincing to anyone who is interested in this subject.

For the next few months, I was on a high. I couldn't believe how fortunate I was. I was dancing and singing from joy. My husband, didn't know what was happening. He didn't let me listen to the phone messages when he was home, and he was not happy that people were entering our home at all hours of the day. He didn't understand why so many people were coming. I finally told him God was speaking to me. "That claim would attract people." He said, "but I doubt very much that it is true." When he tried to test me to see if I really knew things and was receiving messages from Hashem, everything I said was inaccurate. Hashem gave me the wrong answers purposely because He didn't want Jacob to believe and respect me. He wanted him out of my life.

As I became more independent emotionally and financially, Jacob started to become even more aggressive. I believe he was angry that I was gaining more and more self-confidence. Sometimes, I even answered back. He started hitting me physically in retaliation. At first it wasn't dangerous. With twisted logic, he tried to convince me that a good wife shouldn't even whimper when she is struck by her husband. I remember how he once told a friend that a woman is like a sandal; the more you step on it, the better it becomes. When a person has conceit for his own wife,

Hashem has conceit for him. Our sages say that there is no place for Hashem among the arrogant.

The battering escalated, and my six-year-old son, Jonathan, started copying his father and began striking me too! At that point I said to myself, "I'm getting divorced! I won't sacrifice my children's character and well-being for anyone."

One day I decided to be brave. I yelled at Jacob for daring to raise a hand to me. He reacted with the worst physical violence that he ever did. Jacob clasped both of his hands together and banged them on my head! Until now none of the beatings that I received were severe. They left no marks or injury. After these blows, I became very scared. *"This guy is dangerous!"* I thought. I had to do something fast.

By this time, I had already been back in contact with my parents. I told my mother what happened, and she informed her sister in America. Arrangements were made, and I boarded a plane with my two children on a flight to the United States of America.

It wasn't easy to be in America alone with two children. My aunt and other relatives didn't turn out to be as generous as I expected. I traveled to different people's homes every week in order to have a proper *Shabbat*, because my aunt wasn't religious. I really didn't feel comfortable in America. One day while saying the prayer after meals, I read a prayer of thanks to Hashem for giving us the Land of Israel. At that moment, I knew that I wanted to go home.

After being away from Jacob for a few weeks, several people tried to mediate between us in order to make some kind of settlement. When someone offered me a prospective future match, I realized that besides my will to live in Israel, I had to go back home in order to have a Jewish divorce, called a "get."

Jacob arranged the plane tickets for us to return home. The trial reunion didn't succeed. Jacob wasn't abusing me as much as before, but the separation made me realize that we were not meant for each other. I didn't love him anymore. He didn't behave like a real partner and He was a very unrefined person. Only by leaving the house was I able to see that.

On My Own

I decided to rent my own apartment before the divorce court proceedings were over. With pure faith I took a loan from a friend in order to pay the first month's rent. I told Hashem that I would be like Nahshon and jump into the sea.

The story about Nahshon comes from the Midrash. The Midrash is a compilation of rabbinic literature that includes stories that expound upon what is written in the Torah. The Bible says that after the Israelites left Egypt they Israelites stopped at the bank of the Red Sea. There the Egyptians were catching up to them (Exodus 14:9). The Israelites panicked. Moses called out to God, and He told him to stretch out his staff over the water so it would split. The Israelites were crying from fear because they heard the Egyptians approaching as they viewed the bank of the sea ahead. The Midrash says that a righteous man named Nahshon Ben Aminadav decided to trust God and jump into the sea. Once he was up to his nose in the water, the sea parted. The Israelites walked onto the dry seabed and the Egyptians followed in their chariots. Hashem told Moses to again stretch out his staff over the water and this time the water reverted and covered the Egyptians (Exodus 14:9–29).

Nahshon was not suicidal. He simply had so much faith that he was certain beyond a shadow of a doubt that

Hashem would not let His people perish. Like Nahshon, I also jumped, taking a leap of faith. I knew that God would be with me. The following is a song about my faith. I place it here to show you how strong I truly was.

Truly Titanic

It's a lonely world,
But I can console you
Because Hashem is with you
Through the darkest night.
With His help,
You will find your truth.
The day will come,
When all is right.

To believe is ecstasy,
To believe in prophecy,
To believe the Holy One,
Blessed Be He.
I'll begin to sing a song,
A song and prayer to Thee:

Every day in my mind,
I hear You,
I feel You;
That is how I know who You are.
In a life of learning Torah
And keeping the Mitzvot,
You guide me like a shining star.

Near, far,
Everywhere You are.

I believe You create time and space.
Once more,
You open the door,
And You're here in my heart,
And Your presence will fill every place.

Love can touch me one time,
But God lasts a lifetime,
And He never lets go,
Nor lets you down.

Truth was when he found Him.
Abraham was the first Jew.
You gave his offspring your crown.

Near, far,
Everywhere You are,
I believe You create time and space.

Once more,
You open the door,
And You're here in my heart,
And Your Presence will fill every place.

You're here;
There's nothing to fear,
And your Godliness will never end.

You'll be,
Forever with me.
I feel safe in my heart, and
I trust that you'll always
Be my friend.

Divorce

While we were waiting for the divorce to finalize, I initially rented an apartment on the block where Jacob lived. I was worried that my son Jonathan would be too far away when he would go to visit his father. My daughter Gila stayed with me. She didn't want to see her father at all. In Israel, children have rights; not even the authorities nor the police can force a child to see his or her parent against the child's will. Eventually she did have visits with him but in the beginning she was very angry at him. Even though she was only three and a half years old she had a mind of her own.

The new beginnings were not easy. I had to start from scratch. Initially, I didn't even have a phone. There were no cell phones in those days and the apartment that I rented was new and did not have phone lines set up yet. I called people and told them to contact my parents if they had any questions or wanted appointments until I could acquire a phone. I started to acquire regular clients and continued working to pay my rent and bills. In Israel in those days, due to lack of supply and an overabundance of bureaucracy, it took about six months to receive a phone! I also had a hard time with all the procedures that were needed to obtain a legal divorce as well as a Jewish divorce, a "get." However, I did succeed and with the help of my rabbinical council, Jacob agreed to let me have custody of the children as long as he could visit them twice a week and have them sleep over every other Sabbath. I was quite happy.

For the first time in my life, I felt free. I visited my parents regularly and we had boundless fun with my children. My father was sincerely sorry for the way he treated us as children; he cried about it for months. He gave my children plenty of undivided attention that they were lacking from a father figure.

When parents argue they waste so much precious time and energy that their children can go unnoticed. Now that marital conflict did not distract me I had time to take the children on trips. We visited different museums and the zoo. I gave them the best care that I could, including private English and piano lessons for both children.

I had very little money, but I had no fear to spend it. I trusted that Hashem would provide, and He did. My calendar was booked for almost a month ahead. People gave me a good name as a healer. I told a few of my patients the story of how God started speaking to me. Hashem would instruct me about what they should do for their health, every step of the way. Many people felt intuitively that the guidance I gave was special and I started getting a good reputation.

I attended classes to augment my knowledge. As I mastered skills in iridology, kinesiology, and herbal medicine. I felt Hashem's divine wisdom constantly guiding me. Hashem really saved me. The difference between the past and the present was like the difference between a blind and a sighted man. When Hashem initially revealed himself to me, I realized that He had always been there with me. He watched and listened to me my whole life long. I never was alone, and I never will be. Thank you, Hashem, for giving me so much more than I ever dreamed.

I wrote the following poem for my readers, in appreciation of the unbelievable gift that Hashem gave me; His friendship.

Quite A Bit More

If you read this carefully,
You'll see the truth.
It's my greatest pleasure,
Just to write to you.

The gift God gave me,
Is the best of all.
His presence, His kindness, His call.

Not so long ago,
I was a lonely girl;
I was shy and small,
In a great big world.

It was Him I'd think of;
I was yearning for,
And I received quite a bit more.

Every day I'm with Him,
Every day I pray,
That He'll come to help me,
And He'll tell me what to say.
Every day I set myself another goal,
Just to help another soul.

You teach me so much about our history,
And sometimes you tell me,
Just what's going to be.

I love you so much,
I can't believe it's true.
And I know that You love me too.

We must love Hashem,
With all our heart and soul.
It's a mitzvah for the young,
And for the old.

That's the biggest thing,
Hashem is yearning for.
And he'll give back,
Quite a bit more.

Every day He's with you;
Every day He sees,
Every one you anger,
Every one you please.
When you keep the Torah,
And the Laws of old,
You'll be amazed at how your life will unfold.

There's really just too much to learn,
Too much to do.
The main thing to remember is
He's watching you.

He loves you oh so much.
You've got to believe it's true.
Do you?

It's a lonely world,
But you're not alone.
God created man;
He's not on his own.
If you notice Him
In everything you do,
He never will disappoint you.

CHAPTER 2

In the Beginning

Modern scientific discoveries point to the evidence of an intelligent creator who designed this beautiful world in which we live. There is a set of DVDs on this subject called *Intelligent Design Collection* by the Illustra Media. They are so convincing that even a sworn atheist will have trouble keeping his beliefs. Some of the scientists who contributed to this DVD were Darwinists that set out to prove the theory of evolution. However, they eventually came to completely opposite conclusions. If you check Amazon for *Intelligent Design*, you will find many books to help you understand more.

The *Intelligent Design* DVDs show evidence of different time periods of species that do not exist today. No missing links were found. These species suddenly came into being and suddenly disappeared, disproving Darwin's theory of a godless evolution.

For some years now, scientists have been making discoveries that disprove evolution. Dr. Colin Patterson wrote a book about evolution, but he admitted that he gave no examples of any fossils that are in between evolutionary stages. In 1977, Dr. Steven Jay Gold wrote, "There are no fossils of trees that are evolutionary stages to today's trees. Even though they are illustrated in our children's school books, they were never seen in reality." There was even a theory by Professor Niles Aldridge in 1972 that there was no evolution. Species popped up suddenly in different stages. He had to dismiss evolution theory because of the scientific findings.

Aldridge's theory is correct. The fossils that were discovered are from other worlds that inhabited this planet. Hashem created worlds, and after many years he destroyed them. Every world was more advanced than the next.

I asked the Creator, "Did you really create the world in six days?" He answered, "Whatever happened millions of years ago shouldn't bother you. The world as it is today, was created in six days."

God meant to say this world, where we have talking, walking men, with the animals that exist today and not those that existed in prehistoric worlds was created in six days. The Talmud says that before this world, God was creating worlds and destroying them. He kept on changing his mind. Hashem was not happy with his creations until He created this current world with its inhabitants.

This doesn't mean that the earth was destroyed many times. The worlds of creatures that lived on earth were destroyed. What scientists call evolutionary stages do not have thousands of stages of developmental changes between them. They are actually animals and plants from different worlds. No matter how similar different species seem, each one has its own DNA, which does not mutate.

This earth had different species living on it for many generations until Hashem decided that it wasn't good enough. Genesis begins with the last world that Hashem created; our world. The Torah doesn't start from nothingness; it describes, "In the beginning God created the heavens and the earth. Now the earth was formless and empty, darkness was over the surface of the deep, and the Spirit of God was hovering over the waters" (Genesis 1:2).

Water is the first thing scientists look for when they search for life on other planets. The Torah opens with a description of God hovering over the waters. There was water before the six days of creation because there was life before Genesis. The words formless and empty is a translation from the Hebrew *Tohi Vavohu* which really means, "a mess". The mess was the chaos of destruction of the world before ours.

Hashem made a mess of everything but the waters. The water was a good invention in Hashem's eyes as well as the fish. When Hashem created sea animals and birds on the fifth day it says:

> Genesis 1:21
> So God created the great creatures of the sea and every living thing with which the water teems and that moves about in it.

The exact translation of this quote is:

"And God created the big alligators and every living creature that crawls around the water."

When God created the land insects on the sixth day the scripture uses the same word for "crawl" and says, "living creatures that crawl on the ground." This word describes creepy crawly things like lobsters and bugs. Fish don't crawl, they also are in the water and not around it.

The reason the spirit of God was hovering over the waters is because He was giving life to the fish. On the fifth day the fish were blessed to be fruitful and multiply but they were initially designed in the world before this one, maybe for the world of the Neanderthals. Many of the animal species that we have today were existing in the previous world or worlds but Hashem created them again on the sixth day, some animals have some differences and some were exactly the same.

Hashem showed me that they all died because there was a big tsunami that destroyed everything and left only water covering the earth. The creation scientists that say they have proof of a global flood are studying the after-effects of this tsunami that happened before Genesis, not the flood of Noah. The flood of Noah was local, as you will learn in the chapter entitled, *The Flood*.

After each day of creation, Hashem said, "This time whatever I have done is good." In other words, "I am satisfied with this world and I am going to stop creating new worlds."

This is the first world that was created with a Sabbath. The significance of Sabbath is very important. It is a sign that Hashem took a rest from creating worlds. He may get angry at us sometimes but Hashem will not destroy the world. God is willing to be patient with us until we make it perfect. In my book *God Meets the World,* I have a whole chapter on the meaning and importance of the Sabbath.

Hashem cherishes our world where love and communication are a possibility. He tried different alternatives to our world so that if we do fail He will have patience for us. If Hashem compares us to the accomplishments of any previous worlds, He feels proud of us and has patience to wait for us to improve.

Time, the Very First Creation

Before God created anything, He had to design simpler things such as light, sound, and time. Before God invented time, there was just present—no past or future.

If there is no time before God, there is no possibility of establishing life, heavenly bodies, or anything that moves. Nothing can be fashioned before the formation of time, God's first creation. Therefore, there is no God before God, there is no before and after without time.

Dr. Steven Hawking, a great scientist of the past and the twenty-first century, found mathematical proof that time had a beginning. Time did not always exist. There is a movie about his life called *The Theory of Everything*. It is fascinating. Even though he was an atheist, his mathematical confirmation that time had a beginning is a discovery of creation.

Sound and light were certainly existing before this world. Hashem destroyed the atmosphere of the previous world so that only darkness resided, until Hashem said, "Let there be light." I discuss what happened of the six days of creation in detail in my first book called, *Who is God?*

Without atmosphere, sound and light cannot travel. The words "Let there be light," really mean, "Let there be an atmosphere to catch the sunlight to allow the light to shine through." The sound of Hashem saying, "Let there be light," traveled in the atmosphere as it was being created. It's a good thing that there were no people or animals because they surely would have not been able to withstand such powerful sound. The planet earth is never full of light in its entirety so I asked Hashem, "How much time did it take for the words 'Let There be light' to travel around the world?" He answered, "About sixteen hours, to give a chance for the world to turn on its axis and absorb the rays of the sun."

If you are sharp you may be asking how can there have been sunlight if the sun was created on the fourth day?

Genesis 1:16-17
> God made two great lights—the greater light
> to govern the day and the lesser light to govern the
> night. He also made the stars. God set them in the
> vault of the sky to give light on the earth.

Hashem made the celestial orbs a long time ago but on the fourth day he, "set them in a vault in the sky." We are the only planet that has a clear sky. All the other planets are surrounded by icy rocks and meteors that block the view of anyone who would theoretically be standing on the planet. The planet Earth didn't have a clear sky either. The dinosaurs didn't have the ability to gaze at the astronomical wonders of the night. When Hashem decided to create an intelligent man he wanted to give him a window to outer space. Our ability to see the stars has given mankind a basis for many scientific findings. On the first three days there was light but the sun was not in full view. Only on the fourth day did God clear the view which made the sun much brighter.

I used to wonder why Hashem needed a whole day to fashion any of His creations. Now I understand that when Hashem designed creatures all over the world, he wanted to make the diurnal animals and plants during the day so they would be able to enjoy the sunshine as soon as possible. The nocturnal animals were created at night. The parting of the seas from land was done during the day so Hashem would enjoy the beauty of the sunset over the waters. Hashem waited for daylight in each and every time zone in order to complete his daily task. When the scripture says after every day of creation, "It was evening and it was morning," it is referring to an evening and a morning numerous times during that day all over the earth.

Perspective

Maimonides says that without movement, there is no time; if everything is static, no time passes therefore nothing that moves could have been created before there was time. In order to create time God created His spirit hovering over the waters. The movement of that spirit creates time. The speed in which His spirit moves generates the dimension of timeline that we live in.

We move in slow motion compared to any other prior world made by Hashem. He slowed down the speed of His master computer to produce a world that He thought would finally succeed.

The experience of a dog's sense of time elapse is different than that of a human. A fifteen-year-old teenager feels like the whole world is ahead of her. A nine-year-old dog feels old and by the time she's twelve she may begin to suffer from old age. On the other hand, as humans get older they can feel that time moves faster.

There was no need for Hashem to wait millions of years to see if the dinosaur's world would be good. The dinosaurs may have aged for millions of years in their perspective but if we could watch them they would be moving at warp speed. They only existed for as much time as Hashem needed in order to check them out.

Hashem ended the existence of that world and removed dinosaurs because he saw nothing worthwhile would come of it. Evolution didn't account for their extinction; it was Hashem's decision. The other worlds went a little slower. We learn that the Neanderthals lived for about 200,000 years. That is compared to their timeline but for Hashem it may have been just a few thousand years.

In Hashem's perspective, time can pass at whatever pace He would like it to pass. There is a DVD from NOVA all about time and space in consideration of the theory of relativity. In that DVD, the scientist explains that time is a unit. You can see parts of the DVD on You Tube to get a general idea.

It is theoretically possible to jump ahead in time, but there is no leaping back. If Hashem wills he can skip ahead even though the fossils appear as if they have existed for millions of years.

The Race Against Time

When Hashem created this world he was pleased with his creation and He wanted to observe every moment. Therefore, he made our timeline very slow. Even though you may think that time flies, consider that in the past fifty years there have been inventions that superseded the inventions of the entire history of mankind. We have created a whole new world of computer technology in only fifty years. The reason that we are succeeding in doing so is because time is slowing down. We are all under tension in order to accomplish more every day. Sometimes we can feel totally overwhelmed, as if we are racing against time.

Hashem gave me a few hints in order to relieve this tension:

1) Change activities often. If you do the same thing for many hours you start slowing down.
2) You must give yourself quality rest time. If you just sit home and watch TV or talk on the phone you waste time. If you sit in the park or at the beach and enjoy a picnic with a friend you relax and recuperate.
3) When planning an excursion add a half an hour to your departure time to make extra time for traffic

or parking difficulties. You drive will be much more relaxing if you know that you have time to spare.

4) Concentrate on what you are doing and not on what you must do. If you cannot get your mind off of what you must do in the future, then do it right away if at all possible. For example, if you are worried about a phone call that you must make to a government office by next week, just call them right away, the tension of worrying about it is very draining and time consuming.

5) If you feel that you have too much to do, don't get overwhelmed. Start step by step and praise yourself for what you did accomplish. If you really have so much work that it will take away from quality of life, then get help, even if you have to pay for it.

6) Do not give up your right to spend time with your children. They grow up fast and they need their parents. If you tell Hashem that you are willing to survive on less in order to spend time with your children He will provide. In my experience as a healer I have interviewed many women with large families. The women that work outside of the house are miserable from the tension of coming home after a day's work to a dirty house with laundry and cooking and other chores that they have to do. The children that they are working so hard for, become a burden. If you have young children it's best if you can work in the house. If you must work outside of the house get household help. You come home to be with your children and husband, not with the dirty laundry. The mothers that I met that worked part time were the happiest. They don't feel isolated from the world and they still have time to be a Mom.

7) Take care of your health. Exercise and good nutrition give you strength to do whatever you want to do. Don't say that you don't have time to go to the gym, you don't have time not to go.

8) When you are worried about time just say to yourself that time is really going very slowly, slower than any generation before this one. This belief will make you realize just how much you do accomplish. If you look at what you did rather on what you have to do you will get more done.

9) Do not watch TV, it is a time monger. You can watch a DVD that you choose or a You Tube video but commercial television has so many advertisements and propaganda that you become mesmerized, and lose days, weeks and years of your life. For children the television must be monitored closely. Some shows can be educational. However, many children's cartoons just mesmerize young children and inhibit their development.

10) If you are tired, go to sleep. Working at night just makes the same job take longer. If you get a fresh start you will get much more done and you will have greater success in your endeavors.

Human Communication Skills

This world was carefully planned to be fit for intelligent human beings created in God's image. I asked Hashem a curious question. "What were you doing for all those millions of years before creating Adam?" I got the most surprising answer! Hashem said, "I was figuring out a way for people to communicate." I was quite shocked with this answer. Why would it take millions of years to create language?

At the time I didn't know that millions of years could be just a few years for Hashem. I understood that while He was watching all these creatures that He made, Hashem was studying how they communicate with each other. He had to devise a way that this communication would be as advanced as is needed in order to plan, discuss, discover and build the world physically, mentally and spiritually.

It takes an adult a few years to learn a new language fluently. Children learn new languages even faster than adults. For Hashem it took much longer because he had to first figure out the ideas of sound, of speech, and of words. It was God's desire to communicate that drove Him to create humans with a magnificent brain, mouth and vocal chords to perform our speaking capabilities. After He finally invented language, Hashem was so excited to say something that He screamed out into the empty abyss, "Let there be light."

Words are special because they help you to think. They are also very powerful. Hashem gave humankind brains with the potential to speak. Still He wanted us to develop a language on our own. Before humankind spoke properly, people were very simple and primitive in their thoughts and feelings.

When Does Genesis Begin?

Genesis begins after Hashem already figured out language and speech, and He had the layout of how to create an intelligent man. The man that was made on the sixth day did not know how to speak. He had the brain to learn and the vocal chords to enunciate words but he was not successful. Even though he did develop some level of communication above the ability of animals it was not even close to what Hashem planned for all humankind.

Man Needs Help

Even with all the proper apparatus and intellect, man was not able to evolve language on his own. After tens of thousands of years, ancient humans could hardly say a few syllables. Hashem had to help him to progress and achieve language skills.

Genesis 2:7, "And God created man from the dust of the earth and He breathed into his nostrils a living soul." After this verse, we read about Adam giving names to the animals. This means that not only is Adam speaking, but he can be innovative and imaginative.

Thus there are the two creation stories about man. The first account says, "God created man in His image in the image of God, a male and a female, he created them" (Genesis 1:27).

The second version of the story of creation begins in Genesis 2. In this creation story, God gives Adam his name. Adam has conversations with God, and God creates a wife for him. These are obviously two very different stories.

A Special Soul

From a scientific point of view, it is not physically possible for all the races on earth to evolve from a single prototypical couple. It is impossible to have the DNA components represented for the diversity of all the races, including African, Chinese, Irish, and Indian, Eskimo, Scandinavian and all others stemming from one original couple.

Our genetic lines are permanent. A Chinese man will not give birth to an Irish redhead or to any other race. Different people with diverse genetics were created in various places during the period between the first creation story and Adam. I understood from Hashem that the Native Americans were the last men to be created before Adam. That's why they have their own creation stories; many of them have a heritage and belief that they were created on American soil.

Archeological evidence shows that the Native Americans were in America over ten thousand years ago, but not much more. Popular theory holds that the Native Americans migrated from Mongolia. Hashem told me that even though there were some ancient civilizations which migrated from place to place, the Native Americans were created in America just as their heritage asserts.

In the beginning, at the start of the Bible, primitive humans were first created, men and women were formed at the same time. Hashem created many different species of humans: Africans, Chinese, and even Irish redheads. He waited thousands of years for man to evolve and mature enough to advance language and speech on his own, as mentioned above. He designed human vocal chords, a special mouth to speak with, and all the structure of the ear to hear—a high level of sound system apparatus unique to the human body—but there was very little development of communication.

When humans didn't perfect a language that was sophisticated enough in order to talk about deep thoughts, plans, and ideology, Hashem decided that they needed a little help. That help from Hashem was the extra soul called *Neshama*.

> Genesis 2:7 reads, "Then the LORD God formed a man from the dust of the ground and breathed into his nostrils the breath of life, and the man became a living being."

"The breath of life" is the translation of the word *Neshama* in the Hebrew text. The *Neshama* is the part of our soul that gives us the power of speech. Of all God's creations, the creation of the soul is the most miraculous of all. No evolutionary process is evident whatsoever. The intelligence of man so far exceeds that of the most intelligent of the animal kingdom that in no way can it be a slow progressive process. A human baby almost magically learns language and communication, even in two languages. This can only be a gift from God.

The first man to receive this gift called the *Neshama* was Adam, of the second creation story. Genesis 2:7, "Then the LORD God formed a man from the dust of the ground and breathed into his nostrils the breath of life, and the man became a living being."

The word *soul* here is *Neshama* in Hebrew. In Ayurveda, a system of medicine with historical roots in India, it is the fifth chakra. Before mentioning the *Neshama*, the Torah uses the word *Nefesh*. *Nefesh* is the part of the soul that has feelings; the fourth chakra. Many animals have a *Nefesh*, as some people recognize the developed emotions of their pets. The first man that was created had a *Nefesh* but not a *Neshama*. We learn in Kabala that the *Neshama* is the part of the soul that gives wisdom and speech. The *Neshama* not only gave man the capacity for verbal speech but also for increased intelligence to understand a multitude of various concepts, to develop different spoken languages and finally, written language.

In the second creation story the Torah says:

Genesis 2:5
Now no shrub had yet appeared on the earth and
no plant had yet sprung up, for the LORD God had

not sent rain on the earth and there was no one to
work the ground.

Did you ever ask yourself how it is possible for man to
suddenly go from being a gatherer to a farmer? Who taught
man how to till the soil and plant the seeds?

It was all intuition, stemming from Hashem's gift of the
Neshama. Adam and his descendants knew from intuition
and instinct which plants are poisonous, which are edible
and what plants heal. Human beings also had the intuition
to invent innovative ways of cooking and food preparation.

If you think that this was just trial and error, just watch
a baby grow. Babies know that you are eating before they
ever tasted solid food and they want to taste. When I took
my one-year-old baby to the supermarket and sat her in the
shopping cart for the first time, she knew that all that stuff
was food, and she wanted everything. Babies even know
that when you are talking on the phone there is a person
there communicating and it's different than their toy phone
even if the toy phone talks back. I'm sure that parents of
young children can tell endless stories about their children's
innate intelligence.

Among the other amazing capabilities of the *Neshama*
are the abilities to organize, plan ahead, think intuitively,
learn new things just by observation and practice, invent,
develop deep relationships with true love, laugh, sing and
play music, think philosophically or scientifically and so
much more. The *Neshama* also gives us the capacity to enjoy
and write stories, jokes, poetry and music. All these talents
of the soul come from the sixth chakra, or what is called
our third eye in Eastern terms.

In Kabala, this part of our *Neshama* is called *Chaya*.
This word translates loosely into "living being." That
is why Genesis 7:7 says, "And the man became a living

being." In my new book, *Choose Life*, I will provide a deeper explanation of the various parts of the soul—God's most amazing design.

The second Adam, the man that was placed in the Garden of Eden, was truly a creation closer to the image of God than anyone before him. Adam was blessed with the capability to speak to God. Hashem wanted very much to have a friend. Originally Hashem wanted humans to discover Him all by themselves. When He created Adam, Hashem blessed him with a direct connection to God. In Ayurveda philosophy this level is considered the seventh chakra and in Kabala it is called *Yechida*.

The Sons of God and the Daughters of Adam

Genesis 6:2, "And the sons of God saw the daughters of Adam, saw how good they were and they took wives from whoever they chose." The sons of God were the men in the first creation story that were created before Adam and Eve. This is why they are called children of God. The non-verbal children of God were created before speaking humans like Adam and Eve. God made different races of the non-verbal children of God depending on where they lived on earth as He created different animal species in different places. I contest any scientist to show me evidence of the evolutionary process that led from primitive man in Ethiopia to talking redheads with freckles in Ireland!

The word Adam comes from *Adama*, meaning soil or land. Adam was created from soil. Genesis 7:7, "Then the LORD God formed a man from the dust of the ground." This is the second creation story of humankind. It is not a continuation of the first primitive non-speaking humans for whom there is no mention of originating from the ground. Adam was created from the ground in order to make him feel humble. He looked and moved similarly to the humans who preceded him. The big difference is that he received a Neshama.

> Genesis 2:20, "So the man gave names to all the livestock, the birds in the sky and all the wild animals. But for Adam no suitable helper was found."

God blessed Adam with the ability to speak right after he was formed. He spoke an ancient Semitic language and he could understand deep concepts such as planning for the future and regretting the past. He could not converse in speech with the existent nonverbal humanoids or with any of the animals he named. He had no human partner with whom he could communicate in language so he was quite lonely.

The first man was created with his female counterpart; Genesis 1:27 says, "Male and female he created them." Adam was created alone. Genesis 2:20 says, "But for Adam no suitable helper was found."

Hashem wanted Adam's *Neshama* to feel that he was missing someone and He gave him the ability to fall in love. God doesn't give Adam his soul mate immediately. He wanted to watch the love story. The reason why we are so excited to see and hear love stories is because it is such a spiritual part of us. It's so sad that modern man has abused this wonderful gift in countless ways.

Adam realized that he needed another entity with whom he could communicate in depth. Hashem took a part of his soul, of the *Neshama*, and not his physical rib. With that spark, Hashem created a woman with similar abilities and needs. Together, the man and woman constituted a full single soul.

Mother of All

If Adam was not the only human and there were other people in the world at the time, then why would he call his wife "Mother of all the living?"

> Genesis 3:20
> Adam named his wife Eve, because she would become the mother of all the living.

The true translation of this verse is, "Adam named his wife *Chava* which means life, because she was the mother of all living creatures."

Adam didn't name Eve or Chava in honor of the future; he named her because of his observation. Chava was taking care of the animals in need with the tender loving care of a mother! Adam was impressed. He saw the feminine touch that Chava had and wanted her to be the mother of his children.

Husband and wife are not related to each other by blood. However, your spouse is the closest person to you in the world, even closer than your own parents. God wanted to create a couple that will relate to each other even more than they are related to their blood relatives, so that they could bond in the closest eternal union possible. The rib that Hashem removed from man is a part of his soul, not of his body. Men don't have fewer ribs than women. When a man finds this part of his soul that belongs to him, he knows it. He falls in love and decides to live with his soulmate forever.

> Proverbs 20:27

> The human spirit is the lamp of the LORD that sheds light on one's inmost being.

The following is a more accurate translation:

Proverbs 20:27, "For the candle of God is the *Neshama* of mankind. Looking through all the chambers of the emotions."

When you light a candle with another candle, you have two full flames. The *Neshama* is like a candle; it gives its light and is not lacking. Adam was the first man to receive a *Neshama*. Together with Eve and their descendants, they taught others to speak and feel. They gave others more and more wisdom, until the Tower of Babel in the next generation.

The Tower of Babel

Genesis 11:4–9

Then they said, "Come, let us build ourselves a city, with a tower that reaches to the heavens, so that we may make a name for ourselves; otherwise we will be scattered over the face of the whole earth." But the Lord came down to see the city and the tower the people were building. God said, "If as one people speaking the same language they have begun to do this, then nothing they plan to do will be impossible for them. Come, let us go down and confuse their language so they will not understand each other." So God scattered them from there over all the earth, and they stopped building the city. That is why it was called Babel because there, God confused the people. (*Babel* in Hebrew means confusion.)

By attaining a name for themselves, the people of Babel would be in an advantageous position over other humans by using their language to advance themselves, instead of sharing their language and progress with others. They didn't want to disperse their knowledge and wisdom throughout the world. When Hashem gave the ability to develop language and all other human endeavors as a by-product, He wanted His gift to be distributed by man with other humans.

In the story of the Tower of Babel, the speaking humans wanted to dwell together to make a name for themselves, maybe even rule the world with their outstanding talents instead of disseminating them. God didn't like this at all, so He forced these people to roam the earth and instilled different languages in their minds.

The people of the Tower of Babel were forced to spread out all over the planet and began speaking new languages. This way, languages could be taught, developed and established throughout the world. By speaking different languages, it would assure that no one culture will totally control the others. They would also subsequently create different customs, foods and music. Each nation would be proud of themselves for their own uniqueness.

The people of Babel dispersed and taught new languages to others. Even if the inhabitants of Babel didn't arrive to every country on earth, Hashem was so pleased with his new invention that he gave a *Neshama* to all humankind.

Many humans, like the people of the Far East, which were not visited by the inhabitants of Babel developed their own cultures. Maybe that's why their native tongues are so different than the European languages, which have an alphabet based on the first Hebrew alphabet. The Chinese, Japanese, and Koreans all developed their speech and culture just from their own imagination. They used their newly acquired *Neshama* to think freely and create. Hashem also gave them a special gift—Chinese medicine, a gift of brilliance that is so complex it could not have come from trial and error alone.

The more advanced we are in technology and philosophy, the more we can understand the Torah and the whole Bible.

There are many hints in the Bible that have been encoded waiting for someone smart enough to decipher. Just as Adam needed help to be able to speak, humankind needs help to understand the Torah. Hashem has blessed people throughout the ages with a *Neshama* that can even reach the level of prophecy.

CHAPTER 3

The Tree of Knowledge

Genesis 2:16–17
    And the Lord God commanded the man, saying: Of every tree of the garden thou may freely eat but of the Tree of the Knowledge of Good and Evil thou shall not eat of it; for in the day that thou eat of it thou shall surely die.

Hashem gave only one commandment to Adam and Eve, "Do not to taste from the Tree of Knowledge of Good and Evil." The serpent introduced Eve with the idea that she could be like God, and it tempted Eve to eat from the fruit.

Genesis 3:5 says, "For God knows that when you eat of it your eyes will be opened, and you will be like God, knowing good and evil."

The newly created couple did not keep this one commandment. God subsequently expelled them from the Garden of Eden. Their sin was that they wanted to taste from the tree that would enable them to decide and to have the wisdom to choose between good and bad.

What's so bad about knowing what's good and what's bad? Why would Hashem prohibit eating from that tree? Did Adam and Eve really gain the knowledge of what is truly good and truly evil?

The Neshama Gets Smart

The Neshama that God gave Adam was full of potential, but it was still innocent. When Adam ate from the Tree of Knowledge, he didn't just become smarter, he became more sure of himself. He felt certain that he knows what's best. Humans are sometimes so sure that they are right that fiery discussions, disputes and fights erupt, and even reach the level of wars.

No creation in the animal kingdom argues over what's right and what's wrong. When the bees do their dance, do any bees protest that the better pollen is on the other side of the orchard? Imagine what would happen if a flock of birds would be hawking about which way is the fastest way to fly.

It's only mankind that has this urge to be right. Ask any parent; it starts very early in life. Two-year-olds already know exactly what they want.

Adam's Punishment

Genesis 3:17–19
Cursed is the ground because of you; through painful toil you will eat food from it all the days of your life. It will produce thorns and thistles for you, and you will eat the plants of the field. By the sweat of your brow you will eat your food until you return to the ground, since from it you were taken; for dust you are and to dust you will return.

The punishment Adam received was to work the soil with the sweat of his brow. Originally he was supposed to till the soil in the Garden of Eden. Everything he did would be fruitful. Now he would have to work and not always be successful. Sometimes he will grow thorns and weeds. Why?

When Adam ate from the Tree of Knowledge, he didn't gain knowledge; he gained pride—he became sure about himself and his ability to succeed. His punishment was that he can't always succeed. He had to see that he isn't always right.

We win some; we lose some. The more we try, the bigger the possibility that we will have failures. However, if we stay in bed all day, we won't have any successes at all. So, don't be distraught if you have had losses and don't give up; it's the way of the world since Adam.

The other problem with humans deciding what is good or evil is that they are personally invested in their decisions. Lawmakers under the influence of dominant and biased parties have established laws and customs throughout the ages. Individual or collective preferences and desires often determine what is moral. "It's good because I said so or because it is good for me." Established values and rules based on personal advantage are egotistical, corrupt, and oppressive. Rationalizing and justifications replace honest evaluations.

> Malachi 2:17 reads, "You have wearied Hashem with your words, but you say, 'How have we wearied Him?' By saying, 'Everyone who does wrong is good in the eyes of Hashem, and He favors them; Oh! Where is the God of justice?'"

In the days of Malachi, Hashem had grown tired of hearing people say that what is bad is good.

Everything is Subjective

We judge things by comparison. In the nineteenth century, women would never leave the house without a bonnet. A woman would be arrested for wearing clothing that women wear today. In my own lifetime, the understanding of what is good and bad has changed drastically. When I was growing up, there was this commercial on TV:

"You've come a long way, baby.

You've come a long, long way.

You've got your own cigarette now, baby,

You've come a long, long way."

It was a jingle that gave pride to women because they used to have to hide in order to smoke. It advertised a special cigarette just for women. A woman smoking changed from being bad to being great. Today any cigarette smoking for men or women is considered bad. What was bad became good and then in turn became bad again, so bad that advertising cigarettes is now illegal.

Today people also do things that cause their own demise. Teenagers get involved with smoking or even drugs. From the time of Adam's exile, people have been deciding for themselves what good and evil are. There's even a movie called *Bad Boys*. The most famous line in the movie is, "Bad is good!"

Another example of cultural change of what is good and bad is slavery in the United States. Slavery in the South was considered good. Prayer in public schools has gone from good to bad. Murdering Jews throughout millennia was considered a necessity in the holy wars of the Crusaders. Even today, suicide terrorism is considered a very holy deed by terrorists and their leaders. We all live under the illusion that we have the ability to differentiate right from wrong.

If you are careful not to be certain that you know what's right and what's wrong, you will have peace in your home. Marital peace comes from mutual decision-making. Most arguments between couples are about what's wrong and what's right. If you agree to allow your spouse to fully voice his or her opinion and both parties are flexible, peace resides.

Grandparents have a very hard time with this because after so many years of experience, their grown children don't always respect their views on child-rearing. When you're all upset about this, remember that both parent and grandparent are under the spell of the Tree of Knowledge. You both are sure that you're right! The only way that we can know what is truly good and evil is from Hashem's point of view. That is why He decided to write the Ten Commandments and the Torah. Any argument about what is right or wrong can be resolved by following the Bible.

The Punishments

The punishments of Adam and Eve are not eternal decrees. They are the result of eating from the Tree of Knowledge. If you break that spell, then you don't suffer the consequences that are written in the Bible.

> Genesis 3:14–15
> And the Lord God said unto the serpent, 'because you have done this, you are cursed above all cattle, and above every beast of the field; upon your belly you shall go, and dust you shall eat all the days of your life. And I will put enmity between you and the woman, and between thy seed and her seed; it shall bruise your head, and you shall bruise his heel.'

The snake is anyone who is sly, tricky, and out to get you. The snake already ate from the Tree of Knowledge and spoke to Eve from his own experience. Why wasn't he expelled from the Garden of Eden immediately?

The snake was never warned not to eat from the Tree of Knowledge. The snake represents all those sly and sneaky evil people. Hashem doesn't destroy them because he created a world with free choice. He wants us to see the good and evil and choose between them.

"And I will put enmity between you and the woman, and between thy seed and her seed." The snake will be hated by the woman and her children. This is what is happening today with many abusive or sly men and women who act like deceptive talking snakes. They lose their spouses and their children. Even if a partner is not physically abusive and is only dishonest or angry, he loses his family's love and trust.

Some women are snakes too; that's why the Torah doesn't say if the snake was male or female. The snake was a human from those who were created before Adam. He or she was called a snake because after eating from the Tree of Knowledge the snake used its newly found wisdom to be sly and wicked. I assert, Genesis 3:14 in a more accurate translation, would read as

> "So the LORD God said to the serpent, 'Because
> you have done this, cursed are you above all livestock
> and all wild animals! You will crawl on your belly and
> you will eat dust all the days of your life.'"

Sometimes we see how wicked people get their way and seemingly win in this world, but they will always crawl on their bellies and eat the dust of the earth, which means they will never reach any kind of spirituality and their souls will be starved for love, wisdom, and godliness.

The Woman's Punishment

"Your lust will be for your man and he will rule over you" (Genesis 3:16). Eve ate from the Tree of Knowledge. If your husband has earned the name "your man," then he has earned your respect, but if you argue with him about who's right, then he will become domineering. The secret to a happy marriage is to let each other voice his or her opinion. As a woman, I know that this is hard because in a household, "Mother knows best," or at least she thinks she does. You must believe that what happens is for the best. It is not what you think is best, but rather what Hashem knows is best.

This is true especially if the argument is over an important issue, like what school your child should attend. If you praise your husband for his good ideas, you will be much more convincing than if you are forceful with your voice. When arguing about a small thing, let it go, give in. If you give in sometimes your spouse will learn from you to do the same.

Eve's curse of having difficulty giving birth isn't only for the birth itself, but for the whole eighteen or more years of rearing the child. You cannot succeed in rearing a child properly if you don't listen to their point of view. When children feel respected by their parents, they in turn will trust and honor them. When children feel that their parents listen to each other's opinions, they will do so in their own marriages. Children exposed to egalitarian parental unions will not be so affected by deceptive or sly models that they see in others. This mother will not feel pain when it's time to let her children have their independence. She will enjoy seeing her children build their own beautiful homes.

I can also tell you that many orthodox Jewish women who live in Jerusalem have very easy births. They look forward to giving birth for the spiritual uplifting experience. Of course there are also some very difficult deliveries but the righteousness of these woman is so great that even in the hospital they don't complain and are grateful for every moment.

The man is punished to have to work by the sweat of his brow (Genesis 3:19). If you are insistent that you know what's right you can never advance in your job. If you are set in your ways, you can't learn from others. "I know what I'm doing" is a common statement. With an attitude of haughtiness, you cannot learn and advance in your career and you will have to labor physically or mentally, "with the sweat of your brow," in order to make ends meet.

Modern man has learned this lesson very well. We are open to the opinions of others more than in any generation. As a reward, God has blessed us with freedom of the sexes. A man doesn't have to take the whole burden of financial responsibilities, and a woman doesn't have to be ruled by her man. God also blessed our world with advanced technology to help us free up from labor-intensive chores like doing the laundry by hand on a washboard. That's on the large scale, but we still have to beware of the illusion we all feel that individually we know what's right.

A Taste of the Tree of Knowledge

In the Garden of Eden story, God creates Adam and then creates Eve. Genesis 2:25 reads, "They were both arumim, the man and his wife, and they were not ashamed." *Arumim* is traditionally translated as naked in this verse. It also appears in Genesis 3:7, 3:10, and 3:11:

"Then the eyes of both of them were opened and they realized that they were naked (arumin); and they sewed a fig leaf and made themselves belts."

"And he (Adam) said, 'I heard Your voice in the garden, and I was afraid because I was naked, so I hid.'"

"And He (God) said, 'Who told you that you are naked (arum)?'"

When the snake is described in Genesis 3:1, he is called the most cunning of any beast of the field that Hashem had made. *Arum* here in Genesis 3:1 is traditionally translated as cunning or sly. Genesis 2:25, as above: "They were both *arumim*," is spelled the same way as the next verse to describe the snake. Certainly the snake was sly and cunning, even the most cunning of any beast of the field. So Adam and Eve were also cunning and sly, but not as cunning as the snake. Yes, "They were both cunning (*arumim*), the man and his wife, and they were ashamed of their sin!" The cunning excuses are what got them and us into trouble.

Today there are endless amounts of cunning email and telephone scams and many businesses with their operators that are corrupt. Corruption abounds in both the public and private sectors. The value of self-advancement is so overvalued that the cost to others is overlooked. Like the snake, they think they know better than God.

Why did Adam and Eve sew themselves belts of fig leaves after "their eyes were opened?" They were not ashamed of their bodies. They were by far the most beautiful creatures on earth and they knew it. They were ashamed of their attitude.

In order to eat humble pie, they decided to cover up their bodies with the leaves of the fig tree so they wouldn't feel so proud of their beauty. Also, they would be reminded of their sin. The forbidden fruit couldn't have been a fig, because at that point the young couple would have been afraid to even go near the forbidden tree.

Regardless of what kind of tree was forbidden, the fig leaves were used. Fig leaves are a remedy for fertility. Adam said to himself, *"Let's not try to be like God as the snake suggested. Let's have offspring just like mortals should."* Soon after this episode Eve bore her first son.

A Parable

The Garden of Eden is a parable for the Land of Israel. After the destruction of the First Temple, the Jews were expelled from their land and endured many hardships. This was foreseen in the prophecies of Moses at the end of Deuteronomy, thus connecting the beginning and the end of the Torah.

The Israelites of the First Temple Period decided that it was right to worship idols. Archeologists found thousands of idols all over the land of Israel, which proves how rampant idol worship was.

Hashem didn't forbid the viewing or touching of the Tree of Good and Evil. Eating its fruit was forbidden. But Adam told Eve not to even touch the tree. Some educators make the mistake of forbidding their disciples to look at or learn about other cultures. They also forbid them to ask questions. They are just like Adam; they prohibit you from touching the forbidden fruit. This causes young people to leave the right path. For example, when a religious teenager of any strict religious family goes to see an R-rated movie or ask questions about Darwin's theory of evolution and he is subsequently ostracized. A friend of ours told us that as a teenager he was told that he would burn in hell because he masturbated, so he said to himself, *"If I'm going to hell anyway, I might as well enjoy life in the meantime."* This boy left his religion but subsequently returned to Judaism as an adult when he met loving people who were open to help him search for the truth.

For centuries many Christian religious leaders forbade anyone to ask questions. Asking questions is like touching the forbidden tree; it was considered blasphemy. The religious hierarchy and its representatives controlled the less learned masses. If something or someone is true, why fear questioning in order to have an understanding?

As a matter of fact, asking questions is the only way to really get to the truth. All advances in technology and science began with inquisitiveness, curiosity, and imagination.

Nowadays the tables have been turned. The American establishment doesn't allow the questioning of science. Students are not even allowed to learn any theory that opposes the Theory of Evolution. They are not permitted to learn about the theory that the polio vaccine did not end the disease. (See https://healthimpactnews.com/2013/the-real-history-behind-the-polio-vaccine/)

The schools are very fundamentalist for their own religion which is the mainstream scientific establishment. Alternative medicine or alternative scientific findings are all taboo.

A Parable

The Garden of Eden is also a parable for the Land of Israel. When the children of Israel transgressed the prohibition that God gave them and worshiped idols, they were expelled from the Promised Land.

A main theme of Deuteronomy is Moses' prophesy about the future sins of Israel. They would stray and forsake their God. This is the God who changed nature in order to make miracles and take them out of bondage and slavery. God would subsequently severely punish the Israelites and expel them from their land. The Torah begins with a parable to this prophesy, the story of Adam and Eve.

Don't Add, and Don't Subtract

The original commandment from God to Adam was to eat all the fruit of the Garden but not the fruit of the Tree of Knowledge. It was commanded to him before the creation of his soul mate. Eve was not part of the prohibition. Adam told Eve that she couldn't eat from the fruit of the tree or touch it. He knew that he was allowed to touch the tree, but he added another rule just to be on the safe side. He also decided on his own that Eve was part of the prohibition. If he had told Eve that God prohibited him from eating the fruit, but he would like for her not to eat from the tree so that he wouldn't, she would have never shared the fruit with him after she succumbed to the snake. Eve would not have believed that eating from the fruit would make her into a god because God had not prohibited her from eating it.

Adam added to God's original instructions and that's what got him into trouble. The Torah prohibits us to add or subtract (Deuteronomy 13:1–2) Hashem made the law perfect. He doesn't need any wise guys trying to make it better.

Eve

Adam's mistake was that not only did he add to the commandment of God, he also made it sound like the reason not to eat was because it was poisonous.

> Genesis 3:4-6
> You will not certainly die," the serpent said to the woman. "For God knows that when you eat from it

> your eyes will be opened, and you will be like God,
> knowing good and evil." When the woman saw that
> the fruit of the tree was good for food and pleasing
> to the eye, and also desirable for gaining wisdom,
> she took some and ate it. She also gave some to her
> husband, who was with her, and he ate it.

When the snake said, "You will certainly not die" he meant that she won't die naturally because the fruit is not poisonous. She didn't understand that God told Adam that he will die as a punishment for disobedience. Had Adam explained to Eve that God doesn't allow him to eat from the Tree of Knowledge because of reasons unknown to him, and that there will be a death sentence for disobeying Him, Eve would have never succumbed to the snake. Adam had the responsibility of teaching her that we listen to God whether it makes sense or not.

We sometimes tell people to do or not to do things because of a natural outcome, as an excuse to avoid the true reason. For example, tell your child the truth. He cannot eat a certain food because it's not healthy, not because "he'll get in trouble." You can't buy him this toy because it's too expensive, not because he doesn't deserve it. Do not foster a fear like Daddy will punish you or you will call her teacher. Your child is smarter than you think; she was also created in God's image and she will respect you more if you say the honest truth.

Modern society has taught youth to obey the law because they must be a law abiding citizens, or otherwise they will end up in jail. This is not the best reason. The reason to be honest and obey the law is because there are societal laws that are also God's laws. The police might not catch you stealing but God will. The experiment to eliminate God from the lives of the citizens of the Western world failed.

When we teach convicts to believe in God we will be able to control crime and violence. All that Hashem is asking from us is to obey the Ten Commandments and then only good things will follow.

When man-made laws are against the Ten Commandments like the laws of the SS army, then we must disobey. The SS army is an extreme example. Nevertheless, in today's generation many high ranking officials lie, steal and cheat "legally" in order to keep their jobs or advance from within. We are called upon to choose between good and evil. Likewise, any man, woman or child that has the guts to stand up to their superior for the truth is beloved and respected in the eyes of Hashem. If your job forces you to transgress one of the Ten Commandments, it is better to quit. God will provide you with a better job and He will never forget your loyalty to Him.

The Original Sin

The first sin has nothing to do with sex, as some might say. The couple did not have sex until after they were outside of the Garden of Eden (Genesis 4:1). The original sin was disobeying God's orders.

> Genesis 4:4-5 read, "You will not certainly die," the serpent said to the woman. "For God knows that when you eat from it your eyes will be opened, and you will be like God, knowing good and evil."

The snake was right Adam didn't die. What's the score?

Adam got this commandment when he was alone, without a wife. Had he eaten from this tree before he had Eve and received the punishment to work the soil for his bread he certainly would have died.

How can a man alone work all day tilling the soil and then come home, grind the wheat and bake the bread? He would have died of fatigue and starvation. He also would have died of loneliness and depression. When we come to hard times the best way to survive is to stay together, to continue to love one another and comfort each other. Hashem saw that if Adam doesn't obey him he will not survive the punishment so he said to Himself, "It is not good for man to be alone."

Genesis 2:16-18

And the LORD God commanded the man, "You are free to eat from any tree in the garden; but you must not eat from the tree of the knowledge of good and evil, for when you eat from it you will certainly die."

The LORD God said, "It is not good for the man to be alone. I will make a helper suitable for him."

At face value, Eve's curse seems worse than Adam's, but in reality her punishment was much lighter. She didn't really understand that the main reason not to eat from the fruit is because Hashem forbids it.

Women have a hard time giving birth; however, it comes together with many blessings. Women get to enjoy the experience of a life being created inside their womb. They enjoy the miracle of breast-feeding, and they enjoy spending time with their children all day long. Is that really such a curse?

The question I asked Hashem is, "Why do women have to have painful childbirth?"

He explained, "The sin of Eve was not disobeying God because God never spoke to her. Her sin was the will to be like a god. When the snake gave Eve the idea that she can be like a god she took the bait. Hashem realized that giving birth is a very divine experience. Every woman can feel like a god after the see the beautiful baby that comes her womb. Therefore, He gave women pain when she is giving birth in order to remember that she is not so powerful.

> Genesis 3:16
> To the woman he said,
> "I will make your pains in childbearing very severe;
> with painful labor you will give birth to children.
> Your desire will be for your husband,
> and he will rule over you."

Hashem gave Eve a need to feel her husband's emotional support so he will feel important too. Sometimes fathers feel very left out in the first months after the birth of their children. Make sure that the father takes an active part in caring for the child so he won't feel left out. The mother shouldn't take over the entire responsibility of the child's care so as not to be like a god in her household.

Adam's Curse

Adam lost his paradise. He would not be able to live off fruit trees and relax all day; he would have to work for a living. Modern women seem to be jealous of their husbands' curse and run out of the house to help them make a living. It can be a good idea for a single woman but children that are left with a babysitter every day suffer. Today it is sometimes impossible to support a family on only one salary, but if it is at all possible to stay home with your child, do so.

Every woman should take pleasure in the joy of rearing the children. Please don't complain that having kids is too much work. It's the biggest blessing that you will ever have. Give that message to your children and they will grow up loving you and loving family life. They will bring you grandchildren in pride and happiness, so you can see the fruits of your labor" (every pun intended).

From my experience with working mothers I realized that the housework is a much bigger burden then the children. If you must work get household help for cleaning, laundry and even cooking, so that you can give the time you do have, to your children. If you have a cleaning lady come twice a week you will be amazed at how much more relaxed and happy you will be. The clean house and cooked food will give you a good mood and opportunity to play with you children and teach them.

When you eat from the Tree of Knowledge and decide that bearing children is difficult, it will be. If you feel that you are in seventh heaven with every smile and coo of your child, you won't suffer the punishment of Eve. You'll be in paradise for all the days of your children's growth and development, even if you do have to help Adam.

The Tree of Life

Adam's main transgression was that he added to the words of God. Hashem saw that if Adam can't even keep one rule straight, then He would not be able to trust him with any more divine information. After the couple was expelled, God wanted to protect another tree, "The Tree of Life."

> Genesis 3:22–24
> And the LORD God said, 'The man has now become like one of us, knowing good and evil. He must not be allowed to reach out his hand and take also from the tree of life and eat, and live forever.' So

the LORD God banished him from the Garden of Eden to work the ground from which he had been taken. And He expelled the man and He stationed east of the Garden of Eden the Cherubim and the flame of the ever-turning sword to guard the way to the Tree of Life.

The word *Cherubim* is a giveaway. This word proves that the whole story was a parable. Cherubim, a golden image of two babies, a male and a female with wings facing each other, were in the Holy of Holies on top of the Ark of the Covenant. The ark contained and protected the Ten Commandments and all the Five Books of Moses, which were at its side.

Proverbs 3:1 and 3:18 say: "My son, do not forget my Torah and let your heart guard My commandments … It is a tree of life to those who grasp it, and its supporters are happy."

The Tree of Life is the Torah, the Five Books of Moses. Hashem was very disillusioned by the people of Israel and didn't want them to learn the Torah while they were still drenched in idol worship.

In this parable, the Garden of Eden is the Land of Israel and the Torah is the Tree of Life. After the children of Israel worshiped the golden calf, it was not safe to let them have the Torah, the Tree of Life. They would just turn that Torah into an idol itself. After the sin of the golden calf, the first thing that God tells Moses to do when he goes up Mount Sinai is to make an ark, a golden ark. The Cherubim were placed on top of the ark. God knew that an engraved image was the only thing that the Israelites would really respect. The wings show that the Cherubim would fly away or disappear when they are not needed.

Were man to learn Torah at that early point in history, the sly and cunning would interpret the Torah to their liking and form a new religion. The true meaning of the Torah would be masked by the pagan priests. That is why He had the Levites hide the Torah that Moses wrote in the Holy of Holies. Before Moses died, he commanded the Levites to place the Torah that he wrote next to the Ark of the Covenant inside the Holy of Holies. The Holy Ark was protected by the Cherubim.

> Deuteronomy 31:26–27
> Take this book, the Torah and put it next to the Ark of the Covenant of God, it will be for a witness. For I know your rebelliousness and stubbornness, even when I was living amongst you were rebellious of course you will be after my death.

I found another hint that this story is a parable:

> Genesis 3:19 KJV
> In the sweat of thy face shalt thou eat bread, till thou return unto the ground; for out of it wast thou taken: for dust thou art, and unto dust shalt thou return.

The curse to eat bread cannot possibly be for the whole world. Most of the whole world eats rice as their staple. How would Adam even know what bread is? He didn't have a flour mill or an oven. The NIV translates *lechem* as food, but this is a common Hebrew word that means bread. There is no question about it.

Bread was a staple for the Jewish people even since they left Egypt and ate the bread of affliction, matzo. The curse that Adam will die is not a curse of death for all humanity; it is a curse for the future Israelites that worshipped other gods. They died by the thousands; the streets of Jerusalem were flooded with blood.

> Ezekiel 28:23
> For I will send into her pestilence, and blood into her streets; and the wounded shall be judged in the midst of her by the sword upon her on every side; and they shall know that I am the Lord.

The Israelites were curious to know what their neighbors were doing. They tried out the different cults in the area because they had to "taste." Hashem told them not to sample from the different religions. It was not for their benefit. They did investigate the Canaanite nations and worshipped their idols. This ultimately caused their expulsion from the Land of Israel.

Why did Hashem ask Moses to make Cherubim?

The Cherubim not only covered the Holy ark but God's voice came out from them.

> Exodus 25:22
> And there I will meet with thee, and I will commune with thee from above the mercy seat, from between the two cherubim which are upon the ark of the testimony, of all things which I will give thee in commandment unto the children of Israel.

This goes back to the theme of having children. The Cherubim were figurines of a baby boy and a baby girl. This symbolizes the future generations. Hashem spoke to Moses for the purpose of the future babies. He spoke for us; we are the generation that can fully understand the Torah in every way.

Huldah the Prophetess

Many generations after Moses died there lived a prophetess named Huldah around 640 BCE. When King Josiah cleaned up the Temple from idols a copy of one of the books of Torah was found in the temple. Even though the Torah was given over a thousand years beforehand, no one had a written copy or even recognized the copy that was found. Only Huldah, the prophetess, knew that it was the real thing. Huldah knew that this was the actual Torah because she knew how to read, a very rare skill in her time.

> 2 Kings 22:13-16
> Go and inquire of the LORD for me and for the people and for all Judah about what is written in this book that has been found. Great is the LORD's anger that burns against us because those who have gone before us have not obeyed the words of this book; they have not acted in accordance with all that is written there concerning us. Hilkiah the priest, Ahikam, Akbor, Shaphan and Asaiah went to speak to the prophet Huldah, who was the wife of Shallum son of Tikvah, the son of Harhas, keeper of the wardrobe. She lived in Jerusalem, in the New Quarter. She said to them, "This is what the LORD, the God of Israel, says: Tell the man who sent you to me, 'This is what the LORD says: I am going to bring disaster on this place and its people, according to everything written in the book the king of Judah has read.'"

Josiah wanted everyone to see what the Holy Torah looked like and feel its holy energy. After a tour of the country, the holy scripture was returned to the temple.

Was Adam Destined to Live Forever?

Genesis 3:22

And the LORD God said, 'The man has now become like one of us, knowing good and evil. He must not be allowed to reach out his hand and take also from the tree of life and eat, and live forever.' So the LORD God banished him from the Garden of Eden to work the ground from which he had been taken.

The Jewish religion believes in reincarnation. When you die, you go up to heaven and are judged. If you don't do well, it is possible to get another chance. I wrote about this in my book called *Who Is God?* in the chapter entitled, "Life after Life."

In Genesis 3:23, Hashem is worried that if Adam would receive the Torah before he is ready, he would never be able to reach heaven. Man would take the Torah and change it. If society is not yet literate, no one will ever know that it was changed. Man would live on but never accomplish his mission on earth, because he would have a Torah that has been changed many times over. There would be no way of knowing what really happened at Mount Sinai and what Hashem truly wants from mankind. People would have to just come back to earth in a reincarnation again and again forever. Hashem would lose hope in man ever discovering the truth.

The Tabernacle and the Holy Temple would be a house of protection. It would guard the Holy Torah for the future. After the Temple was destroyed, the Cherubim and the Holy Ark disappeared. However, the Five Books of Moses were found. The goal of this book is to explain how, when and where, The Holy Torah, "God's Hidden Treasure," was discovered and taught to the Jewish people in the format that we have today.

A Generation of Literacy

We don't sufficiently appreciate one of God's most important gifts: the ability to read and write. With this ability, we can learn God's work for ourselves and develop our own personal relationship of love and understanding with the Almighty.

Even today, people try to change the meaning of the Torah, but because we know how to read and write for ourselves, we have the ability to learn it in the original text. Men, women, and children can read the Torah for themselves and check the primary verses. We can discover what was added or subtracted from religious teachings. Today we are able to reveal the deep secrets of the Torah and what it wants to teach us about life. Translations from the original Hebrew are improving and those learning Biblical Hebrew are increasing in numbers and fluency. The Hebrew language is very much alive in Israel. Even young children know enough Hebrew to read and understand the Bible in its original tongue.

Psalm 97:11, "Light is planted for the righteous and the one who has an honest straightforward heart will be happy"

When a righteous person learns Torah, he can reveal the light that God planted in it. If you learn Torah with an honest objective, you will be able to discover the truth.

I asked Hashem questions with a clean slate, no preconceptions or expectations, just like Psalm 97:11, "a straightforward heart." With Hashem's help, I have discovered some fascinating truths that cannot be denied.

CHAPTER 4

The Flood

In my previous books *God Meets the World* and *Who is God?* I wrote a lot about Noah and the Flood. Sometimes I feel that my ideas are so mind boggling, that I don't want to upset my readers too much and write everything in one book. I'm giving you time to absorb the new ideas before I come up with more disclosures.

> Genesis 6:5–8
> The LORD saw how great the wickedness of the human race had become on the earth, and that every inclination of the thoughts of the human heart was only evil all the time. The LORD regretted that he had made human beings on the earth, and his heart was deeply troubled. So the LORD said, 'I will wipe from the face of the earth the human race I have created—and with them the animals, the birds and the creatures that move along the ground—for I regret that I have made them.' But Noah found favor in the eyes of the LORD.

As we described in the previous chapter, Adam wasn't the only man or even the first man. Hashem says he was the first speaking man. Even though the story of Adam and Eve in the Garden of Eden was a parable, Adam was a man, and he was the forefather of Noah, who was the forefather of Abraham. Genesis chapters 5, 10, and 11 write the names of the family line. One of the reasons the Torah writes the details of these family trees is to show that this is not just a fable. It's a story of a man who had children, grandchildren, and great-grandchildren and what their names were.

Noah was living in a world of corruption. There is no mention of idolatry in this story. There were other cities at the time of Noah and their inhabitants were idol worshipers. Hashem wasn't so bothered by them; He was patient. It would take time for man to discover God.

However, when Hashem saw the city of Noah and how people were hurting each other, He was steaming! Finally, there was a group of people who did away with idol worship, and they became corrupt. Noah was six hundred years old when the flood started. Many of the other people of his city were also very old. The people of Noah's generation abandoned their pagan worship. However, after many years without idolatry, they started cheating, stealing, and killing.

These were the first people who were intelligent enough to realize that stone idols are not gods with supernatural powers. Without spending so many hours a week worshipping idols, they had too much time on their hands. Without a systematic religion or government, they invested themselves in new evil behavior. When Hashem saw this, He declared that man should only live 120 years (Genesis 6:3).

This shortened lifespan that God planned was not helping. The corrupt ancestors taught their offspring how to be evil. Hashem wanted to start all over again! Noah was not the only one who was spared. His wife, three sons, and the spouses of those sons were welcome passengers on the ark he built. A family of moral monotheists was chosen to begin a new world. Noah's world was destroyed, but not the whole world. There were many other civilizations all over the planet but they were all idol worshippers. How do I know this? Because of another passage in the Torah that may seem unrelated.

430 Years in Egypt

> Exodus 12:40–41
> Now the sojourning of the children of Israel, who dwelt in Egypt, was four hundred and thirty years. And it came to pass at the end of the four hundred and thirty years, even the selfsame day it came to pass, that all the hosts of the LORD went out from the land of Egypt.

The Torah says that the length of time the Israelite people lived in Egypt was 430 years. The commentaries say that 430 isn't really 430. They assert that for only 210 years the Israelites were in Egypt and that 430 years is to be calculated from the birth of Isaac. This is what I learned as a child and what all Jewish children learn. This commentary always bothered me. How can you teach a child that what the Bible says is not the truth? How can God-fearing people change the simple meaning of the words of the Torah?

Simple Arithmetic

The reason that the commentaries say it was only 210 years is because there just weren't enough generations to account for more. However, my strong faith that the Bible is true to the letter, kept me questioning.

I am glad to tell you that we figured it out. This one was a joint effort between my husband and me. Whoever said that there were only 210 years looked over a major calculation problem.

Take a closer look at the family tree of Moses as an example. Moses was the son of Amram, Amram was the son of Kehat, and Kehat was the son of Levi; then there are only four generations from Jacob to Moses. The three children of Amram are the current generation. Multiply that by four for the four sons of Levi, and you get twelve. Add the children of Moses and Aaron, and you get another generation of 12 x 4. Are there only forty-eight adult Levites?

> Numbers 3:39 says, "The total number of Levites counted at the LORD's command by Moses and Aaron according to their clans, including every male a month old or more, was 22,000."

We learn from Numbers 3:39 that there were 22,000 Levites, and you can double that number because the women were not counted. Even if there were more children per family than are mentioned in that Torah, it still cannot add up. The tribe of Levi was a small tribe. The tribe of Judah had over one hundred thousand able-bodied men. Even if each woman had six children, it is still impossible to arrive at these numbers in only two hundred years. If there were 430 years as the scripture says, then there is a possibility. So what happened to all the down lines? Why don't we see more generations recorded?

The answer lies in a discussion that Moses had with Hashem after the sin of the golden calf.

· Blot Me Out

Exodus 32:31-34

So Moses went back to the LORD and said, 'Oh, what a great sin these people have committed! They have made themselves gods of gold. But now, please forgive their sin—but if not, then blot me out of the book you have written.' The LORD replied to Moses, 'Whoever has sinned against me I will blot out of my book. Now go, lead the people to the place I spoke of, and my angel will go before you. However, when the time comes for me to punish, I will punish them for their sin.'

In summary, Moses said to Hashem, "Forgive their sin or erase me now from your book that you wrote." Hashem answered, "Those who sinned against me I will erase from my book."

When the children of Israel sinned with the golden calf, Moses was very upset. I never heard any rabbi or commentary ask if Hashem really did erase anyone from His book. Hashem told me that He erased the names of entire generations in reaction to Moses wanting his name erased.

Hashem didn't write their names in the Torah because they worshipped idols in Egypt. Hashem also erased the names of the sinners of all the generations who worshipped idols. The names were removed from the Torah, and therefore the calculations are all wrong. The Torah considers a grandchild a child, so a direct descendant can still be considered a son. For example, we call Abraham, "Abraham Our Father."

I always questioned why the names of the children of Ishmael and Esau are written in the Torah. Now I have the answer. They didn't worship idols! The whole world was drenched in idol worship since the creation of the world. But the children of Esau and Ishmael didn't go in their ways; they stayed loyal to Abraham, to Isaac, and to God.

Archeologists have found idols all over the planet that are more than ten thousand years old. They even found an idol that was carbon dated thirty-two thousand years old. The rabbis' whole calculation of the age of the world since Adam is inaccurate because they mistakenly used an incorrect understanding of the Torah as a measure. Hashem didn't write about the idol worshipping civilizations in the Torah. He blotted them out.

Noah's Ark

This also explains why the story of Noah's ark is included in the Bible as the humans living in Noah's time and place were not idol worshippers. The DVD *The Bible's Buried Secrets* shows that there is an ark underground on the mountain range of the Ararat Mountains, exactly the size and shape of Noah's ark as written in the Bible. It's hidden underground and was discovered by very modern technology. The following picture is the place near Mount Ararat that the Ark was discovered with the exact measurements as stated in the Torah. The rims are made of petrified wood. Please see arkdiscovery.com for this and other wonderful discoveries.

http://www.arkdiscovery.com/noah's_ark.htm

Hashem told me that there really was a flood and there was a man named Noah who survived because of his righteous ways. The bigger problem with this story is that we were taught to believe that the flood covered the entire planet earth. If it were a global flood, there would be no koala bears or polar bears left in the world because there would be no way for them to get to the ark. How could Australian animals get to Noah's ark? What about the Native Americans? They were around before and after Noah's ark with no reports of any global floods. The answer is in scripture. It's just a matter of one simple word.

Genesis 7:4–5
Seven days from now I will send rain on the earth for forty days and forty nights, and I will wipe from the face of the earth every living creature I have made. And Noah did all that the LORD commanded him.

The word in Hebrew that is translated to mean "every creature that I have made," is *Yikum*. In modern Hebrew, this word means universe. The reviver of the Hebrew language, a man named Eliezer Ben Yehudah, learned the word from this chapter about Noah and gave it a new meaning.

Yikum

Before we look into the word *Yikum*, I would like to translate the other words in the sentence word for word: "And I will erase all the Yikum that I created from the face of the land."

The word *Yikum* is a rare word in the Bible; it comes from the word *Kum*, which means to stand. In biblical times, a test to determine if people were idolaters was that you brought them to a body of water to drink. If they prostrated themselves to drink, that was considered a sign that they were pagans. Gideon used this system to choose himself an army that had only God-fearing soldiers in Judges 7:5–8.

> So Gideon took the men down to the water. There the LORD told him, 'Separate those who lap the water with their tongues as a dog laps from those who kneel down to drink.' Three hundred of them drank from cupped hands, lapping like dogs. All the rest got down on their knees to drink. The LORD said to Gideon, 'With the three hundred men that lapped I will save you and give the Midianites into your hands. Let all the others go home.' So Gideon sent the rest of the Israelites home but kept the three hundred, who took over the provisions and trumpets of the others.

The civilization of Noah was not a civilization of idol worshippers. They were the descendants of Adam. They learned from Adam that there is one God and He decreed that they work and toil by the sweat of their brow.

At this time there were people in other parts of the world that did not learn that there was one God. Many of them worshipped idols or deified nature. Before the flood, Hashem says that He regrets creating the world. Of course! When the one civilization that didn't believe in idols consisted of a bunch of hoodlums and killers, Hashem felt totally discouraged.

When Hashem says that He will erase the whole *Yikum*, He means that He would destroy the whole civilization of people that are standing and do not prostrate themselves to other gods. The flood was a decree on a civilization of robbers and murderers, not idol worshipers. "The land is full of robbery" (Genesis 6:13).

Another Definition

> Genesis 7:3 says, "Every living thing on the face of the earth was wiped out; people and animals and the creatures that move along the ground and the birds were wiped from the earth. Only Noah was left, and those with him in the ark."

Most of the places that the word *Yikum* is found, it is read *Yakum* meaning he will stand. I did find one other place where the word *yikum* was used:

> Deuteronomy 11:5–7
> It was not your children who saw what he did for you in the wilderness until you arrived at this place, and what he did to Dathan and Abiram, sons of Eliab the Reubenite, when the earth opened its mouth right in the middle of all Israel and swallowed them up with their households, their tents and every living

> thing that belonged to them. But it was your own eyes
> that saw all these great things the LORD has done.

The above NIV translation defines Yikum as the true definition of the word, "everything that belonged to them." In the flood, not only the people were killed but everything that they owned. That is to say that the generation of the flood was destroyed together with their belongings—their cattle, their birds, and even their children.

The flood in Noah's generation was not a flood of the planet earth. It was a local disaster of a very evil place. Hashem wanted Noah to save the animals in order to build a new village with livestock, horses and donkeys for all of his family's needs. However, there was no reason to destroy all of nature all over the world. Any evidence of a global flood is related to the destruction of life on earth before Genesis as I mentioned in the chapter called *In the Beginning.*

Imagine All the People

John Lennon wrote a song, "Imagine," about a world that in his imagination would be a utopia: a world without religion, countries or possessions. Noah's world was just that. They didn't worship idols, and they had no religion. There were no countries yet, so there were no armies. They had no money or valuable possessions such as gold and silver, but still the people were bad. They stole and murdered. They even attacked pregnant women and killed their unborn fetuses.

Religion, politics, and wealth are not the cause of evil in the world; people are. Noah could have been evil just like his friends, but he was a man who thought for himself. The only way there will be a good world is when each and every person thinks for himself. Most people are worried of what others will think of them and their actions reflect those fears.

It's not enough to be good. Hashem gave us laws so we know what good is. The Ten Commandments outline the laws that the Creator of the world decided are the most important in order to have a just and good world. In my book *God Meets the World* I go into the details of every commandment.

We must believe that Hashem loves us and that He is watching. If you don't have that awareness, then you think that people are watching you, even if they aren't. This invites anxiety and paranoia. When you predominantly act on what is acceptable to others, you can never find yourself and develop a strong ideology.

Most governments take the responsibility of determining what is good and what is evil into their own hands; that is why they have not succeeded to make a just and good world. Controlling people through fear and punishment will not change the world but faith in Hashem will. We observe the commandments out of love for Hashem.

My husband wrote the following song, to the tune of "Imagine," asking us to imagine a world where people really believe in God and follow His law.

A World Like Heaven by David Shemesh

Imagine a world like heaven,
People following God.
No more hell on earth,
Truth without any fraud.
Imagine all the people
Living by Torah law.

Imagine there's no wars,
No more blood to spill.
Nothing to kill or die for,
People having just good will.
Imagine all the nations
Living together in peace.
You may say I'm a dreamer,
But I'm not the only one.
I hope we'll all soon follow God's rules,
And the world will be as one.

Imagine no stealing possessions,
I wonder if you can.
No more abominations,
A brotherhood of man.
Imagine all God's creatures,
Respecting life and limb.

You may say I'm Hashem's friend,
But I'm not the only one.
I hope all cruelty will soon end,
Then God and His name will be One.

Each person will be unique,
And have freedom to choose.
The loving respect we seek
No one should abuse.
Imagine knowing that God is above.
That from Him we get our love.

You may say Hashem gives and takes life,
And we can imagine anything.
Let's choose Torah and end strife;
Hashem will take care of everything.

———

The theme of this book is the Torah, God's Hidden Treasure. God decided to write the Torah after he viewed the generation of the flood. He saw that without guidelines, human beings would not develop a good ideology on their own.

He gave the Torah to a generation that wasn't able to fully understand it. The Israelites learned Torah in the desert by heart. They didn't know how to read or write, but they memorized the Torah in order to pass it down through the generations. Hashem knew that the Israelites would sin and forget the oral tradition, so He hid the written Torah until people were educated enough to learn it on their own from the written text.

The people of ancient civilizations were not able to read or write or even to afford to have a book of their own. They followed their leaders. In the case of the Israelites, they followed their neighbors the Canaanites. For centuries people followed their religious hierarchy. Just in the last century, millions followed a madman blindly and approved the murder of millions of others in the Holocaust.

Independent Thinkers

Modern education claims to teach children to think for themselves. That message is not enough to really produce independent thinkers. The school curriculum in America removes the religious factor from all history lessons. Young Americans never heard of the Spanish Inquisition; they don't learn about Crusaders or the history of Buddha and Islam. Many children never heard a Bible story in their life!

When you purposely prevent children from learning specific subjects it doesn't encourage free thinking; it is a continuation of the brainwashing of the masses that began with the Dark Ages. In Israel, the students of public schools learn all of the above. They also allow children to form their own ideas and share them.

In America the public schools don't even allow the students to learn other alternatives to the theory of evolution. Just watch the video called *Evolution Verses Intelligent Design*.

If there were a top quality piece of literature that was so popular that it was translated into 500 languages and now up to 100 million copies were sold and distributed for free every year, year after year, every school would teach their students about this special book. There is a prejudice against the Bible. Even though it is the best seller of all times, public schools in America will not teach it or anything about it. Why?

The original law to form a separation between church and state was because there were many Christian factions and there was prejudice between them. America was founded on the concept of freedom of religion. People came here to escape prejudice and persecution. The Founding Fathers wanted to form a government body that believed in God but without law being determined on the basis on any particular religion in order to promote their ideology.

Is the Bible Religious?

The Old Testament Bible is more like a universal doctrine than a religious one. The Bible relates stories of people who were not perfect. It teaches morals and advice on how to live in this world. The strong prohibition against idol worship is meant to pull you out of religious doctrine. The important commandment to observe Shabbat is not in order to worship on the Sabbath but to rest for our own physical and emotional wellbeing.

The Torah preaches trust in God and prayer. The prophets discouraged the importance of sacrifices in the Holy Temple that were meant to be temporary. All in all, the Old Testament does not give an outline of a religious doctrine. There are many holidays for our enjoyment but not so much for the purpose of worship. These holidays are our celebrations intended for the Jewish people in memory of the Exodus of Egypt, just like Independence day is celebration for the Americans in memory of the victory of the War of Independence in 1776.

The religions of the world have added customs, laws and even books to the Old Testament. Religious proponents seek to control our lives. If we just take the Old Testament Bible at face value, we will not feel that we are being hypnotized into a certain faith. So why not learn it in school?

We are not even allowed to teach the children that there are hundreds of millions of people worldwide who believe in this book. The American youth is so naïve in the subject of religion that they can easily be taken advantage of by different cults. Teenagers looking for spiritualism may turn to taking LSD in order to "get high." The whole drug scene is a result of this godless culture. The best way to get high is to go into the forest and scream out to God with all your soul. Talk to Him about your troubles with a full heart and you will surely feel His presence. That will be a real high not a result of a toxic hallucinogenic. The more you do so, the closer you will get to Hashem and your life will turn around for the best.

When we teach children and adults how to learn the Bible they develop their own ideas and insights. When children develop their own insights, they grow up to be more and more creative and then you can hope for a better world, free of mass hypnosis. It's never too late.

If you prohibit your child from reading a particular book that is your right. You don't want children looking and pornographic magazines at any age. However, a book that is clean and full of famous stories can only open their minds to understanding more about life.

Everyone can benefit from God's wisdom and teachings and pass them to their children and grandchildren even if they are not affiliated with any religion. It is the most honest book that you will find. The Bible has infinite divine intelligence that develops the human brain at any age.

My books are meant to encourage adults and youths to ask questions, see the beauty of the Bible, become inspired to learn, apply what they learned and to teach others. Please send any questions to batyashemesh@gmail.com.

CHAPTER 5

The Everlasting Torah

When we were young, we learned about Moses and how he wrote the Torah on Mount Sinai. In our minds, we saw a man writing on leather parchment. According to modern archeology, we only see some evidence of leather parchment from the end of the First Temple about 500 BCE, and even then it was not popular yet. Habakkuk is a prophet who lived in the seventh century BCE.

> Habakkuk 2:2 says, "And Hashem answered me and said, 'Write the vision and clarify it upon tablets, so that a reader may read it swiftly.'"

Habakkuk is writing and prophesizing before the destruction of the First Temple. He was still chiseling the letters onto stone tablets.

When Did Writing on Parchment Begin?

The oldest evidence of leather parchment found by archeologists appears at the end of the First Temple period, around 586 BCE. The parchments are on display in the Israel Museum in Jerusalem. These findings were very small fragments measuring up to an inch in width and five inches in length. The letters of the ancient Hebrew alphabet are written on them. These fragments appear to be remnants of someone who was learning how to write on parchment. Some of them have the blessing of the high priest (Numbers 6: 24). It has been assessed that these parchments were remnants of a religious article to safeguard a child.

In the Land of Israel Museum in Tel Aviv are bowls and pieces of pottery on which there are writings, including a slate of stone with chiseled inscriptions that mention Nebuchadnezzar, the king of Babylon. He was king in 605 BCE. There is a bowl with ink writing encircling the inside. In the bowl is mentioned in its text as being a book. A *book* in ancient times was a slate of stone, clay, or a vessel of pottery on which ink was written or engraved upon before drying.

The Torah mentions the word *book*, or in Hebrew *sefer*, many times. Deuteronomy 31:24 and 26 mention that Moses finished writing the Torah on a *sefer*, and he put it next to the Holy Ark in the Holy of Holies. The Torah doesn't specify on how many books it was composed, aside from Deuteronomy that Moses calls a book. When the Bible was canonized in the year 200 CE the Torah was divided into five sections and named *The Five Books of Moses*.

The books of the prophets were written on special vessels and placed in the Holy Temple for safekeeping by their authors but, of course, not in the Holy of Holies, where it was forbidden to enter.

The Assyrians and the Babylonians wrote cuneiform on clay tablets using their ancient letterings; they also wrote on parchment from the sixth century BCE. Writing on animal skins only started to be common in Asia Minor in the fifth century BCE as well. The wider use of parchment in the shape of a scroll began in Pergamum in what today is northwest Turkey. A great library was built in Pergamum that compared to the Library of Alexandria. Parchment was then substituted for papyrus; whose prices rose because the reed was overharvested toward extinction in the Nile River area.

There was some writing on animal skin in ancient Egypt for the records of the pharaohs, but it wasn't nearly as popular as papyrus. Papyrus use begins around 3100 BCE. Some Egyptian Fourth Dynasty (2613 to 2494 BCE) royal texts were written on parchment, but like the architectural genius of Egyptian pyramids, was not recorded. The system of writing on parchment had also been forgotten. As mentioned earlier, the popular use of parchment for writing began at the end of the first Temple period around 560 BCE.

Papyrus and parchment are both perishable. In the Museum of the *Hechal Shlomo* synagogue in Jerusalem old parchments from a hundred and even two hundred years old are exhibited. They are very discolored and brittle. The Dead Sea Scrolls were kept intact for two thousand years because the Essenes preserved them in clay vessels in mineral-rich dry air within caves near the Dead Sea. Shortly after these parchments were removed from that environment, they began to crumble. Today those scrolls are preserved in special controlled conditions of heat and low humidity in the Israel Museum in Jerusalem.

We learn from this that writing on parchment is not a strong and permanent way of preserving holy words. When Hashem told Moses that the Bible would be a witness, Deuteronomy 31:26, He had in mind that it would last for about a thousand years until the Israelites would be able to write their own scrolls. Therefore, Moses wrote on stone, the standard way of writing at the time. Very few Israelites knew how to read and write, but Moses was brought up in the palace of the king receiving a full education of reading, writing, and arithmetic.

Moses taught his educational skills to Joshua. When the children of Israel entered the Land of Israel, Joshua taught them the Ten Commandments and the Torah. He wrote the words of the Torah on stone.

> Joshua 8:32 says, "There, in the presence of the Israelites, Joshua wrote on stones a copy of the law of Moses."

Mount Sinai

Exodus, 19:10–13

And the LORD said to Moses, "Go to the people and consecrate them today and tomorrow. Have them wash their clothes and be ready by the third day, because on that day the LORD will come down on Mount Sinai in the sight of all the people, put limits for the people around the mountain and tell them, be careful that you do not approach the mountain or touch the foot of it. Whoever touches the mountain is to be put to death.

Exodus, 19:16–19

On the morning of the third day there was thunder and lightning, with a thick cloud over the mountain, and a very loud trumpet blast. Everyone in the camp trembled. Then Moses led the people out of the camp to meet with God, and they stood at the foot of the mountain. Mount Sinai was covered with smoke, because the LORD descended on it in fire. The smoke billowed up from it like smoke from a furnace, and the whole mountain trembled violently. As the sound of the trumpet grew louder and louder, Moses spoke and the voice of God answered him.

At this point, the Israelites heard all the Ten Commandments from the voice of God. After the last commandment, they begged Moses to ask God to speak to him silently and that Moses should then tell them what He said.

> Exodus 24:3–7
>
> When Moses went and told the people all the LORD's words and laws, they responded with one voice, "Everything the LORD has said we will do." Moses then wrote down everything the LORD had said. He got up early the next morning and built an altar at the foot of the mountain and set up twelve stone pillars representing the twelve tribes of Israel. Then he sent young Israelite men, and they offered burnt offerings and sacrificed young bulls as fellowship offerings to the LORD. Moses took half of the blood and put it in bowls, and the other half he splashed against the altar. Then he took the Book of the Covenant and read it to the people. They responded, "We will do everything the LORD has said; we will obey."

The Book of the Covenant did not include the words of the whole Torah, because many of the events in the Torah had yet to occur. It included the whole book of Genesis and the first half of Exodus until the end of chapter 23.

The Mountain

Moses was in a cloud for six days before he went up to the mountain for an additional forty days. The following picture is a photograph of the true Mount Sinai that was discovered in Saudi Arabia. Right near Midian, the home of Jethro, Moses saw the burning bush on this mountain when he was tending the sheep of his father-in-law.

Above - Aaron Sen a contemporary explorer stands in the encampment area of Mt. Sinai with the blackened peak in the distance. See:
http://www.arkdiscovery.com/mt sinai found.htm

When Moses came to his destination on Mount Sinai, what do you think would be the first thing that God would talk about?

Maybe the first commandment? Maybe other important ideology?

No, the first thing that Moses learned was how to make the Golden Ark.

Exodus 25:10 says, "Have them make an ark of acacia wood—two and a half cubits long, a cubit and a half wide, and a cubit and a half high. Overlay it with pure gold, both inside and out, and make a gold molding around it."

Moses went up to Mount Sinai to receive the Tablets of the Ten Commandments. Before he receives them he must learn how to prepare an ark for their safe keeping. God knew the future; He knew that the Israelites would not keep the commandments. He knew that they would serve other gods, until a time when idol worship would go out of style. God also knew that eventually the children of Israel would be intelligent enough to appreciate the Torah. The Torah was written in stone so that it would last for almost two millennia. Before Moses completed the Torah, God wanted to provide a sanctuary to keep the Tablets of the Covenant and place the Holy Torah adjacent to it.

It took Moses over forty years to compile and transmit the Torah, from the site of the burning bush and throughout the experiences in the wilderness. Before Moses died, he told the Levites to place his completed book in the Holy of Holies next to the Ark of the Covenant.

> Deuteronomy 31:26–27
> Moses commanded the Levites the bearers of the covenant saying, "Take this book of Torah and place it at the side of the Ark of the Covenant of Hashem your God, and it shall be there for you as a witness. For I know your rebelliousness and your stiff neck. Behold while I am still alive with you today, you have rebelled against Hashem and surely you will do so after my death."

When writing the Torah, God had to consider the future. Moses said that the children of Israel would stray, forsake the Torah, and be severely punished.

Deuteronomy 31:28–29
> "Gather to me all the elders of your tribes and your officers, and I shall speak these words into their ears, and call heaven and earth to bear witness against them. For I know that after my death you will surely act corruptly, and you will stray from the path that I have commanded you, and evil will befall you at the end of days, if you do what is evil in the eyes of Hashem, to anger Him through your handiwork."

Thus, Hashem knew that the children of Israel would sin. Then Hashem planned accordingly. The children of Israel had to go through a many trials and tribulations until they were intelligent enough to read, write and understand the Torah.

The Golden Calf

After all the miracles that Hashem did for the Israelites, and after all the warnings, they still needed an idol, the golden calf. When Moses was late in returning from the mountain after the Ten Commandments were given the Israelites gave up hope that he would ever come down and built an idol to replace him. Moses was furious when he descended and saw the golden calf.

Exodus 32:19–20
> When Moses approached the camp and saw the calf and the dancing, his anger burned and he threw the tablets out of his hands, breaking them to pieces at the foot of the mountain. And he took the calf the people had made and burned it in the fire; then he ground it to powder, scattered it on the water and made the Israelites drink it.

Aaron's Sin

Exodus 32:21-24

He said to Aaron, "What did these people do to you, that you led them into such great sin?" "Do not be angry, my lord," Aaron answered. "You know how prone these people are to evil." They said to me, "Make us gods who will go before us. As for this fellow Moses who brought us up out of Egypt, we don't know what has happened to him." So I told them, "Whoever has any gold jewelry, take it off." Then they gave me the gold, and I threw it into the fire, and out came this calf!'"

Did the golden calf really come out of the fire all by itself? Let's bring in the evidence.

Exodus 32:1-4

When the people saw that Moses was so long in coming down from the mountain, they gathered around Aaron and said, "Come, make us gods who will go before us. As for this fellow Moses who brought us up out of Egypt, we don't know what has happened to him." Aaron answered them, "Take off the gold earrings that your wives, your sons and your daughters are wearing, and bring them to me." So all the people took off their earrings and brought them to Aaron. He took what they handed him and made it into an idol cast in the shape of a calf, fashioning it with a tool. Then they said, "These are your gods, Israel, who brought you up out of Egypt."

The above verses relate that Aaron carved the idol himself. Why is he lying to Moses?

The answer that we learned in school was that Aaron was afraid that the Israelites would kill him and then he was afraid of his own brother.

Hashem chose Aaron to accompany Moses in Egypt because he was brave enough to face Pharaoh. He was no scaredy-cat. Aaron also heard the Ten Commandments. He heard God say that if is forbidden to bear false witness. If the leaders cannot keep the covenant of God, how can the simple people do any better?

A year after the golden calf, the tabernacle was built and Aaron was still the high priest. Why would Hashem allow Aaron such a prestigious position after such a grave sin? Aaron had a cousin, Korach, who fought for his right to be the high priest. He witnessed Aaron in action, and that's why he protested that he was really more worthy than Aaron was for the job. You can read the full story in Numbers chapter 16.

The reason Hashem forgave Aaron was because he was so special. Aaron was beloved by the people. He didn't want to become their enemy even when they wanted to sin. It says in *Ethics of the Fathers* 1:12, "Be like the students of Aaron, love people, chase after peace, love mankind and bring them closer to Torah."

The Israelites were going wild when Moses was absent and they demanded a golden calf replacement for him. Aaron wanted to calm them down by stalling them until the gold melted and the craftsmanship was completed. He knew that fighting them would not help. Hashem forgave Aaron for his act of mercy even though it was the wrong thing to do because that type of fear can really compromise a person. However, at a later date when Aaron yelled at the Israelites at the Waters of Meribah, then God said, "You are not going to enter the land! If you can yell now when the Israelites are dying of thirst and legitimately crying for water, then you certainly could have yelled when they demanded an idol!" (See Numbers 20:1)

I have another question about this episode. How can Aaron possibly suppose that Moses would believe such a story? Is Moses, the greatest prophet that ever lived, going to believe in the magical eruption of a golden calf?

Aaron's intention in creating this idol was to stall the people. He was an expert at gold craftsmanship, the best in the camp. The problem was that it didn't work and time flew. He was getting so much pressure from the Israelites that he couldn't proceed slowly. They wouldn't allow him time to perfect his work. Time went so fast that it felt like the gold just turned into a calf.

Aaron was also punished for this sin. He was very talented in the art of gold craftsmanship but the hands that created the golden calf would not create the holy vessels of the Tabernacle. Hashem found new young talents.

> Exodus 31:1-6
> Then the LORD said to Moses, "See, I have chosen Bezalel son of Uri, the son of Hur, of the tribe of Judah, and I have filled him with the Spirit of God, with wisdom, with understanding, with knowledge and with all kinds of skills— to make artistic designs for work in gold, silver and bronze, to cut and set stones, to work in wood, and to engage in all kinds of crafts. Moreover, I have appointed Oholiab son of Ahisamak, of the tribe of Dan, to help him. Also I have given ability to all the skilled workers to make everything I have commanded you."

Bezalel and Oholiab were appointed to make the golden cover for the Holy Ark in addition to the Menorah and the other holy vessels. For this task he chose two people who were pure. Free of sin. The most important accomplishment of the miracles of Exodus was the preservation of the Torah. That is why Hashem's first words to Moses on Mount

Sinai were the detailed description of the Ark that would preserve the Torah, the law of Moses.

An altar was discovered at the site of Jabal al-Lawz, which I believe is the true Mount Sinai in Saudi Arabia. The Saudis found gold dust in the area left over from the remnants of the golden calf that Moses commanded the Israelites to destroy and turn to powder. There is a gate around it because the Saudis forbid entry into the site.

Aaron Sen stands next to government sign at base of Mt. Sinai acknowledging this archaeological area. http://www.arkdiscovery.com/mt_sinai_found.htm

http://www.arkdiscovery.com/mt__sinai_found.htm

This altar was actually a pedestal for the golden calf. There are drawings of calves on this altar.

http://www.arkdiscovery.com/mt__sinai_found.htm

The drawings on the stones of the altar are very elementary. They reflect a simple people very far below the level of intelligence of their leaders. In Egypt the art was full of intricate details. These pictures are appropriate for a six- or seven-year-old child. The Israelites were intelligent enough to understand the teachings of Moses. If they had drawn these figures they would probably be more artistic.

Saudi archaeologists who did the survey of the area found that there were about three hundred rock art sites in northwest Saudi Arabia and about fifty rock art sites with bovine in the al-Bad'/Jabal al-Lawz area. Hashem told me that native graffiti artists had sketched them as they roamed the desert after the Hebrews left the area because they were so excited to find runaway cattle or even some meat that was left behind from the sacrifices. That would also explain the primitive level of the sketches. These pictures served the purpose of giving other Nomads a sign that they were there. It might have been their emblem or marker for direction. Nomads roaming the desert would have had rudimentary education at best, so they would use pictures instead of a written language.

There is a lot of information about Jabal el Lawz on line and even on YouTube. There are also many books and videos to purchase that prove that the stories of Exodus really happened. Timothy Mahoney wrote a beautiful book and documentary of these archeological findings called *Patterns of Evidence*. Go to their website for more information and literature at patternsofevidence.com.

The Torah Is a Witness

Deuteronomy 31:26, "Take this book of Torah and place it at the side of the Ark of the Covenant of Hashem your God, and it shall be there for you as a witness."

The Torah was placed in the Holy of Holies next to the Holy Ark. How can the Torah be a witness or a proof? The Holy of Holies was off-limits completely. Only the high priest could enter the Holy of Holies on Yom Kippur, the holiest day of the year. He went there to pray for the nation and exited promptly. He didn't read the Bible when he was inside.

God knew that the Torah had to be protected, so he made strict laws about where and how to keep it. The Torah was still whole and intact when Nebuchadnezzar took it to Babylon with the rest of the holy vessels at the time of the destruction of the First Temple but the Holy Ark with the tablets was never found.

The Next Generations

Since the Israelites were in Egypt, they never really ousted their idols. Joshua reprimands the Israelites to do away with their idols before his death.

Joshua 24:19-24

Joshua said to the people, "You are not able to serve the LORD. He is a holy God; he is a jealous God. He will not forgive your rebellion and your sins. If you forsake the LORD and serve foreign gods, he will turn and bring disaster on you and make an end of you, after he has been good to you."

But the people said to Joshua, "No! We will serve the LORD."

Then Joshua said, "You are witnesses against yourselves that you have chosen to serve the LORD."

"Yes, we are witnesses," they replied.

"Now then," said Joshua, "throw away the foreign gods that are among you and yield your hearts to the LORD, the God of Israel."

And the people said to Joshua, "We will serve the LORD our God and obey him."

After the death of Joshua, the Israelites sinned even more. They worshiped idols and assimilated with the non-Jews in the Land of Canaan. Throughout the First Temple Period, even when the Israelites observed the Holy Temple services, they forgot most of the other commandments.

Ezekiel 20:27-31
   Therefore, son of man, speak to the people of Israel and say to them, "The Sovereign LORD says: In this also your ancestors blasphemed me by being unfaithful to me: When I brought them into the land I had sworn to give them and they saw any high hill or any leafy tree, there they offered their sacrifices, made offerings that aroused my anger, presented their fragrant incense and poured out their drink offerings. Then I said to them: What is this high place you go to? Therefore, say to the Israelites: 'This is what the Sovereign LORD says: Will you defile yourselves the way your ancestors did and lust after their vile images? When you offer your gifts—the sacrifice of your children in the fire—you continue to defile yourselves with all your idols to this day. Am I to let you inquire of me, you Israelites? As surely as I live, declares the Sovereign LORD, I will not let you inquire of me.'

The Holy Temple was made to serve as a safe storage place for the Torah and the holy tablets as well as a place where people could feel Hashem's presence. When the people stopped worshipping Hashem and sacrificed their own children to idolatry, Hashem decided to destroy the temple.

Nebuchadnezzar, the king of Babylon, entered the Holy Land with his armies and commenced what would be the first major massacre of Jews in history. The streets were flooded with blood and the refugees were taken to exile for seventy years as the prophets foresaw.

> Jeremiah 29:10-11
> This is what the LORD says: "When seventy years are completed for Babylon, I will come to you and fulfill my good promise to bring you back to this place. For I know the plans I have for you," declares the LORD, "plans to prosper you and not to harm you, plans to give you hope and a future.

Ezra the Scribe

A few years before the seventy years are over, the Bible introduces a new character, Ezra the scribe. A scribe was a scholar, was highly literate and had the knowledge and skill to write on parchment. Ezra was a court Jew. He worked for King Cyrus the Great, one of the first humane kings in history.

King Cyrus conquered Babylon in 539 BCE. On a clay cylinder, he described how he captured the city and it describes his three main principles of freedom; religious equality, return of slaves and displaced peoples to their national homes, and the restoration of destroyed temples. This cylinder is situated in the British Museum in London. A replica of the Cyrus cylinder, the first written charter of human rights, was placed at the United Nations Headquarters in 1971 in New York City and translated into the six official UN languages. See the following website for more details about this amazing king.

www.iranchamber.com/history/cyrus/
cyrus_charter.php

The policies of King Cyrus mark the beginning of modern society. The King gave Ezra written permission to return to Jerusalem with all of the Jews of the Babylonian exile and rebuild the Holy Temple in Jerusalem.

> Ezra 6:3–5
>
> In the first year of King Cyrus, Cyrus the king issued a decree: "Concerning the house of God at Jerusalem, let the temple, the place where sacrifices are offered, be rebuilt and let its foundations be retained, its height being 60 cubits and its width 60 cubits; with three layers of huge stones and one layer of timbers. And let the cost be paid from the royal treasury. Also let the gold and silver utensils of the house of God, which Nebuchadnezzar took from the temple in Jerusalem and brought to Babylon, be returned and brought to their places in the temple in Jerusalem; and you shall put them in the house of God."

Thus, King Cyrus directed Ezra to Babylon to collect all the vessels of the Holy Temple. Among them were the original tablets of the Five Books of Moses. King Cyrus was very excited to let Ezra rebuild the temple. The book of Ezra starts with the story of Cyrus, ruler of Persia.

> Ezra 1:2–3
>
> This is what Cyrus king of Persia says: "The LORD, the God of heaven, has given me all the kingdoms of the earth and he has appointed me to build a temple for him at Jerusalem in Judah. Any of his people among you may go up to Jerusalem in Judah and build the temple of the LORD, the God of Israel, the God who is in Jerusalem, and may their God be with them."

Among these findings was the first original Torah that was written by Moses. Ezra 7:14 reads, "concerning the Torah of your God that is in your hands."

How did it get into his hands?

King Cyrus asked Ezra to read the Torah and translate it for him. When he learned about the God of Israel the king was happy to give permission for Ezra to build a Temple for god and for the safekeeping of the Holy Torah. Ezra took the original Torah that was written by Moses to Jerusalem. When the Jews saw the Torah in its original format, they immediately bowed down and accepted to fulfill its contents.

> Ezra 3:3 says, "And they built an Altar of the God of Israel ... as written in the Torah of Moses."

The scripture continues with all the details of the commandments that the Jews started keeping in accordance with the Torah. They were so excited that the Torah was found that they wanted to do everything that is written in it.

> Nehemiah 8:5–8
> Ezra opened the book. All the people could see him because he was standing above them; and as he opened it, the people all stood up. Ezra praised the LORD, the great God; and all the people lifted their hands and responded, "Amen! Amen!" Then they bowed down and worshiped the LORD with their faces to the ground. The Levites—Jeshua, Bani, Sherebiah, Jamin, Akkub, Shabbethai, Hodiah, Maaseiah, Kelita, Azariah, Jozabad, Hanan and Pelaiah— instructed the people in the Law while the people were standing there. They read from the Book of the Law of God, making it clear and giving the meaning so that the people understood what was being read.

The nation didn't understand the Torah, so the Levites were explaining it to them. The following passage gives more evidence that the Jews did not know what was written in the Torah.

> Nehemiah 8:1–3
> All the people came together as one in the square before the Water Gate. They told Ezra the teacher of the Law to bring out the Book of the Law of Moses, which the LORD had commanded for Israel. So on the first day of the seventh month Ezra the priest brought the Law before the assembly, which was made up of men and women and all who were able to understand. He read it aloud from daybreak till noon as he faced the square before the Water Gate in the presence of the men, women and others who could understand. And all the people listened attentively to the Book of the Law.

Hashem had Moses write the Torah on stone so that it would last for many centuries without any special treatment. The minute the Jews saw the Torah in its original form, they felt its powerful energy and bowed down. They didn't need proof that it was from God. They just felt it in their souls.

The people were very sorry that they hadn't kept the Torah. Ezra told them not to cry:

> Nehemiah 8:9 "Do not mourn and do not weep, for all the people were weeping as they heard the words of the Torah."

It is obvious that the people did not know anything about the Torah. However, they trusted Ezra one hundred percent that the Torah that they were shown was from Hashem.

Nehemiah 8:13–17

On the second day of the month, the heads of all the families, along with the priests and the Levites, gathered around Ezra the teacher to give attention to the words of the Law. They found written in the Law, which the LORD had commanded through Moses, that the Israelites were to live in temporary shelters during the festival of the seventh month and that they should proclaim this word and spread it throughout their towns and in Jerusalem: 'Go out into the hill country and bring back branches from olive and wild olive trees, and from myrtles, palms and shade trees, to make temporary shelters'—as it is written. So the people went out and brought back branches and built themselves temporary shelters on their own roofs, in their courtyards, in the courts of the house of God and in the square by the Water Gate and the one by the Gate of Ephraim. The whole company that had returned from exile built temporary shelters and lived in them. From the days of Joshua son of Nun until that day, the Israelites had not celebrated it like this. And their joy was very great.

"Temporary shelters" are really *Succoth*, or tabernacles. The Jews did not keep the holiday of *Succoth* since the days of Joshua. This means that all those years of the kings of Judah and Israel the chosen people did not observe the holidays. They were too busy worshipping idols. What they did preserve was the system of kosher slaughter, circumcision and laws of burial. Those laws were passed down from father to son through the holy priests and Levites.

The most important purpose of the sacrifices was to make sure that people don't kill animals viciously. God knew that the skill of kosher slaughter could not have simply been written down to be remembered; it must be taught through apprenticeship. The sacrifices in the temple were observed daily even in the worst of times until the actual destruction of the temple. That's why we still know how to slaughter animals painlessly. Those same priests also performed the circumcision, another ritual that was practiced and never forgotten.

There were always some scholars and prophets who knew the Torah by heart but they were scarce. Ezra was a Cohen, his forefathers worked as teachers and priests. His family learned the Torah by heart and passed it down from generation to generation. The system for learning was by chanting. When words are studied through a melody they are memorized forever. When Ezra got a hold of the written Torah he knew exactly how to enunciate every word.

Ezra made one copy of the Torah to read in the temple court, and the original was placed in the Holy Temple. Ezra also started building houses of assembly in Jerusalem. These buildings were meant for the people to gather together to learn Torah from the wise men of the community. Each building had a Torah scroll for the community to share. In English we call this structure a synagogue. The Torah Scroll consisted of all the Five Books of Moses.

The following photograph is a picture of an open Torah Scroll. When the Torah scroll is opened the congregation rises in respect.

An Israeli holding up a Torah Scroll in Jerusalem next to the Western Wall.

It was centuries later, after the Hasmonean victory, that these synagogues appeared in every village across the country. Every synagogue had at least one Torah scroll for the whole congregation from which to read and learn. Today the synagogue is a center for communal worship as well as a place to learn Torah.

At the time of Ezra and Nehemiah, there was a minority of Israelites living in the land of Israel. The few Jews that remained were mostly in Jerusalem and had married women from the heathens. Ezra came to Jerusalem with an entourage of 42,000. Most Jews remained in Babylon even though the Holy temple had been rebuilt. Three hundred years later bring us to the time of the Hashmonean rebellion and Chanukah.. By that time, the land was populated with Jews from North to South. In the next couple of chapters, I will go back in time to explain how the population increased so dramatically.

CHAPTER 6

The Women's Role

When the Torah was given at Mount Sinai, it was given to men, women, and children. Judaism encourages women to be brave and strong. Our sages say, "In the merit of righteous women our forefathers were freed from Egypt." In the First Temple era, the Israelite fathers sinned. They worshipped idols, sacrificed their children and cheated on their wives. This chapter will teach you that in the merit of righteous women, the Second Holy Temple of Jerusalem was built and the Torah was saved forever.

Before we discuss the Second Temple Period, I would like to review the stories of a few righteous women in the Bible. Let's start with Sarah, the first matriarch, the wife of Abraham.

Sarah

> Genesis 21:12, "Everything that Sarah says to you listen to her, because your descendants from Isaac will be called your seed."

In ancient times, a woman was obligated to obey her husband, not the other way around. God told Abraham to listen to Sarah on everything. He could have said, "Sarah is right; you should send away Ishmael." Instead Hashem said, "Everything that Sarah says listen to her." Hashem respected Sarah's judgment. He wanted Abraham to trust her in every way and to let her be his guide. Sarah was not blinded by Abraham's worries. Her decision was based on the urgent need to protect her son.

Hashem would like men to listen to their wives' intuition before making decisions. As a woman she spends more time with the children than the father does; her opinion is very important. When a woman knows that she can make decisions she can be a much stronger and more responsible parent. The father should let his wife make family decisions if he trusts her and knows that she is only considering the best for the children and the family. There is a certain intuition that good women have that is above the natural wisdom of man.

Rachel

> Genesis 30:1–2
> When Rachel saw that she was not bearing Jacob any children, she became jealous of her sister. So she said to Jacob, "Give me children, or I'll die!" Jacob became angry with her and said, "Am I in the place of God, who has kept you from having children?"

We learned this story when we were in sixth grade. Our teacher asked us, "Why was Jacob so angry at Rachel?" She told us that it was because Rachel said, "I will die." We cannot live only for the purpose of having children.

Rabbi Amnon Yitzchak from Israel once asked a secular Jew, "What do you live for?"

"My children," he said.

So the rabbi asked, "What will they live for?"

"For their children" the man retorted.

The rabbi then asked, "If you live for your children, and they live for theirs, then why doesn't Hashem skip all the generations and create the children that live for themselves?"

We are created in God's image not just to have other children but to cherish our own special souls. You are your Mommy's baby. She didn't give birth to you merely so that you should bring her grandchildren. She had you, for you.

Of course, men and women want children of their own, but if we feel that we would die without them, we may overprotect them, not always to their benefit. We should want to have children in order to give life, happiness, and of course, love.

Being a mother was the best career a woman could have when Rachel was alive. Jacob understood that Rachel couldn't face her sister Leah or the world if she didn't have a baby. He was angry that she was even willing to give up on her own life, which would have caused him great suffering.

As it worked out, Rachel died after the birth of Benjamin. As a result of that loss Jacob became overprotective. He favored Rachel's sons Joseph and Benjamin, causing jealousy and the eventual kidnapping of Joseph.

When Rachel said, "Give me children, or I will die," she was interrupted by her husband. If he had let her finish her words, he would have heard her say, "Give me children or I will die barren, for I foresee that I will die young." Instead of getting angry, Jacob should have just listened to what she had to say and then prayed for her, as his father and mother, Isaac and Rebecca, prayed when they didn't have children.

When Jacob and his family decided to return to Israel from Haran, Rachel had stolen her father's idol. Jacob said that anyone who has the idol shall die.

Genesis 31:31–32

Jacob answered Laban, "I was afraid, because I thought you would take your daughters away from me by force. But if you find anyone who has your gods, that person shall not live. In the presence of our relatives, see for yourself whether there is anything of yours here with me; and if so, take it." Now Jacob did not know that Rachel had stolen the gods.

From that day on, Rachel knew that she would die young. If Jacob had been more understanding, Rachel might have admitted stealing her father's idols. If Jacob's curse could kill, his blessings could be the antidote. Jacob made her feel so badly that she didn't dare confess to what she had done.

As I mentioned above Rachel died at the childbirth of her second son, Benjamin. At the time of birth, she called him *Benoni*, the son of my affliction. Benjamin was the name given by Jacob, which means son of my right hand. (Genesis 35:16).

Jacob named his son Benjamin to remind him that Rachel was close to him like his right hand. He was sorry that he yelled at her. Jacob jumped at her and made her feel so bad that she never told him of her vision. All along she kept the secret that she knew she would die young.

Why did Rachel steal the idol? Our sages tell us that she didn't want her father worshiping this idol. She knew that her father would be very upset when they left and he would resort to idol worship for consolement.

Mama Rochel

The Lord says in Jeremiah 31:15, "A voice is heard in Ramah, mourning and great weeping, Rachel weeping for her children and refusing to be comforted, because they are no more."

Rachel wept for her husband's children. Rachel was the mother of Joseph and Benjamin, two of the twelve tribes. Most of her children were stepchildren and nephews. It doesn't matter; she is called "Mama Rochel" (Rochel is Rachel in the Yiddish language). She is considered the mother of the whole Jewish people for her devotion and prayer for all her children. Today, every day, two busloads of Israelis travel in armored buses to pray at Rachel's grave, which is in Arab Territory. The following picture is a photograph of her burial place.

Moses Is Saved by Three Women

Yocheved, or Jochebed in the English Bible, was the mother of Moses. She was quite independent. At a time when baby boys were being drowned in the Nile, she had the guts to place little Moses in a basket on that same river.

Her daughter Miriam was also very brave. She spoke to the daughter of Pharaoh, who at the time was also like a queen.

Excavations show that Pharoah's daughter had her own palace. Miriam had wit and self-confidence. In Exodus 2:5–10, Miriam decided, on her own, that her mother would nurse her baby brother for Pharaoh's daughter. This young girl took steps to protect baby Moses and offered her mother's services to the distinguished princess.

Pharaoh's daughter knew that the baby was a Hebrew; she saw his circumcision. Bravely she decided to adopt him anyway. The Israelite people named Pharaoh's daughter Batya, which means the Daughter of God. She was a praiseworthy woman in the eyes of Hashem. This act of Batya showed that even though she wasn't the biological mother of Moses, she had the motherly instinct to protect a helpless baby. If you are not a biological mother, you still can use your feminine strength to care for and protect a child that you adopt or care for.

Inheritance

In Numbers 27:1–11 there is a story of the daughters of Zelophehad. This is an account of a family of five daughters with no sons. When the father died, the girls came to Moses and said, "Our father died. … Give us an inheritance with the brothers of our father."

In those days, women did not inherit land. It was quite brazen for the daughters to have any demands. However, God understood them and said in Numbers 27:7–8,

> You must certainly give them property as an inheritance among their father's relatives and give their father's inheritance to them. "Say to the Israelites, 'If a man dies and leaves no son, give his inheritance to his daughter.'"

That was the first time in history that women's property rights were considered. Many years will have passed before women would have full rights of inheritance. Moses under Hashem's guidance was the first leader to extend a father's inheritance to his daughters.

Job and His Daughters

Job 1:1-5 KJV

There was a man in the land of Uz, whose name was Job; and that man was perfect and upright, and one that feared God, and eschewed evil. And there were born unto him seven sons and three daughters. His substance also was seven thousand sheep, and three thousand camels, and five hundred yoke of oxen, and five hundred she asses, and a very great household; so that this man was the greatest of all the men of the east. And his sons went and feasted in their houses, everyone his day; and sent and called for their three sisters to eat and to drink with them. And it was so, when the days of their feasting were gone about, that Job sent and sanctified them, and rose up early in the morning, and offered burnt offerings according to the number of them all: for Job said, "It may be that my sons have sinned, and cursed God in their hearts." Thus did Job continually.

In the above passage we see two hints that the girls were not treated like the boys. In Job 1:4, the sons call the sisters to come feast with them. The women don't own houses themselves and are merely guests. In 1:5, Job sacrificed burnt offerings for his sons but not for his daughters.

Even though it was accepted practice not to leave any inheritance to girls, Job felt that all his suffering was because he didn't appreciate his girls enough. He wasn't planning on including them in his inheritance, and he was a very wealthy man. Job's girls were not the owners of the wealth; therefore, the brothers could have felt powerful compared to them and abused them accordingly. If they got drunk, the girls would be susceptible to even more abuse. That's why Job said, "It may be that my sons have sinned, and cursed God in their hearts." He was afraid that his sons were abusing their sisters, but Job was not brave enough to crash the party and investigate.

This goes to show that it isn't enough to be good. You have to be strong enough to fight evil. Job's children were punished because of the evil that they were doing. Job himself was reproved because he had the opportunity to oppose that evil but didn't.

After Hashem gave Job a second chance, he made sure to give his girls rights equal to their brothers. Job must have made the right decision, because not only was he subsequently free of troubles, he prospered more than ever and lived until he was 140 years old.

> Job 42:12-17 KJV
> So the LORD blessed the latter end of Job more than his beginning: for he had fourteen thousand sheep, and six thousand camels, and a thousand yoke of oxen, and a thousand she asses. He had also seven sons and three daughters. And he called the name of the first Jemima; and the name of the second Kezia; and the name of the third Kerenhappuch. And in all the land were no women found so fair as the daughters of Job, and their father gave them inheritance among their brethren. After this lived Job 140 years, and saw his sons, and his sons' sons, even four generations. So Job died, being old and full of days.

Job had sons and daughters and he bequeathed his wealth to his sons and daughters in order to repent his former sin of leaving his first daughters out of his will.

This statement is written at the end of the whole story of Job after all the tragedy that happened to him.

The Maternal Line

Today Judaism is passed down through the maternal line. If your mother is Jewish and your father is not, you are considered Jewish by Jewish law and by Israeli law. If your father is Jewish and your mother is not, you are not deemed Jewish. However, every Jewish father has an obligation to give his children a Jewish education. If their mother isn't Jewish, the father should try to convert his children to Judaism after they are old enough to understand.

If your parents are both Jewish, but come from different ethnic backgrounds the father's tradition is followed. The priesthood also is transferred through the paternal lineage. This is the custom that is followed to this day. If we thus follow the traditions of the father, why do we follow the nationality of the mother?

The Paternal Line

Before the return of the Jews to Zion in the year 539 BCE, the Jewish line was paternal. Genesis 25:19, "And these are the generations of Isaac, Abraham's son: Abraham begat Isaac." Abraham was willing to take Hagar, an Egyptian woman, in order to have offspring from his seed. King Solomon was married only to non-Jewish women, yet all his children were considered part of the nation of Israel. Rehoboam, his son became king.

There is a law in the Torah that a soldier is allowed to take a beautiful girl from the enemy camp and marry her (Deuteronomy 21:10–14). This law shows that if the father were an Israelite, he could build a home with a single girl from the gentiles after she mourned her parents, agreeing to leave them forever. It seems that it was perfectly acceptable to marry a woman from another nation because the nationality was determined according to the father.

How did things change?

Well, let's start from 2 Kings, chapter 17. The chapter explains how bad the children of Israel and of Judah were. They worshipped idols and trees and even brought their children as sacrifices to the gods.

> 2 Kings 17:14–15
> But they would not listen and were as stiff-necked as their ancestors, who did not trust in the LORD their God. They rejected his decrees and the covenant he had made with their ancestors and the statutes he had warned them to keep. They followed worthless idols and themselves became worthless.

Notice that there is mention of fathers and not mothers; seed and not eggs or womb. Well, maybe Hashem can overlook that seed if the eggs are good.

The Righteous Women of Israel

Malachi 2:11, "The nation of Judah betrayed, and an abomination was done in Israel for Judah desecrated God's Holiness and loved and cohabited with a daughter that worships another god." Now Hashem got mad. He didn't agree that it was acceptable to marry idol-worshiping women. When he wrote in his Torah that it was permissible for an Israelite soldier to take a woman captive from another nation, it was on the condition that the prisoner had to mourn her parents and change her alliance, before he took her as a bride.

Deuteronomy 21:10-13
When you go to war against your enemies and the Lord your God delivers them into your hands and you take captives, if you notice among the captives a beautiful woman and are attracted to her, you may take her as your wife. Bring her into your home and have her shave her head, trim her nails and put aside the clothes she was wearing when captured. After she has lived in your house and mourned her father and mother for a full month, then you may go to her and be her husband and she shall be your wife.

The Covenant of Marriage

Malachi 2:14: "And you said, for what reason? Because you betrayed the wife of your youth and she is your friend, the woman of your covenant."

This is a very interesting passage. It presents proof from the Bible that marriage with a proper covenant, or marriage contract, is to be revered. The verse further provides the reason for the destruction of Jerusalem; the men cheated on their wives. That was their first sin. All the other sins and abominations followed.

When I bought a new piano about twenty years ago, I was very excited. As I sat beside it, I heard Hashem singing a song to me from Jeremiah. This was a song that I remembered from high school. I had no idea why, but Hashem kept on singing that song every time I sat down to play. The words of the song come from Jeremiah.

Jeremiah 31:3–4
The Lord appeared to us in the past saying: "I have loved you with an everlasting love; I have drawn you with unfailing kindness. I will build you up again, and you, Virgin Israel, will be rebuilt. Again you will

take up your timbrels and go out to dance with the joyful."

How can the prophet say an everlasting love? We just read in 2 Kings 17:14 that Hashem was disgusted with the seed of Israel. There were times that Hashem didn't love them at all! This is not an isolated passage; all throughout the prophets Jeremiah, Isaiah, and Ezekiel we read about God's anger at the children of Israel.

Everlasting Love for the Women

This whole verse in Jeremiah 31 is written in female gender, as if to say, "An everlasting love, I've loved you, my daughter." The women did not sin in the desert. They didn't participate in the golden calf or in the sin of the spies. The prophet is saying that throughout the hardships of the children of Israel, Hashem always loved the women. Jeremiah goes on to say, "I will build you up and you will be built O virgin of Israel. You will drum on your drums and you will go out dancing and playing."

The commentaries say that the virgin Israel is the whole Jewish people. Is this truly the meaning the prophet Jeremiah wishes to convey? On the contrary, the people of Israel were likened to an unfaithful wife or even a harlot. There are many examples of this allegory in the prophet's writings. For example, Jeremiah 3:20, "But like a woman unfaithful to her husband, so you, Israel, have been unfaithful to me, declares the LORD."

Even if the Jewish people are destined to repent, they cannot be compared to a virgin. It is the women of Israel who never worshiped idols who are likened to a virgin. The virgin of Israel also means real virgins. When the Jews returned to Zion, Ezra the scribe demanded from the men to leave their heathen wives; they subsequently took young virgins of their nation to start new families.

The Feminine Way to Pray

1 Samuel 1:13–16
> As she kept on praying to the LORD, Eli observed her mouth. Hannah was praying in her heart, and her lips were moving but her voice was not heard. Eli thought she was drunk, and said to her, "How long are you going to stay drunk? Put away your wine. Not so, my lord," Hannah replied, "I am a woman who is deeply troubled. I have not been drinking wine or beer; I was pouring out my soul to the LORD. Do not take your servant for a wicked woman; I have been praying here out of my great anguish and grief."

Silent prayer was unknown at the time. It was devised by Hannah. Hannah invented a way of worshipping God from the heart, and that's what kept her close to Him. She prayed silently with her lips moving.

Until this day the Jewish people, men and women say a special prayer every day in silence. This form of worship found favor in Hashem's eyes, and He told His prophet Hosea that this will be the way of devotion in the future.

Hosea 14:1-2
> Return Israel because your sins have been your downfall. Take words with you and return to Hashem. Everyone should say to Him, "Carry away our sins and take our good qualities, and our lips will replace the calves of our sacrifices."

In some Christian translations it says "fruit of our lips," instead of "replace the calves of our sacrifices." This is an error. The word for *calves* is *parim* and the word for *fruit* is *pri*; in plural it would be *Pairot*. Any other definition for *parim* would be a mistake.

The Prophet Hosea is stating that sacrifices were not necessary any more. Hashem doesn't want any sacrifices, especially not human sacrifice!

Amos joins in Hosea's words of Hashem's disregard for sacrifice.

> Amos 5:21–22
> I hate; I despise your religious festivals; your assemblies are a stench to me. Even though you bring me burnt offerings and grain offerings, I will not accept them. Though you bring choice fellowship offerings, I will have no regard for them.

> Hosea 13:1-2
> When Ephraim spoke, people trembled; he was exalted in Israel. But he became guilty of Baal worship and died. Now they sin more and more; they make idols for themselves from their silver, cleverly fashioned images, all of them the work of craftsmen. It is said of these people, "They offer human sacrifices! They kiss calf-idols!"

This despicable act of sacrificing children was God's last straw. It made Him angry and he decreed destruction of Jerusalem and of the Holy Temple within.

> Jeremiah 7:31, "They have built the high places of Topheth in the Valley of Ben Hinnom to burn their sons and daughters in the fire, something I did not command, and I didn't even contemplate such a thing."
> In Jeremiah 32:35 he adds: "I didn't even contemplate such a thing to cause the people of Judah to sin."

After centuries of animal sacrifices, Hashem saw that the ceremonial sacrifices led to the most horrific sin that He never even contemplated; the sin of sacrificing one's own children. Hashem decided that he abhors sacrifice and we should replace sacrificial service with prayer. Not only that, but Hashem's approach totally changed.

> Hosea 14:4–5
> I will heal their mischievousness; I will love them regardless because I am not angry at them anymore. I will be like dew to Israel and they will blossom like a rose and their roots will become as strong as the roots of a Lebanese cedar wood tree.

Hosea lived in the beginning of the Second Temple Period. In the books of other Second Temple prophets, there is more evidence to show that Hashem did not want animal sacrifice.

> Zachariah 11:4–5
> This is what the LORD my God says: "Shepherd the flock marked for slaughter. Their buyers slaughter them and go unpunished. Those who sell them say, 'Praise the LORD, I am rich!' Their own shepherds do not spare them."

> Amos 5:22
> Even though you bring me burnt offerings and grain offerings, I will not accept them. Though you bring choice fellowship offerings, I will have no regard for them.

Hashem didn't want any more sacrifices for the Second Temple. In the latter part of the Second Temple, sacrifices were reinstated by the Pharisees but it was not Hashem's true will. Ultimately it stirred up chaos on the Temple mount which caused a rift within the nation and a civil war which weakened Israel so much that they were defeated by the Roman enemy and sent into exile.

Deuteronomy

> Hosea 14:1-2
> Return, Israel, to the LORD your God. Your sins have been your downfall! Take words with you and return to the LORD.

Hashem wasn't going to give up on his Torah. He wouldn't abolish the rewards or the punishments. The blessings and curses of the Torah remain, but the people of Israel must see for themselves how the Torah way will give them success; not so much through reprimand, but more through study and learning as people became more literate and educated.

In the above passage from Hosea 14, "Take words with you" the word *words* in Hebrew is *Devarim. Devarim* is the Hebrew name for the fifth book of the Bible, Deuteronomy. If so, then the prophet is saying take Deuteronomy with you and return to Hashem.

If you can only learn only one book of the Bible Deuteronomy is the one.

The last book of Moses is essentially his last speech. It reviews all the basic laws, including the Ten Commandments and all the blessings that result from adhering to the Torah law. The most important theme of Deuteronomy, *Devarim*, is the mitzvah to know God, fear Him and love Him.

> Hosea 14:9
> Who will be smart and understand these things? Who will be wise and know them? The paths of

Hashem are straight, the righteous will walk on them and the sinners will stumble.

Here the prophet wants to say that the words of the Torah are there; threatening and yelling aren't necessary. You can read God's instruction manual for life for yourself. If you are righteous you will know what to do and if you are a sinner, learning the sacred scriptures in the Torah and Old Testament Bible will help you repent. Hashem won't send out prophets to frighten the people anymore. There will be only gentle and encouraging prophesies like those of Zechariah and Hosea.

This also hints that there will be a day when the whole nation will be able to read. Individuals will be able to read the scourges themselves in the book of Deuteronomy and take those words seriously for their own advisement. Literacy was very rare at the time of the Second Temple, but it increased slowly when the Greeks entered the land. Literacy on a large scale from early childhood is less than a hundred years old. The words of the prophet Hosea have much more meaning today in our generation— the generation of multimedia where everyone can learn anything on their own.

Fear of God

Deuteronomy 10:12
    And now Israel what does Hashem your God ask of you? Just to fear Him and go in his ways. Love Him and worship the Lord your God with all your heart and all of your soul.

You must fear Hashem in order not to fear man. Do you know anyone who got panic attacks from fearing God?

I don't think so. But many fear man and become very sick from dread, especially women.

Women's biggest weakness is fear. I was very afraid of my ex-husband and too timid to file for divorce. When I saw my son imitating and attacking his sister and me physically, I realized that my trepidation was selfish. I must fear the consequences of staying in the marriage. God will not be happy with me if I don't save my child from growing up in a home of violence. I started yelling at myself to stop being frightened of a man. This thought gave me the courage to see a lawyer and start the process of changing my life for the better.

Fear of God gives you strength. Switch fear of man with fear of heaven; it is much easier than taking away the fear. When you fear God, you become brave; you feel proud that you are doing Hashem's will and not letting anyone else terrorize you.

The Next Generation

> Hosea 2:19–20
> I will betroth you to Me forever, and I will betroth you to Me with righteousness, justice, kindness and mercy. I will betroth you to Me in faithfulness, and you shall know Hashem.

Betroth means engaged to be married. This is when Hashem decided to take the women as the ones to continue the Jewish faith. He still didn't make the switch, but He decided that He would. The decision to make the women the givers of the Jewish soul is like an engagement. The marriage was scheduled to occur with Ezra the scribe as the orator. When the Jews returned to Zion and left their non-Jewish wives, Hashem gave the legacy of the keepers of the souls to the women permanently. Giving the responsibility to the women was the condition that Hashem made in order to agree to forgive the whole people and make a new covenant.

> Ezra 10:3–5
> Now let us make a covenant before our God to send away all these women and their children, in accordance with the counsel of my lord and of those who fear the commands of our God. Let it be done according to the Law. "Rise up; this matter is in your hands. We will support you, so take courage and do it." So Ezra rose up and put the leading priests and Levites and all Israel under oath to do what had been suggested. And they took the oath.

From that day on under Ezra's leadership, the Jews left their non-Jewish spouses and took only Jewish women as their wives. The children of the non-Jewish women were to be considered gentiles from that day forward. Hashem would give another chance to the children of Israel if they would go by the female line. In order to protect the next generation from falling into idol worship again, the Jewish women would have to take over the education. Ezra had the Jews promise to leave the heathen women and take Jewish wives in order to start new families. The new covenant would also be part of a new marriage covenant. The women would not be passive as in days of old. They will lead, teach and guide the family in Torah law and Jewish values.

A woman gives a spark of her soul to her offspring. Her child is a Jew regardless of the father. A man cannot give his son his heritage of belonging to a certain tribe unless the mother is Jewish. There is interdependence between mother and father.

Ezekiel 39:25-29

Therefore, this is what the Sovereign LORD says: "I will now restore the fortunes of Jacob and will have compassion on all the people of Israel, and I will be zealous for my holy name. They will forget their shame and all the unfaithfulness they showed toward me when they lived in safety in their land with no one to make them afraid. When I have brought them back from the nations and have gathered them from the countries of their enemies, I will be proved holy through them in the sight of many nations. Then they will know that I am the LORD their God, for though I sent them into exile among the nations, I will gather them to their own land, not leaving any behind. I will no longer hide my face from them, for I will pour out my Spirit on the people of Israel, declares the Sovereign LORD."

In this passage the "fortunes of Jacob" is a translation from the literal words that mean the refugees of the House of Jacob. The House of Jacob denotes the women. The people of Israel is a translation from the literal "sons of Israel" and denotes the men. The refugees that survived were saved in the merit of their mothers. In the future God will "be proved holy through them" and "pour out His spirit on the people of Israel" through the women as stated in the above passage.

After a child is born, the baby stays with his mother and she continues to give him or her spiritual energy through her physical and emotional affection. Her love teaches the baby that he is not alone in the world until he can grow up and learn to trust Hashem. The passion of the Jewish mother comes from this blessing that Hashem gave her to pass on the Jewish soul.

All mothers of the world are blessed with this same responsibility. The women of today are increasingly stronger and stronger in their ability to influence their family. Without any formal instruction, young mothers accept the job of mothering with a passion. This is a blessing from God and when the father sees that the mother of their children is proceeding on the path that he wants for his children, then he should support and follow her lead. When a father allows his wife to be a spiritual guide to the family, the couple proceeds in the ways of the blessings of the prophets.

Balaam the Gentile Prophet

In scriptures, every time the word "tent" is mentioned, it is connected with the home and the family. For example, the prophet Balaam exclaimed, "How good are your tents Jacob" in Numbers 24:5. Balaam, a gentile prophet, was sent by the king Balak to curse Israel. Israel had already done many sins such as the golden calf. However, when Balaam saw the women of the Israelites, he couldn't curse them; they were pure as pure could be. What did Balak do? He sent prostitutes to the Israelite men to make them sin. He knew that he didn't have a chance with the Israelite women but if he could entice the men to leave their wives, then they would sin.

The Israelites sinned with the heathen women and Phinehas caught the leader of the tribe of Shimon lying with an idol-worshiping prostitute and stabbed them both together. He lifted his sword with the two of them on it and paraded around the camp, to show all what happens to someone who desecrates the Ten Commandments. This brave soul did something that no woman would be able to do. We need our men to stand up against evil, protect us and to defend God's name.

Back to Eden

When Hashem created Eve, He said that she would be a helper parallel to Adam. When Adam complained and blamed Eve for causing him to sin, he forfeited accepting her capability to help him and suffered the consequences. God created something in the anatomy of a woman's soul to help Adam keep his faith. Eve failed the first time, but she wasn't given a fair chance because Adam didn't tell her the truth (See the chapter entitled "Tree of Knowledge"). Adam told Eve that it was forbidden to even touch the Tree of Knowledge even though God told Adam not to eat from the tree. Had Adam confessed, asked her forgiveness and given her a second chance, she could have protected him, and they might not have been expelled from Eden.

When the Jewish people repented and agreed to take good Jewish women to be their wives, Hashem decided that He would give the women permanent authority in the home. It is also an allegory for every couple. A man must respect his wife, for she is the mother of his children. When she is not faithful to God, like the pagan wives of the Israelites, of course she must be divorced. However, if she is a good person with faith in God, she merits being placed into the position of authority for issues of belief and faith.

Just like the woman has the power to instill faith in her family, she has the power to influence her family to neglect the faith. I have seen many families that keep the laws of the Torah and send their children to good Jewish schools. However, some mothers have children that eventually leave the faith and sometimes have even deteriorated to drugs and promiscuity. For years I have pondered on this phenomenon, and I even bought a book about it called *Off the Derech*, by Faranak Margolis. She describes in numerous stories how Jewish offspring have left their faith.

This book enumerates many reasons for Jewish teenagers to cease being religious. Sometimes the school and family were too strict. Sometimes children did not get adequate answers to their questions on faith. Some children were ridiculed for even asking!

One thing that is in common with these teenagers is that none of these children admired both of their parents. These adolescents ridiculed them for different reasons causing a will to escape from the religious upbringing presented at home. A loving home is even more important for a child than a good school. When children feel loved they want to go in their parents' path. Either parent can instill faith in his child but the way to do it is through love and not through reprimand.

I don't believe that the mother is the only one to have faith in the home, but she has been given the responsibility. She is called upon to give her husband faith and encouragement. She shouldn't rely predominately on others to teach her children.

Fathers and teachers have a responsibility to help to properly rear children. However, the woman's ability to maximally influence is enhanced when the children feel loved by a motherly love that is irrevocable and everyone else involved respects her for her special role and position. Sometimes the mother is very loving but she is not very knowledgeable in Torah. In this case the children may leave the religion because the father did not get involved enough in the children's education.

Therefore, the education of girls is vital. They must learn everything including laws that only pertain to men as she will be the mother of boys and girls in the future. My father taught us Torah for hours every Shabbat. He gave us a strong base for faith; however, he would have been a much happier man and an even better educator had he had my mother's support.

You don't have to be an atheist to live a godless life. If you don't mention God in your daily speech in your plans, hopes, and actions, then you are essentially living without God. Some teenagers who stray away from God may even have heard Torah and Bible ideology from their fathers and teachers, but they did not have discussions about faith with their mothers. Many women are so preoccupied with food, laundry, and financial worries that they don't discuss faith with their children. The youngsters should hear about their Creator as soon as they are able to talk, and even before that, through songs and stories. That will ensure the faith of the next generation.

The Female Gender in Biblical Texts

There are many examples of poetry in the female gender that are traditionally explained as parables for the entire nation of Israel. The truth is that many times the prophet is really referring to females. Sometimes the prophet is referring to Jerusalem the city, because cities have a female gender in Hebrew. When the text mentions Jerusalem and Zion in the same verse, then Jerusalem is the city and Zion is the name given to the righteous people of Jerusalem, as illustrated in the following verse:

> Isaiah 30:19, "People of Zion, who live in Jerusalem, you will weep no more. How gracious he will be when you cry for help! As soon as he hears, he will answer you."

The people of Zion are the righteous men and women who were living in Jerusalem. This verse is referring only to the righteous of Jerusalem and not all the people of Jerusalem who at the time had a majority of idol worshippers. The next verses are famous.

Isaiah 4:3-4
Those who are left in Zion, who remain in Jerusalem, will be called holy, all who are recorded among the living in Jerusalem. The Lord will wash away the filth of the women of Zion; he will cleanse the bloodstains from Jerusalem by a spirit of judgment and a spirit of fire.

The women of Zion need to be cleansed not because they worshipped idols but because they didn't stop their husbands from worshipping idols. This is akin to Job's error in ignoring his sons' wanton actions. Nevertheless, the mothers are still called women of Zion because they did pray for their families and maybe even brought sacrifices in the temple for them as Job did for his sons.

The following verse is actually a prophecy for today:

Jeremiah 31:22, "How long will you wander, unfaithful Daughter Israel? The LORD will create a new thing on earth—the woman will return to the man."

A more exact translation from the Hebrew is:

"For how long will you procrastinate o' naughty daughter of Israel? God created a new thing in the land; a woman will turn around a man."

Hashem told me that this verse means that the women will turn the men toward Hashem and far away from idol worship. They were naughty because they had delayed reprimanding their husbands for their sins and mistakes. The previous verse says, "God created a new thing." This is also a prophecy for today when the woman can have a strong positive influence on her man and even "wrap him around her finger."

The main point of the prophet is that the women will be the spiritual leaders of the family. The Torah laws involve family living and the women have to help their families keep the Torah. When the women take care of their homes and create a holy atmosphere, they will make sure that the new generation will be a holy one and will never turn to other gods or profane pursuits. When a man allows his wife to be the spiritual guide of the family, the household will be blessed with a peaceful home for the couple themselves and for their progeny as well as for their families in the next generation.

> Psalm 9:13-14, "LORD, see how my enemies persecute me! Have mercy and lift me up from the gates of death, that I may declare your praises in the gates of Daughter Zion, and there rejoice in your salvation."

In the above psalm, the man can only rejoice when he can exult at the gates of his home with his wife, a daughter of Zion, meaning a woman who has the spirit of Zion, the spirit of closeness to God.

Woman of Valor

Proverbs 31:10 begins with a song of praise to the woman of the home. It is a custom for the whole family to sing this song to the woman of the house on Friday night, before the Sabbath meal.

Proverbs chapter 31:10-31

A wife of noble character who can find?
She is worth far more than rubies.
Her husband has full confidence in her
And lacks nothing of value.
She brings him good, not harm,
All the days of her life.
She selects wool and flax
And works with eager hands.
She is like the merchant ships,
Bringing her food from afar.
She gets up while it is still night;
She provides food for her family
And portions for her female servants.
She considers a field and buys it;
Out of her earnings she plants a vineyard.
She sets about her work vigorously;
Her arms are strong for her tasks.
She sees that her trading is profitable,
And her lamp does not go out at night.
In her hand she holds the distaff
And grasps the spindle with her fingers.
She opens her arms to the poor
And extends her hands to the needy.
When it snows, she has no fear for her household;
For all of them are clothed in scarlet.
She makes coverings for her bed;
She is clothed in fine linen and purple.
Her husband is respected at the city gate,
Where he takes his seat among the elders of the land.
She makes linen garments and sells them,
And supplies the merchants with sashes.
She is clothed with strength and dignity;
She can laugh at the days to come.
She speaks with wisdom,
And faithful instruction is on her tongue.
She watches over the affairs of her household

And does not eat the bread of idleness.
Her children arise and call her blessed;
Her husband also, and he praises her:
"Many women do noble things,
But you surpass them all."
Charm is deceptive, and beauty is fleeting;
But a woman who fears the LORD is to be praised.
Honor her for all that her hands have done,
And let her works bring her praise at the city gate.

This song is known by the name "Woman of Valor." The exact translation of the first two words of the song is woman of strength. The woman in the above song is very resourceful. Aside from caring for her family, she also makes money! She is generous to the poor, speaks words of wisdom, and is known in public. She is certainly not an old-fashioned lady!

This song praises the Jewish woman and encourages an eternal bond. When the composer says that "Charm is deceptive and beauty is fleeting," he didn't mean to say that she is not beautiful, but that the woman of valor doesn't put an excessive effort into her beauty and charm. She doesn't load up on makeup and jewelry like the pagan women whose intention was to lure the men. For the "Woman of Valor" fear of the Lord is much more important than beauty. She is praised for not giving importance to external beauty.

A woman who has fear of the Lord automatically receives a gift of grace and beauty, but she does not have the type of beauty that lures men. Men and merchants can do business with her, without a thought of infidelity. She has a holy aura protecting her. Only for her husband is she sensual and attractive.

As a healer I cannot resist giving women who are reading this some herbal advice. Spirulina is a nutritional supplement that enhances your true beauty. 1000mg or two pills in the morning makes your face shine and your cheeks rosy. If you are nursing a baby the baby's cheeks will also be beautiful. Spirulina also comes in powder. A teaspoon in a drink of natural juice or a smoothie will give you strength and beauty. It also quiets the appetite and is therefore used for dieting.

Sabbath Is Mother's Day

On the Sabbath day, we eat very fancy meals. Every Jewish religious home enjoys spreads like a wedding, and the parents and children wear fancy apparel in honor of *Shabbat* (the Sabbath in Hebrew). Even if they are poor, everyone has a *Shabbat* outfit.

Shabbat obliges children and grandparents to stay in a family structure because every week they are required to clean the house and help prepare festive meals. The women are in charge of the cooking and cleaning but everyone helps.

Everything has to be on schedule, and the mother is the one to set the tone. Proverbs 31:11, "Her husband's heart relies on her, and he shall lack no fortune." The husband trusts his wife to prepare for *Shabbat*, and she trusts Hashem. The Shabbat table is a spread of the good fortune of that week. Even poor families feel rich on Shabbat. A wise woman can make a luxurious meal with minimum expense.

The mitzvah of Shabbat reinforces family ties not only between husband and wife but also between siblings and even in-laws and cousins. It's a day to get together with no time pressure. This is also a mother's dream come true because on this day there is time for the father to give attention to his children and to her.

The children have time to learn Torah with their parents. They also become involved with preparations for *Shabbat* and learn how to cook and clean. I am amazed how well my children know how to cook, just from what they learned from me once a week, on Friday afternoons in preparation for Shabbat.

The Secret

There is a book called *The Secret* by Rhonda Byme. This book and others focus on the power of positive thinking. They claim that what you say and what you believe can cause events to happen. In many cases, such belief and positive reflecting does work. However, I would much rather believe that an all-caring, all-loving God is taking care of us more than just an anonymous power of words or thoughts. If you trust Hashem, things will usually work out for the best. It is only when you ignore Him that you succumb to the powers that be. A wife and mother has the ability to put faith and happiness in the home. When women use that gift, their children and husbands will be just like the tree in Psalm 1:3. This same verse is also found in Jeremiah 17:8.

Marital Sex

God gave humans more hormones than animals in order to have sex for pleasure. We have a reason to live that is more than just being fruitful and multiplying. Mankind has sex not only to have offspring but also to keep the family together. The physical love promotes unity and loyalty.

Shabbat is a day that is designated not only for family time but also as a day to be together sexually. Religious Jewish couples as a rule keep a healthy sex life well into old age because it is a mitzvah to be together on Shabbat, unless the woman is menstruating or near the time of menstruation.

Family Purity

Shabbat keeps the men and women away from idolatry by affording them a day to work for and anticipate. When we are actively exerting ourselves for Hashem, we don't have a need for idleness or idol worship. The Israelites of old were lured into having sex with idol worshippers who lured them into having sex in front of these gods and giving other sacrifices to them. Another way that women help keep the men away from drifting towards idol worship or straying towards other women is by maintaining the laws of family purity.

In the past, women separated themselves during their period of menstruation from physically being in intimate contact with their husbands for seven days every month in accordance with Torah law. This gave women a rest from their usual routines of family care for a week. The woman lived in a community tent for a week with the other women that were menstruating.

Today these laws are still kept, but the women stay home with their families and for the separation period, the parents sleep in detached beds. The separation of beds and bodies concludes with a celebration of a ritual bath in a special bathhouse called a *Mikvah*. This gives the couple an exciting day to anticipate and keeps them very attached to each other. The Talmud says, "Why did the Torah command the woman to be separated for seven days? Because he is used to her and gets annoyed with her. Now she will be dear to him like on the day of her wedding."

In most Jewish religious couples, there is no fear that the husband will stray. Orthodox Jewish men are excited to have their own wives who really love and admire them. The temporary parting makes the heart grow fonder. They yearn for one another when they are young and even after menopause Jewish observant couples continue to enjoy frequent sexual relations well into old age.

Hashem gave women the ability to feel emotions and to feel Hashem. This present is a reward for keeping away from idol worship throughout the generations. Of course, a woman could personally lose that talent if she transgresses any one of the Ten Commandments.

If you are not Jewish, you could still merit that gift of spirituality and pass it on to your young ones. All you have to do is keep the Ten Commandments. Please refer to my book entitled *God Meets the World* where each commandment is explained in depth.

The New Covenant

> Jeremiah 31:31 "The days will come that I will make a new covenant with the Israelites and the tribe of Judah."

The words "new covenant" were translated as New Testament for centuries in the Christian world. Hashem explained to me that the new covenant is an agreement where Hashem includes the woman in the promise. He already tried to give man the reins in the old covenant. Now he will make a contract not only with the Ten Commandments but also with all the Five Books of Moses with the men and the women.

Jeremiah 31:32-33

Not like the covenant that I made with their forefathers as I held their hand when I took them out of Egypt. They broke their covenant and I was their master said the Lord. For this is the covenant that I will make with the house of Israel: I will give the Torah in their midst and I will write it on their hearts, I will be a God for them and they will be a nation for me."

Nowhere does it say that the new covenant is in place of the old one. The old covenant is the Ten Commandments written on "The Tablets of the Covenant." The new covenant includes the Ten Commandments because they are written in the Torah. The Ten Commandments were commanded by God himself, not through a prophet. The entire nation of Israel were the prophets who heard God's voice delivering the Ten Commandments. Millions of men, women and children heard God's voice at Mount Sinai. God forbid should any covenant be switched with the Ten Commandments. Any change in the original pact would have to come from a prophecy of the same magnitude and exposure!

After years of complaining to the prophets about how bad the Children of Israel were, Hashem realized that if the women would be in charge the men might repent. Women can drive their husbands to do good or evil. Jewish women who have devoted themselves to be stay at home moms to rear their children have been exposed to much less outside influence than men. Like a lioness, a woman must be strong in order to keep their unborn and born children alive. Hashem saw the strength of the Jewish women throughout history and decided to make them the cornerstone of the family.

The prophet Jeremiah says that this time the children of Israel will write the Torah on their hearts (Jeremiah 31:33). This also means that they will learn it by heart as for centuries the Jews learned the Torah through memorization. Few had a book of their own, so learning by heart was the only way. Today we know that by chanting and studying, you can have an influence on your soul. During the First Temple Period, only the prophets and scholars studied Torah. In the future, the Torah would be available and learned by all.

Meam Loez is a Bible anthology written in the eighteenth century in Ladino. Ladino is a Jewish dialect of Spanish that was spoken by the Jews of Spain. This language was kept alive even after the Spanish Inquisition, much like Yiddish exists until today. Meam Loez has been translated into Hebrew and English and is available online. It has fascinating Bible stories, parables, historical legends, and commentaries and remains in its original style and format since the year 1760.

My great grandmother who lived in Turkey knew all the available volumes of Meam Loez by heart. She recited them along with her friends when they got together to learn while their children played with each other. My own grandmother learned many passages of Meam Loez and the Torah by heart from her mother.

Two Hearts—One Soul

Deuteronomy 6:5, "You shall love Hashem your God with all your heart with all your soul and all your strength." Just like in Jeremiah 31, *heart* is written in the plural conjugation, *Levavcha*, (plural meaning hearts) instead of *libcha*, one heart. The two hearts are the two spiritual hearts of each half of your soul. Man and wife make one soul; therefore, you as a couple have two physical hearts but just one spiritual heart and soul. Only when you are one with your beloved can true Torah values be kept; only with your soul mate can you really love Hashem with all your strength. Jeremiah's prophecy uses the word *hearts*, "I will write it on their hearts." When the couple is bonded together in their minds and hearts, they will be able to truly fulfill the Torah precepts and values to integrate them into their family life under one unified soul.

The advice of Hashem for modern couples is to learn Bible together. You can also learn by yourself, but at least once a week devote an hour or two to learn together. My husband and I study together for a couple of hours every Sabbath. Joining of the souls by learning Bible together can create a strong bond that lasts a lifetime.

Hashem told Jeremiah that this time the relationship between man and God will be mutual: "I will be a God for them and they will be a nation for me" (Jeremiah 31:33). We are still in the process of receiving this covenant. As our love for Hashem grows, His love for us grows. A woman has the ability to connect the family to Hashem with her gentle love. The new covenant demands the man to respect his wife and be faithful to her, as she is the new cupbearer. With her new role, she will be the link that connects her husband and children, the children of Israel, to Hashem.

Sins of the Fathers

Exodus 20:4–6
>You shall not make for yourself an image in the form of anything in heaven above or on the earth beneath or in the waters below. You shall not bow down to them or worship them; for I, the LORD your God, am a jealous God, who remembers the sin of the fathers on the children for three and four

generations of those who hate me, but showing love
to a thousand generations of those who love me and
keep my commandments.

The above verse in Exodus says that you will suffer for
your father's transgressions. Hashem told me that you will
be punished for your father's sins only if you repeat them.
While you were growing up, you may have had a chance to
see you father and his deeds in an objective way. You may
have seen your grandfather and maybe even your great-
grandfather. That's why it says "three or four generations",
sometimes you see only three generations and sometimes
four.

When you have a bad habit it is very hard to break,
but if that habit was also your father's weakness it is even
harder. Imagine if a person is in a mafia family for three
or four generations. That would make it seem like the evil
his family does is good. Therefore, Hashem must punish
this person if He wants him to repent. A man who's been
in the mafia for three generations is not going to change his
life around unless something very drastic happens to him.

The same goes for all punishments. When bad things
happen to us it is only because Hashem wants us to change
or the better. In the limited time we have in this world we
have to prepare for the next world. Get ready for the day of
judgement where you will see your relatives that passed and
they will see the video of your life. If you asked Hashem
for forgiveness, the sins you have committed in life will be
erased from the records. Your great grandparents won't see
those bad things that you have done.

Jeremiah 31:33-34
"This is the covenant I will make with the people
of Israel after that time," declares the LORD. "I will
put my law in their minds and write it on their hearts.

I will be their God, and they will be my people. No
longer will they teach their neighbor, or say to one
another, 'Know the LORD,' because they will all know
me, from the least of them to the greatest," declares
the LORD. "For I will forgive their wickedness and
will remember their sins no more."

Please note that the Hebrew Commandment says,
"remembers the sin of the fathers," not "the parents" as
in many translations. When the prophet Jeremiah speaks
about the new covenant, he says in Jeremiah 31:29-30,
"In those days, people will no longer say, 'The fathers have
eaten sour grapes, and the children's teeth will become
blunt.' Instead, everyone will die for their own sin; whoever
eats sour grapes—their own teeth will become blunt."

Jeremiah is relating Hashem's prophecy to the people.
In the future the Children of Israel will repent with a full
heart. He will forgive and forget their sins and the sins of
their forefathers too. The Nation will do such a complete
repentance that even if they do sin Hashem will not attach
it to the past. Hashem will write a clean slate as a reward
for their repentance.

The New Covenant with the Mothers

Jeremiah isn't canceling the second commandment; he
is just stating God's new idea. Hashem knew that the new
generation will learn Torah. They won't follow in their
fathers' footsteps of idol worship; especially if they are
educated by their God-fearing and loving mothers.

From Jeremiah until today, Hashem has a covenant
with the women. You are your mother's child. You won't
be punished for your father's sins if your father is an
idol worshipper or violates other directives in the Ten

Commandments, because you will be considered your mother's child.

What if your mother sins? The tendency to go in the way of your father is out of respect and awe. If you follow the sins of your mother it is probably on your own volition. If people follow their mothers' ways, it is usually out of admiration and choice.

Customs were handed down through the paternal line in most ancient cultures. So even if your mother had particular religious custom that her family followed it would not continue after she married. Remember this verse is part of the second commandment, "Do not have any gods before me." The sins that the Torah is referring to are sins of idol worship.

In ancient times, people lived as a group. They followed their family tradition without any independent thinking. Today everyone is allowed to think for themselves and make their own decisions. When Hashem spoke to Jeremiah about how He would change the way He judges people, He also planned to change the ways of the world. Modern society with freedom and individuality is God's blessing. It is part of this new covenant. One of the ways that this will be accomplished is by making the Torah available to all. People will understand the law and not just have to obey blindly. They will be able to change because of what they read even if they come from generations of idol-worshippers.

Literacy gave the people of the world much more free choice after the Second Temple was built, but it didn't stop there. As society becomes more modern we have more information available and we are becoming more and more independent of our parents. We can even teach our parents because of our computer literacy. Therefore, Hashem demands of us to repent on our own and discover

Him for ourselves through history, science, Biblical sources and any other means that are available to us.

Deborah the Prophetess

Deborah the prophetess is an example of how brave a woman can be. She was a general in the army of Hashem. The way she sings to Hashem in praise of victory is emotional and picturesque.

Deborah also takes responsibility for the Israelites. Judges 5:7, "Freedom ceased in Israel until I, Deborah, got up, I Deborah, a mother in Israel." She didn't blame the people of Israel for anything; she was just proud of herself. She felt like a mother giving her love to the whole people of Israel. Deborah was an unbelievable woman as a leader, a warrior, a writer, and a loving mother.

Deborah was one of the first female leaders. It has taken centuries for women to become leaders again. Today women are admired and respected. We can take advantage of that respect to teach men to be softer and more understanding of their young ones. Today's women must grasp the opportunity to teach their family and other families how to love God's children and how to love Hashem.

Twenty-four hundred years ago, Ezra the scribe wanted the woman to have a significant influence on the family. He wanted women to be respected and admired. In the times of Ezra, Jews were very strict about marrying within the faith, and they respected their wives. However, just a couple of hundred years after Ezra, the status of women took a big dive.

Women's Downfall

In Ancient Greece, a lot of Greek goddesses were worshipped and idolized. Nevertheless, the ruling elite in Greece were males who held the powerful positions without so much admiration for women. When Christianity started to become popular, in the third and fourth century CE, the Romans wanted to diminish the value of women so that people would leave their pagan goddesses. This caused the Romans to degrade women, beat them, and take away their rights. Centuries later, there was a craze of real persecution of women by declaring a witch hunt. See Wikipedia, "Witch trials in early modern period."

During the fifteenth to eighteenth centuries the witch hunts abounded. Thousands of women were imprisoned in dark dungeons and killed. The cry for women's rights was at first, just their right to a fair trial.

There is a book called *The Dark Side of Christian History*, by Helen Ellerbe. She writes that St. Peter said, "Every woman should be filled with shame by the thought that she is a woman." He was of the opinion that Eve was responsible for death in the world, and every woman is an Eve. You can find this book on the Internet and for more horrifying details search under "The Witch Hunts; The End of Magic and Miracles."

Slowly women are catching up to the respect they had in the days of Ezra. Until the turn of the 20th century women didn't have the right to own land or vote in the United States. They certainly earned less than men in the same job. I wrote a little poem to describe this change in the women's role from the Dark Ages until today.

A Dark World

When the world was dark,
Only violence could light up a spark.
Where was freedom to give us some light?
Just to handle our plight.

When the world was dark,
Men and women were miles apart.
The mothers' hearts had true faith in Hashem,
Even more than the men.
Then came our turn,
God remembered the prize that we earned.
Mother knows best,
Education will be in our nest.

Now there is light,
Mommy's here, and she'll fight for our rights.
She will teach us to stick to Hashem,
And she'll strengthen the men.

. . . .

Men and Women in Jewish Law

Torah observant Jews respected women throughout history. If there are some laws that women are not obligated to perform, we are taught that it is because they don't need as many laws as men do. For example:

1. Circumcision. The main purpose of circumcision is to remember your conviction to God even when you are going to the toilet or having sex.

2. Phylacteries worn on the head and arm are leather straps to spiritually bind a man to his creator while praying.

3. A skullcap, or yarmulke, is worn on the head to remind every male that God is above him.

Women don't have the same weakness as men do to forget their faith, so they don't need so many extra reminders. I asked Hashem again, "Why were women less prone to idol worship?" He answered, "A woman is a partner with God in creating a child. Men are also part of the process, but they tend to forget. A woman has to carry a new life for nine months and give birth; she realizes that she isn't the creator of that embryo. It's a gift, a miraculous one, not something that can be created by an idol or a mythological being."

A woman feels a creation growing in her body, and outside of her body as she sees her children develop from her breast milk. She can conclude that God is there, and she can feel the holiness and become pious. She feels the big responsibility that God gave her by trusting her with a new life, a newborn for a new generation.

In Ancient Israel, the sinful women that performed all of those sacrilegious orgies were not so weak as to be mesmerized by the pagan idols. They were doing it for financial benefit. They even married the Jewish boys in order to take them away from Judaism and get favors from their own people. This makes their sin much worse.

If a man wants to be righteous, he too must realize the miracles of creation around him and especially the miracle that he has a wife and children. When a husband looks up to his wife, her feminine instincts develop. She will have the talent to know just what he and her children need physically and emotionally.

A woman has a tremendous influence on her man. If a woman has faith, she will give him faith and vice versa.

The man's job is to give his wife the utmost respect so that she can be free to use all her talents and be proud of herself. Years of persecution have implanted a memory in women's souls that they are inferior to men. Sometimes women act with haughty pride because they are hiding their inferiority. If a woman shows off her body, she lowers herself to the level of her physical flesh. When her body is hidden, her wisdom is given more of an opportunity to shine.

Modest dress is very important to Hashem. Of course you must look nice and neat in public, but don't wear gaudy jewelry, a shirt that exposes your belly, or anything that will catch a man's eye other than your own husband's.

A Parallel Helper

Genesis 2:18, "It is not good for man to be alone,
I will make him a helper parallel to him."

When women are downtrodden, belittled, and abused, they can't be the "parallel helper" that they were meant to be. After Adam and Eve sinned, they were cursed. Eve was told, "Your lust will be for your man and he will rule over you" (Genesis 3:16). For generations upon generations, men have ruled women, and women stayed with their abusive men out of weakness.

Esther 1:17, "The story of the queen will become public and all women will embarrass their husbands saying, 'The king called for the queen and she didn't come.'"

In the Scroll of Esther, Vashti the queen was put to death just because she didn't want to come to the king when he called for her.

When Adam and Eve were kicked out of the Garden of Eden, Eve lost her job of being a parallel helper. That doesn't mean that she has to accept the decree permanently.

If she is not influenced by the Tree of Knowledge, meaning her absolute right to be right absolutely, she will be able to be patient with her husband and be his parallel just as Hashem wanted her to be.

Hashem knew from the beginning that it wouldn't be good for man to be alone, but if couples eat from the Tree of Knowledge and they each always think that only they are right, it becomes a tug of war. Many couples sometimes don't even give each other a chance to finish their sentences, let alone give respect to each other's opinions.

Only after the Jewish people went through a major catastrophe, ending with the destruction of the Holy Temple in Jerusalem and their exile, would they realize that "it is not good for man to be alone." Man was alone because the woman wasn't parallel to him; she was his subordinate. She had no power to influence her man. With the new covenant between God and the Jewish people, the women will play a major role in the family and in keeping the Torah. This time the women will have special respect. They will be the down line for the inheritance of religion and education. Only because of the righteous women did God give the Jewish people a second chance.

Abuse in the Family

The type of abuse that women suffered from is depicted in Jeremiah chapter 30. The following verse is written in female gender.

> Jeremiah 30:14
> All your lovers forgot you and won't ask for you, but will beat you like an enemy. You will receive mean reproach on all of your transgressions, your sins have become stronger.

The simple meaning of the above verse is that the Prophet Jeremiah is speaking to Jerusalem. I feel that he is also speaking to the women of Jerusalem who were abused by their husbands. Many women suffer from their man's reproach and criticisms. Their husbands may blow up at any mistake as if it was some horrible sin. Women can do this too; they can wrongly attack their partner for life, but not in those days. In ancient times, a woman could be harshly beaten and expelled from her home if she dared to reprimand her husband.

Women were so looked down upon that even a prophet couldn't complain about the women being abused, nor could he praise the women. Therefore, the women are mentioned allegorically as a city, the holiest city in the world. The prophets sometimes speaks about Israel in feminine conjugation when speaking to the women.

> Jeremiah 30:17, "I will give you more time, I will heal your wounds said the Lord for you have been pushed aside. You were called, 'Zion is her' and no one wants her."

Zion is a nickname for Jerusalem, but many verses in the prophets mention Zion and Jerusalem in the same sentence because Zion is the heart and soul of Jerusalem.

In Jeremiah 30:17, Zion is mentioned as a name, not as a place. "Zion is her" means your woman is likened to Zion; she is the heart and soul of your family and nobody wanted her.

In the prophets' writings there are many verses that mention the daughter of Zion or the daughter of Jerusalem. Here too most commentaries say the daughter of Zion is the land itself. The truth is that these are all hidden messages to the women of Jerusalem or to Jewish women of all times.

Zephaniah 3:14-15

"Sing, Daughter Zion; shout aloud, Israel! Be glad and rejoice with all your heart, Daughter Jerusalem! The LORD has taken away your punishment; he has turned back your enemy. The LORD, the King of Israel, is with you; never again will you fear any harm."

Zephaniah is telling the women to rejoice because "the King of Israel is with you." This is a hint that the Jewish soul will come from the mother. Hashem will be in the hearts, minds and wombs of the Jewish women. Zephaniah tells the women to rejoice and sing for the gathering of the nation of Israel back to its land, because they were much more aware of the horrors of the destruction.

Aside from the prophets and holy men, the women were the ones who mourned the most over the destruction of Jerusalem. Most men were so drenched in idol worship they didn't feel the pain of the loss compared to the women. In Lamentations we can see how the women were focusing on the devastation, lamenting bitterly.

Lamentations 2:10

They sit on the ground they are silent, the elders of the daughters of Zion they have put ashes on their heads and dressed themselves in sackcloth. The maidens of Jerusalem have bowed their heads to the ground.

Cling to your Wife

Genesis 2:24 states, "Therefore a man should leave his mother and father and cling to his wife."

It's a mitzvah for every man to consider his wife's wishes before those of his parents. Why doesn't the Torah stipulate the same obligation for the women?

We mentioned earlier that the story of Adam and Eve is a parable. When the Torah was written, God saw that the Israelite men would sin because they were worshipping idols in Egypt. Therefore, He already wrote that a man should cling to his wife since the women were the ones who were more loyal to God.

Hashem was also thinking about the woman's physical well-being. Women have the job of giving birth and nursing their children. In the delicate months after birth, a woman needs her own Mommy. Hashem didn't want the husband objecting to the interference of his mother-in-law when his wife needed her. Even today in Israel many women go to their parents' house after birth, or if it is too difficult, Mom comes to her daughter's home to be of help and comfort. It wouldn't be so good if the man's parents came over and saw their daughter-in-law in her weak moments, especially if there were any demands that the child bearer rise, serve and honor them.

Hashem says that every married man and woman must respect each other's judgment as to how to relate to their parents. Even before engagement, a couple that is loyal to each other and wants to build a life together already is obliged to put their loyalty to each other above their fidelity to their parents. If your parents are against the marriage and you know in your heart that you found your partner for life, you should cling to each other and marry. Your obligation to your own soul is greater than your obligation to your parents. If you devote your heart and mind to Hashem, when you meet your soul mate you will know it, and no one will be able to talk you out of it. If your parents are good people, they will see your strength and respect your decision.

If your parents love you and only want your best, but they are against your choice for a life partner, do not ignore their cry entirely. Investigate. Ask other people that know your fiancé and discover if there is any truth to your parents' fears. Out of respect for your parents, take their words seriously, but remember, you are supposed to respect your parents, not cling to them.

Start with Your Baby

Let's start from the very beginning, from birth. I advise any new mother who wants her child to emulate her, to nurse her baby. The influence is so much more that way. When you nurse, you bring your child physically close to you and keep him or her in your aura. If for any reason you can't nurse, you still should have the baby be as close as possible when bottle feeding. Physiologically, this promotes the flow of oxytocin, the hormone associated with bonding. The baby learns about human contact and looks up to his or her mother as protector and savior. After your baby learns to trust you, he or she can learn to trust Hashem. From infancy I advise you to sing songs of prayer and praise of Hashem to your children. Their souls will also be comforted by chanting words of the Bible to them twice a day, just like it says in Deuteronomy 6:7, "And you should repeat these words to your children, and speak about them, when sitting in your home, when going on the road, when it is time to go to sleep, and when you wake up."

In the past, women always gave tremendous amounts of love to their children, but they had very little Torah knowledge. The majority of women were not taught to read and write until the middle of the nineteenth century. Modern women are literate and have more knowledge. The possibility to acquire more knowledge is endless. We are called upon to use our acquired wisdom and knowledge to build a generation with strong faith, love of Torah and love for God.

Reprimanding the Woman of Jerusalem

> Lamentations 4:6, "The iniquity of the daughter of my people is greater than the sin of Sodom which was overturned in a moment though no hands were laid on her."

No hands were laid on the daughters of Israel because they were very careful about their modesty. In Sodom, certainly, there were many sexual transgressions. In Jerusalem, the women were untouched. Why was their sin worse than the sins of Sodom? The answer is in Lamentations 4:10, "The hands of merciful mother cooked their children; they became their food in the trauma of the daughter of my people."

Hashem told me that the women didn't really cook their children. However, there was a horrible custom of sacrificing children to a pagan god called Molech. It was done in the valley of Hinom. Today the word for hell in Hebrew is *Geihinom*, which means the valley of Hinom. This valley is situated on the outskirts of the Old City of Jerusalem. If the women didn't rebel, riot, run away, or kidnap their own children to save them from being slaughtered, then surely their sin was greater than the sins of Sodom. It is as if they themselves cooked their own children.

Why didn't they save their children? Fear. Not only distress of divorce, but worry of not having money to live, dread of being abandoned. Many women feared that their husband or the false prophets would chase them and even kill them in order to take their baby. If they would have had greater fear of heaven, they would have fought and even killed to avoid the slaughter of their children.

Make-up and Bells

The Israelite women did not worship idols. In Isaiah 3:16–17, the prophet Isaiah reprimanded the woman for wearing makeup on their eyes and bells on their feet.

> Isaiah 3:16–26
> The LORD says, "The women of Zion are haughty, walking along with outstretched necks, flirting with their eyes, strutting along with swaying hips, with ornaments jingling on their ankles." Therefore, the Lord will bring sores on the heads of the women of Zion; the LORD will make their scalps bald. In that day the Lord will snatch away their finery: the bangles and headbands and crescent necklaces, the earrings and bracelets and veils, the headdresses and anklets and sashes, the perfume bottles and charms, the signet rings and nose rings, the fine robes and the capes and cloaks, the purses and mirrors, and the linen garments and tiaras and shawls. Instead of fragrance there will be a stench; instead of a sash, a rope; instead of well-dressed hair, baldness; instead of fine clothing, sackcloth; instead of beauty, branding. Your men will fall by the sword, your warriors in battle. The gates of Zion will lament and mourn; destitute, she will sit on the ground.

Why do the women get such a serious punishment just for dressing up? Is that such a principal sin? Compare that to the men who were worshiping idols and sacrificing their children to them.

These women were adorning themselves for their husbands; they wanted to lure their men back to them, for they had strayed and gone to the pagan prostitutes. Instead of grabbing their kids and disappearing, they sought to become pretty! The prophet said to the women, "If you are afraid of being alone, I assure you they will die in battle so you'll be alone without them or your children!"

Today some women make the same mistake. If your children are in danger of an abusive father or a horrible marriage, you must save your children, even if you don't have the money to live alone. If you take the first step, Hashem will help you succeed. Otherwise you too will be called a "merciful mother who cooks her children for her food." (Lamentations 4:10)

There was no reason to prohibit the women from learning Torah from day one. On the contrary, if they learned Torah, they would have never allowed their husbands to sacrifice their children or any children to any gods. The original plan was to let the women learn Torah by heart just to keep the faith, and let the men work in the fields until the world would be ready to study a book that needs a high level of literacy to understand it in detail. When Eve got excited at the idea that she can be a god, Hashem changed His plan. Neither Adam or Eve can taste from the Tree of Life until they were ready. Why?

If Eve wanted to be a god she can easily be one. Her body produces offspring and milk for her offspring. She also has more intuition than her man does and can make better decisions accordingly. If the woman would be the one to also learn Torah, that would give her much too much power.

Therefore, Eve was destined to be needy of her man and ruled by him, but only until our generation when everyone is literate and there are equal rights for both sexes. As a matter of fact, today women are better at religious leadership than men.

A Matriarchal Society

I have worked with many religious families in Israel. In the families that the men are in charge of the religious issues, the children are watched and criticized. The fathers left to themselves, can have a tendency to promote a strictness of rules that just make children angry and bitter. I have also seen that when couples allow their rabbis to stringently control their every move, they become very ill, even to the point of needing medication.

In fact, today in Jerusalem and other areas in Israel, there are many homes and even neighborhoods where the women rule. In those homes I have witnessed peace, happiness, and joy. The mothers use their Torah knowledge to instill faith and hope in the next generation. Everyone has fun. All of the children get married at a young age and enjoy being parents themselves.

There are homes that are totally matriarchal. The mothers head the families and are fully respected. The older children care for the younger ones without complaint and all respond to each and every request of their parents. The father models esteem for his wife. There is commonly less discord in these homes than in families with a fraction of the number of children. If a woman is not feeling well, her mother, sisters and maybe even her mother in-law come to the rescue. I have a friend from this community. She has eight children and wanted to come to my classes to learn natural medicine. Three of her sisters volunteered to care for the children once a week to allow her to study.

These large families are admired by welfare services and are often chosen to be foster families for children in need. This supports the notion that difficulties are not ensured due to the number of children or crowded living situations.

What is critical is the respect for the mother to rule the home and her support of Torah life and education.

There is a Jewish expression that says, "One mother can take care of ten children but ten children cannot take care of one mother." That saying comes from the Lower East Side in New York, where the influence of American culture prevailed. In Israel, Jewish religious parents are respected and cared for in their homes until their last day. The large families have the children and grandchildren take turns caring for the elderly grandparent and they all participate in the payment of home health care when needed.

Eve had to suffer the pain of childbirth and child-rearing not because she ate from the tree, but because she gave Adam to eat from the tree when God prohibited it. With the guidance from the Tree of Life, the Torah, the mothers enjoy their lives and their families. The pain of childbirth for them is minor compared to the blessed pleasures and gratification from their irreplaceable position as mothers and educators.

Single Women

If you are single or barren, God forbid, you are still a woman. You are still blessed with the capability of showing compassion and helping others. There is a great need for female therapists, teachers, medical professionals and even lawyers who can help young women and children. Through your good demeanor you can help people feel relaxed enough with you so that they share their worries and request your help. Instead of taking the gratitude for yourself, teach them to thank Hashem. Don't be afraid to mention Him even in the most secular surroundings. Bringing God's name to a God forsaken place gives Him pleasure. By doing this you can fulfil your role as a woman of the world.

Don't Cook a Kid in Its Mother's Milk

One very famous verse in the Bible is, "Don't cook a kid (a baby goat) in its mother's milk" (Deuteronomy 14:21). In my next book, *Choose Life*, I will discuss the dietary laws connected to this verse, but this verse is also a spiritual message to the mothers.

The Torah says not to cook a kid in its mother's milk, meaning not to overwhelm them with love and attention. Even though mother's milk is the best thing for the baby, don't cook him in it. A baby can be overfed or overprotected. There are times we just have to let go and watch those kids grow. Don't overwhelm your children with Torah laws either; they should enjoy themselves with the fun parts of the religion until they ask for more direction. As fate may have it, the word *kid*, which meant baby goat, means child in modern day English.

Don't give your child so much that he is smothered. We have to find the middle way. We must give our children love but also encourage their independence. When our offspring are born they need 100 percent of our love and closeness; that's why Hashem gave us mother's milk. Modern mothers are so anxious to separate from their babies that they want to wean them as soon as possible, and send them to a day-care center as early as two months old.

If for any reason you cannot nurse your baby, it is not an excuse to prop a bottle. Even adults do not like to eat alone; imagine an infant. If you hold your baby as if you are nursing, and look at him while eating, cuddle close for comfort instead of just rocking the carriage, your baby will become attached to you just like a nursing mother.

Hashem's advice is to try to nurse your child until two years old, and even after that not to put any boundaries between you and your child until age five. Children can come to your bed at night; you can give them as much attention and affection as they want. Never leave them alone, even in another room while you are in the house. You should overprotect until that age. They still need your love and closeness as they still can do dangerous things.

After five years old, it is time to let go and watch your child grow; teach him, and see what he needs. He may need discipline for his sake and not because you don't have the patience. Here too we need our men. A father can really help rearing a child in the right path. In the absence of a biological father, it is important to have another male figure of importance in the child's life.

A Man Is Like a Tree

Psalm 1

> Blessed is the one
>   who does not walk in step with the wicked
> or stand in the way that sinners take
>   or sit in the company of mockers,
> but whose delight is in the law of the LORD,
>   and who meditates on his law, day and night.
> That person is like a tree planted by streams of water,
>   which yields its fruit in season
> and whose leaf does not wither—
>   whatever they do prospers.
>
> Not so the wicked!
>   They are like chaff
>   that the wind blows away.
> Therefore, the wicked will not stand in the judgment,
>   nor sinners in the assembly of the righteous.

For the LORD watches over the way of the righteous,

but the way of the wicked leads to destruction.

The man who is like a tree is a man who has a home; he has roots. He has no fear that the troubles of life will dry out his faith. His wife will always support his belief in God and help him keep the Torah laws. He will not stop producing fruit as he and his wife will never avoid having children because they "fear the drought." This means that they are never afraid of not having the funds to support themselves. When a man marries, he sets down his roots. If his wife is God-fearing, then she will give him the spiritual support that he needs in order to fully trust Hashem with everything. Hashem will bless their home with righteous children and financial security.

CHAPTER 7

The Scroll of Esther

Of all the holy books of the Bible, the story of Queen Esther seems to be the most problematic. Many scholars claim that it is a fictional novel and no more. The Scroll of Esther is the only book of the Bible not to be found in the Dead Sea scrolls. The reason for this is because the Dead Sea scrolls were written before the canonization of the Bible. Approximately in the year 200 CE the Bible was canonized. That is when it was finally decided what books would be part of the Old Testament Bible and which ones would be external. The Essenes copied all the books that they thought were important and holy enough to be handed down throughout the generations. They didn't think that the Scroll of Esther was so important as to be part of the Bible because they didn't understand the deeper meaning behind this story, which at first glance seems like a fairy tale.

In this chapter, I am about the reveal a hidden meaning of the story of Esther that is only hinted in the scroll of Esther. Of course, the author of the scroll of Esther used literary license to elaborate and make a narrative with a plot, heroes, villains and a happy ending. However, the minute I reveal the true story, all the various parts of every episode fall into place; all the questions about this event are answered and all the problems are explained.

I am also about to solve an even bigger problem; one that I mentioned in the beginning of the book. This is a subject that has interested scholars and speculators for centuries: What happened to the Ten Lost Tribes?

In order to fully understand this chapter, I recommend reading the story of the Scroll of Esther straight from the Bible. If you have children, read it to them. They will understand and enjoy it. For those who want a shortcut, I will relate the story to you, keeping its fairytale style.

The Story of Queen Esther

Once upon a time in the far away land of Persia in the capital city of Shushan, there was a king who ruled over a hundred and twenty-seven provinces. His name was Achashverosh. One day the king decided to make a very large banquet in Shushan for all his subjects. Many kings and princes came to the feast from all over his lands. But who was missing?

None other than his queen, Vashti. Achashverosh sent messengers to fetch the queen but to no avail. Queen Vashti was making her own party, and she didn't want to leave her guests. The king was quite infuriated that his queen would not come when he asked for her. His ministers clamored, "If you forgive your queen, then all the women of the land will disobey their husbands. You must be rid of her!" Achashverosh was quite drunk from his banquet full of delicious wines so he agreed to their insistence to have the queen eliminated.

In the morning Achashverosh woke up crying hysterically, "Where, oh where is my beloved queen? What did I do?" Achashverosh mourned for his wife Vashti and could not be consoled. His ministers advised to present young maidens of the land to the King so that he would be encouraged to find a gorgeous new replacement. The most beautiful maiden in all the land was a Jewish girl named Esther, whose Hebrew name was Hadassah. She was chosen to be the new queen.

Hadassah was the niece of Mordechai, an educated Jew of the tribe of Benjamin, who adopted her because her father, Avichail, had passed away. Mordechai's wife, who was Avichail's sister, was also deceased, so as they were both lonely, they lived together and took care of each other.

Mordechai was not only learned in Torah but was also a great linguist. He overheard two people talking in ancient Greek plotting to assassinate Achashverosh. He informed the authorities, and the perpetrators were caught and hanged.

Haman was one of the ministers in King Achashverosh's court. Haman was very haughty and wanted everyone to bow down to him. Mordechai refused to bow before him because Jewish people are not allowed to prostrate themselves before anyone but God. Haman was incensed, and instead of just killing Mordechai, he aspired to destroy all the Jews. He told the king, "There is a nation that is dispersed all over your lands, and their religion is different from other nations. They do not obey the law of the king. It is not good for the king to let them live." Haman offered ten thousand blocks of silver to the king so that he could have permission to exterminate all the Jewish people—men, women, and children. Lots were drawn, and the date for the destruction of the Jews was set for the thirteenth of the month of Adar.

Dispatches were distributed to the kingdom's hundred and twenty-seven provinces to instruct all the royal subjects to eradicate the Jews on the fateful thirteenth day of the month of Adar. The letters were all sealed with the stamp of King Achashverosh's ring. All the gentiles prepared for the day that they could slay the Jews.

Mordechai dressed in ash and sackcloth because this was the clothing of mourners and sat by the gates of the palace. He was lamenting the terrible decree that had befallen the Jewish people. Queen Esther heard from her servants that he was attired inappropriately and she was shocked. It was forbidden to sit near the palace of the king dressed in rags. She forwarded her servants with new garbs for him but he refused to wear them. Then Mordechai informed Esther, "Haman has plotted to kill all the Jews. Please plead for us in front of the king. Maybe this is the reason that you reached to your position of royalty."

Esther said, "How can I? It's been thirty days since the king has called upon me!"

Mordechai replied, "If you are silent at this time, salvation and freedom will come to the Jews from another place, and you and the house of your father shall perish!"

Esther answered, "I will do as you say, but please fast for me; do not eat or drink, and my maidens and I will do the same. Whatever happens, will happen!"

Queen Esther came to the king's court after fasting for three days. She was a very brave queen because the king could have chopped her head off for coming to see him without being called. He extended his scepter and invited her to approach. "What can I do for you, my dear queen?" said the king. "Request up to half of the kingdom, and it will be granted." She asked the king to have Haman accompany him to a private feast that she would arrange the next day. Having received his royal invitation, Haman returned home happy and self-assured. At the banquet of three, Esther again asked Achashverosh, "If the king regards me with favor, and if it pleases the king to grant my petition and fulfill my request, let the king and Haman come tomorrow to the banquet I will prepare for them. Then I will answer the king's question."

Leaving the banquet, on the way home Haman saw Mordechai, who continued to refuse to submit and bow before him. Haman told his wife, Zeresh, of his despair over Mordechai's impudence. She suggested he build gallows to hang Mordechai, and so he constructed them.

On that night, the king could not sleep. He was tossing and turning until he called for his Book of Chronicles to be read to him. The king heard the recounting of Mordechai's faithfulness and action to save his life. The king wondered if Mordechai was rewarded. His servants said, "Nothing was done for him."

As the king was feeling bad that Mordechai wasn't rewarded he heard some noise in the royal courtyard and asked his servants, "Who's there? Have him come in." In comes no other than Haman. The king besought his guidance and said, "What should be done to a person that the king would like to honor? Haman said to himself, *Who could the king wish to honor more than me?"* Haman then counseled Achashverosh, "The person that the king desires to honor should be dressed in royal garb and led about the city on the king's horse in a processional with the leader calling out, 'This is how the king honors the one he favors.'" King Achashverosh commanded Haman, "Do this to Mordechai, who sits at the gate of the palace."

Haman was appalled. He returned home to his wife and children so depressed and virtually in mourning after escorting Mordechai through the capital city on the king's horse. His wife declared, "If this is the man against whom you plotted, you will fall before him."

The king's men then arrived to escort Haman to court for the party with the king and queen. At this second banquet, Esther said to the king, "If I found favor in the eyes of the king, and if it feels good to you, grant me my soul and my nation as my request. We have been sold for destruction and murder. If we were sold as slaves and maidservants, I would be quiet because the suffering would not be worth causing damage to the King." The King answered, "Who has plotted to do so?" Esther replied, "This bad and wicked man Haman!" Haman fell into the corner from shame. One of Queen Esther's helpers named Charvona informed the king, "Haman built wooden gallows on which to hang Mordechai, the man that you honored." The king directed, "Hang Haman on it!"

Achashverosh saw that Queen Esther was still not happy. "What's the matter?" asked the king. "The nations of your kingdom are all preparing to annihilate my people, so what can we do?" asked the queen. The king replied, "I will give you and Mordechai my ring, and you can write a different letter to your people. Write whatever you wish, but I cannot take back what had already been engraved because what has been inscribed and stamped with the seal of the king cannot be revoked."

Haman was hanged together with his ten sons and the city of Shushan was joyous. After the hanging ceremony, Mordechai wrote letters to the Jews that they can fight to defend themselves on the thirteenth and the fourteenth days of Adar. The city of Shushan had the worst fighting, so the war between the Jews and the gentiles continued until the fifteenth of Adar in Shushan the capital city of Persia. The Jews prevailed everywhere so there were more celebrations and festivities in all of the empire. Subsequently, many converted to Judaism because they were afraid of the Jews. Mordechai instituted a holiday every year to commemorate the history of the events. It would become a mitzvah to deliver portions of food to friends and presents for the poor.

On the fourteenth of Adar every year we celebrate this big miracle with singing and dancing, distributing allotments of provisions to our comrades and allocating charity for the poor just as it says in the Holy Scroll of Esther. On the fifteenth of Adar the holiday is celebrated in Jerusalem and in every city in Israel that had a wall in the days of Joshua, in memory of the war in Shushan.

Purim

Purim is the name for these days of festivity. Haman cast lots, known as "purim" to fix the date, the thirteenth of Adar, to go to war against the Jews. Nowadays, on the fourteenth and fifteenth of Adar, there is rejoicing in every Jewish synagogue with special prayers and the story of Esther is read from a scroll made of parchment. Schools have plays and everyone dresses up in masquerade. It is a favorite holiday for Jewish children all over the world.

In any Jewish school, when learning this story, the teacher never forgets to say the following, "Every time that it says the King in the Scroll of Esther, it means Hashem." We were also taught that Purim is similar to the Day of Atonement, which in Hebrew is Yom Kippurim or Yom Kippur for short. The syllable *Ki* in front of a word means *like*. Yom Kippurim, the Day of Atonement, is the holiest and most solemn day of the year. On Yom Kippur we pray all day to Hashem to forgive us for our sins. How could Yom Kippur be like Purim? Why would our sages give that type of importance to this fun and frolicsome holiday?

In very tiny hints since early childhood we have been taught that the Scroll of Esther is more than what meets the eye. I would like to relate the true story of Purim as

Hashem helped me understand. It is very important to Hashem that I write it in this book in order to further encourage faith in the entire Bible and to give Esther the respect that she deserves.

Background Check

The story of Esther opens in the palace of the Persian King Achashverosh, the ruler of a hundred and twenty-seven provinces between Ethiopia and India. Some scholars claim that there is no evidence of the existence of an empire with a hundred and twenty-seven provinces at the time of the event, which is believed to begin approximately 550 BCE to 539 BCE. We checked the history of Persia, which is very well documented, and there is no evidence in the entire Persian history of a King Achashverosh. Queen Esther herself is a historical impossibility because, at the time, Persian kings could only marry within seven noble families. Esther was a simple woman from a nation that was taken away from its country and captured into slavery. She certainly was not of royal blood fit for a king.

There are many more problems with the story too numerous to be just unintentional mistakes. Many Bible scholars argue as to how impossible the story actually is. Some say that the story should be deleted from the Bible. To these scholars the following observation will be a shock and a comfort. The importance of this story is paramount and this holiday marks a major turning point in Jewish history.

The story of Esther is a tale that was told in order to give a valid reason for a very special holiday without revealing the actual true events. It is no mistake. It was a narrative intended to be kept secret and whose true meaning would be revealed in a future generation.

Is There any Truth to the Story?

In Jewish folklore, there is a belief that the story of Esther took place in a time period about twenty years before the return of the nation to Zion and before King Cyrus ruled. At this proposed era in ancient Babylon, there was still evidence of writing on clay basins. King Cyrus the Great wrote his first laws on a famous clay vessel. Parchment was still not in full use.

In the story of Esther, scrolls were copied hundreds of times and sent to many locations in all hundred and twenty-seven provinces, as is quoted in Esther 8:9 and 9:30. In order for there to be any truth in the story, it had to have happened at least a few decades later, when writing on parchment was a bit more popular.

King Darius the Great ruled from 522 BCE to 486 BCE. He completed the conquest of a hundred and twenty-seven countries, the same number that Achashverosh ruled as is stated in the Scroll of Esther. In the year 500 BCE, he conquered Egypt, which was inside the provinces that stretched from "India until Ethiopia" (Esther 1:1).

By the time King Darius ruled, the use of parchment was fully developed, and a system of runners announced messages to all the lands just like it says in Esther 8:14: "The couriers, riding the royal horses, went out, spurred on by the king's command, and the edict was issued in the citadel of Susa."

I would like to set the timing of this story somewhere between 465 and 445 BCE, the period of the reconstruction of the Wall of Jerusalem. One proof I have that this is true is that Mordechai, a main character in the story of Esther, is mentioned in the very beginning of the book of Ezra. In Ezra 2:2 and Nehemiah 7:7, Mordechai is listed as one of the people returning from Babylon with Ezra. The Talmud says that this is Mordechai himself. All the Jewish biblical commentaries agree. When Jewish scholars learn this chapter, they teach that Mordechai returned to Israel after the story of Esther. I assert that he is entering the land beforehand.

Artaxerxes and Achashverosh

The King James version translates Achashverosh as Xerxes. Artaxerxes is the king who finally gives permission to the Jewish people to build the Holy Temple and to teach Torah. I would like to give you an overview of historians on the subject.

The Scroll of Esther is set in the Persian capital of Shushan (Susa) during the third year of the King Ahasuerus' rule. The name Ahasuerus in the book of Ester comes from the same Persian term for Xerxes and who reigned between 486 and 465 BCE. The majority of scholars ascribe *Xerxes I* as the ruler most likely connected to the events described in the Scroll of Esther. Other historical sources including Josephus, the Jewish commentary *Esther Rabbah*, the Christian theologian Bar-Hebraeus, and the Greek Septuagint translation of Esther, propose that Ahasuerus was either Artaxerxes I ruling from 465 to 424 BCE or Artaxerxes II ruling from 404 to 358 BCE.

Artaxerxes is also given as the name of a King of Persia in the Book of Ezra.

Ezra 7:1, "After these things, during the reign of Artaxerxes king of Persia, Ezra son of Seraiah, the son of Azariah, the son of Hilkiah."

I would like to claim that the story of Esther happened under the rule of Artaxerxes while Ezra was alive. Ethiopia was one of the countries mentioned in the Scroll of Esther.

Ethiopian writings mention Achashverosh referring to him as Art'eksis. The Israelites of Ethiopia had no contact with other Jews for centuries. Thus, their texts are not influenced by any outside censorship or secular historians. Their opinion should be considered authentic.

There is a mention of an Achashverosh in Daniel 9:1, "In the first year of Darius the son of Achashverosh from the descendants of Mede that ruled over the kingdom of Casdim." Some commentaries say that this is the Achashverosh of Queen Esther. However, this Achashverosh was not a king over Persia, and he definitely didn't live in Shushan, the Persian capital. He was a ruler over Casdim, which was a country in the area of today's Lebanon.

Many of the kings had similar names. There was another Darius. There were three different kings by the name Artaxerxes in later generations. Just like the kings of England, the kings of ancient times had similar names. There is no doubt that the Achashverosh mentioned in Daniel is not the king mentioned in the Scroll of Esther that ruled over Persia, Mede, and 127 countries.

There is another Achashverosh mentioned in Ezra 4:4–6

> Then the people of the land weakened the hands of the people of Judah, and troubled them in building, and hired counsellors against them, to frustrate their purpose, all the days of Cyrus king of Persia, even until the reign of Darius king of Persia. And in the reign of Ahasuerus, in the beginning of his reign, wrote they an accusation against the inhabitants of Judah and Jerusalem.

According to these passages, first came Cyrus, then Darius; next was Achashverosh, succeeded by Artaxerxes. This makes more sense because then Achashverosh ruled after Darius, who conquered the 127 nations. However, this theory is not backed up by historians. It is possible that the rabbis added these words into the book of Ezra later, in order to find a place for Achashverosh in history. If you want to believe that the King Achashverosh in Ezra was the King of the Scroll of Esther, it only strengthens my point. This whole story happened after the return of the Jews to Zion.

The Order of Historical Events

721 BCE. Assyria conquered the northern ten tribes of Israel.

612 BCE. Babylon conquered the Assyrian Empire.

586 BCE. Babylon conquered Judea and destroyed the First Temple.

539 BCE. Cyrus conquered Babylon.

522 BCE. Darius rules and begins the conquest of 127 countries.

520 BCE. The Second Temple building commences.

515 BCE. The Second Temple was completed and dedicated.

485 BCE. Xerxes I rules.

465 BCE. Artaxerxes I rules.

458 BCE. Ezra the scribe comes to Israel from Babylon.

445 BCE. Nehemiah rebuilds the walls of Jerusalem.

Ezra's Mission

When Artaxerxes came into power, he gave Ezra authority to bring the original Torah as well as gold, silver, vessels and any other needs with him for the Holy Temple in Jerusalem (Ezra 7:12-24). Furthermore, Artaxerxes said,

"Sure I'll furnish your temple, but if I find even one person that doesn't follow your faith he will be punished."

Ezra 7:25–28

And you, Ezra, in accordance with the wisdom of your God, which you possess, appoint magistrates and judges to administer justice to all the people of Trans-Euphrates—all who know the laws of your God. And you are to teach any who do not know them. Whoever does not obey the law of your God and the law of the King must surely be punished by death, banishment, confiscation of property or imprisonment. Praise be to the Lord, the God of our fathers, who has put it into the King's heart to bring honor to the house of the Lord in Jerusalem in this way and who has extended his good favor to me before the King and his advisers and all the King's powerful officials. Because the hand of the Lord my God was on me, I took courage and gathered leading men from Israel to go up with me.

A Dispersed Nation

When Nebuchadnezzar conquered Israel he exiled the Jews to Babylonia. The Jews of the Babylonian exile didn't leave Babylon except to go to Persia, the conquering country, or to return to the Holy Land. It says in the Scroll of Esther 3:8, "There is a nation who is dispersed all over the kingdom." The Jews were not dispersed all over the kingdom. The hundred and twenty-seven provinces "between India and Ethiopia" (Esther 1:1) were not inhabited by the Jews of the Babylonian diaspora. These two countries are known today to be countries where the Ten Lost Tribes dwelt for generations.

The Assyrians had a custom of dispersing their captives to foreign countries in order to weaken their ability to revolt.

After their victory in Northern Israel, they dispersed the Israelites of the Northern Kingdom all over the hundred and twenty-seven different provinces. The people of these ten tribes knew no Torah, as they continued to worship idols even in exile. The countries that they dwelt in under Assyrian rule were conquered by Nebuchadnezzar and later by King Darius.

In Esther 3:8, Haman says,

> "There is a certain people dispersed and scattered among the peoples in all the provinces of your Kingdom whose customs are different from those of all other people and who do not obey the King's laws; it is not in the King's best interest to tolerate them."

What he really meant was, "Your majesty the king, these Jews that are in your city have relatives. They are also descendants of the Children of Israel that received the Torah on Mount Sinai. They are dispersed all over your provinces. They are not keeping your decree to keep the Torah. We must destroy them as you decreed." Letters were sent all over the provinces to kill any Israelites who did not keep the Torah.

Queen Esther

Who was Esther? How can Mordechai say to her that the house of her father will be abolished while the Jews are set free?

In the beginning of the story, Esther is mentioned as the daughter of Avichail. Jews always name after their grandparents and great-grandparents. Avichail was the name of the head of the tribe of Naftali in the times of Joshua. Esther's father was named after him just as today many Jewish children are named after righteous people in their families or countries.

Hashem showed me that a group of women from the tribe of Naftali decided to go back to the Land of Israel as soon as King Cyrus allowed it. They were students of Esther, learning Torah with her and working on their spirituality. They knew that the Land of Israel was the place for them. They left their families, who were pure idolaters, and came to the Holy Land with Esther and her family.

Mordechai was related to Esther through marriage. He married the niece of Avichail, and his wife passed away as did Esther's parents on the long trek from Babylon to Israel. That's why it says in the Scroll of Esther, "Avichail the uncle of Mordechai" (Esther 2:15). Esther was very young when this happened, and Mordechai adopted Esther, as it says, "Mordechai took her in as a daughter" (Esther 2:7).

A Prophetess

Rabbi Shlomo Yitchaki known by the contraction of his name as Rashi, the famous commentator on the Talmud and the Bible, mentioned Esther as one of the seven prophetesses (Rashi on Tractate Megillah 14a). Even though there is no evidence for that in the Scroll of Esther, there was a tradition that Esther was a prophetess.

Since I was very young, it bothered me that Mordechai would have allowed his only daughter to marry a non-Jewish king. According to Torah law, marriage to a gentile is forbidden. At the time, I had a theory that Mordechai just wasn't religious. I tried to research this theory, but I discovered that this was not true. Mordechai was part of the first group of Jewish leaders who entered the Holy Land. The Talmud says that Mordechai was a great leader and was on the head council of Jewish lawmakers. He was very religious on all accounts.

How is this possible? How could there have even been a council of Jewish lawmakers? I just finished teaching you how sinful the Israelites were. The Kingdom of Judea was no better. All the horrible sins that the prophets complained about were in the Kingdom of Judea, where the destruction of the Holy Temple occurred. They were devout idol-worshipers!

The answer lies in the book of Daniel.

Daniel

In the generation before Mordechai, there were a few scholarly men in the Babylonian diaspora. Their names were Daniel, Chanania, Mishael, and Azria. They were servants in the palace of King Darius, and they refused to eat non-kosher meat. They asked for beans and seeds and to the surprise of the head of the royal kitchen, they stayed healthy and strong, They may have been the first Jewish vegetarians.

By the way this is further proof that the women were righteous. Jewish boys may have been worshipping idols because they learned that from their father but they would never eat non-kosher food because Mama always did the cooking!

Daniel was the King's right-hand man. He had free access to the entire palace. Daniel was able to examine the books of the royal library and what did he find? The holy book of Jeremiah. It was one of the many writings taken from the Holy Temple by Nebuchadnezzar. Daniel read about how bad the Jews were in the Land of Israel and how much God was angry with them. In those days, most people were illiterate and knew nothing of their past.

Daniel learned how to read but he never read the books of the Bible because they were not available at the time. Daniel was very impressed by what he read in the book of Jeremiah and he started to pray. He prayed with all his heart that the Jewish people repent and he prayed that God should forgive them for their sins (Daniel 9:2-3).

It was against the law of Babylon to pray to any other deity but the god of the Babylonian king. After reading Jeremiah, Daniel began to pray to Hashem. King Darius was told that Daniel was praying to the God of Israel and the king's advisors got very angry. They pressured King Darius to punish Daniel, his best servant.

King Darius cast Daniel into the lion's den to be greeted by a pack of these hungry beasts. The king felt sick. He tossed and turned all night long. He was sorry that he had killed Daniel. However, when he woke up in the morning, he ran to the lions' pit. Lo and behold, Daniel was alive and well, untouched by the lions.

King Darius was in shock. He couldn't understand how this is possible. Were the lions sick? To find out if this was the case, he threw the people who slandered against Daniel into the pit. They were devoured in minutes. The king was in awe; he felt that the God of Israel was with Daniel. He made a proclamation to his entire kingdom.

> Daniel 6:25–28
> Then Darius the King wrote to all the peoples, nations and men of every language who were living in all the land: May your peace abound! I make a decree that in all the dominion of my kingdom men are to fear and tremble before the God of Daniel; For He is the living God and enduring forever, and His kingdom is one which will not be destroyed, and His dominion will be forever. He delivers and rescues and

performs signs and wonders in heaven and on earth, who has also delivered Daniel from the power of the lions. So Daniel prospered during the reign of Darius and the reign of Cyrus the Persian. (Read Daniel chapter 6 for the entire story).

From that day on, the inhabitants of the Median Kingdom, which included Babylon, Mede, and Persia, started believing in God. The Jews that were exiled by Nebuchadnezzar, King of Babylon returned to Hashem after many years of idol worship. King Darius the Mede granted them permission to keep the Jewish faith but they remained under Median rule.

The True Story Begins

Mordechai and Ezra were friends and colleagues. They were both afraid of the decree of Artaxerxes. They knew that most of the ten northern tribes were still worshiping idols. Ezra went up north to the Persian provinces to try to teach Torah to the Israelites in the northern Diaspora, as it says in Ezra 7:28, "I took courage and gathered leading men from Israel to go up with me." Mordechai, who respected his niece Esther the prophetess, visits her to request that she speak to the king, not the King Artaxerxes, but to God, the King of Kings.

It's interesting to know that the numerical value of the king Achashverosh is 1820. Gematria is a system of codes where every Hebrew letter has a numerical value, just like numerology. The numerical value of the Hebrew words "The King of Kings, The Holy One blessed is He" is also 1820. Maybe that's the reason that Artaxerxes' name was changed to Achashverosh. Everything was codified.

Mordechai to the Rescue

Mordechai is in a panic because hundreds of thousands of lives are at stake. Messengers of the king were on a mission to find anyone who was not keeping the Torah, as Artaxerxes commanded. Mordechai begged Esther to speak to Hashem to save the Ten Tribes of Israel from extermination. Esther complained, "The King has not called for me for thirty days." What she means is that the King of Kings did not call on her. She didn't have any prophecies for thirty days. In Esther 4:11, Mordechai answers, "If you are quiet, the salvation will come to the Jews from another venue, but you and your family will be lost."

In Esther 4:14, Esther decides to fast for three days together with her maidens, who were actually apprentice prophetesses. The fasting was for the purpose of receiving prophecy. Fasting doesn't help so much if you have to be beautiful for a mortal king.

What was Esther's problem? Why did she consider this a difficult request?

The Ten Tribes of Israel were still worshiping idols. There were many Jewish people who were also deserving of death according to Torah law. They didn't keep *Shabbat* or other laws that are also punishable by death. Esther didn't know what to say to God. In the Torah it says to kill those who worship idols, so how can she pray to save them?

In the Scroll of Esther, she tells the king, "I am begging you for mercy on my people's children. If they were to be sold as slaves I wouldn't bother you because the suffering that they would endure would not be enough to cause damage to the King." The damage is harm to God's name. Instead of sending the Jewish idol worshipers to their death, Esther is asking God to please change the decree and give a chance for her family and her tribe, who were still in the Diaspora, to live. The reason she said that if they were sold as slaves she wouldn't ask Hashem to save them is because they did deserve some kind of punishment for worshipping other gods. But if they are killed, how can they repent? How could their souls be saved?

The miracle was that God answered:

> Esther 8:8, "And you can write anything you want to in the name of the King and sign it with the ring of the King. For whatever is written in the name of the king and stamped with the ring of the King cannot be retrieved."

The king here is Hashem, the King of Kings. "Whatever is written in the name of the King," is the Torah, and what's "stamped with ring of the King," is the Ten Commandments, which were written with Hashem's finger.

Hashem told Esther, "I can't change what I wrote in the Torah, but you can write another decree in my name." She sent a message to the Jewish people in the name of God that they can fight for their lives. Even though they deserve death, they haven't been tried by a Jewish court.

Anybody who transgresses Torah law cannot simply be executed. It is necessary to have witnesses and warnings. Violators can defend themselves in court, repent from their ways and fight for their lives. Esther prayed that the Jewish idolaters know that God would accept their repentance even though their sins are great. From here we learn that Hashem wants us to fight for our lives, no matter what. We have to do our best to live. We cannot say, "We sinned and therefore we deserve the punishment that has come to us, so let's accept it without a battle." Esther learned that no matter how great our sins are, there is always a possibility for repentance and forgiveness.

The message to fight cannot simple be sent through runners who would warn the enemy. Therefore, Mordechai wrote his messages in fairy tale form so that his brethren would understand. The Book of Esther is an anthology of all the messages that were sent back and forth to the Israelite population in the guise of a beautiful fairy tale.

Hashem told Esther that He would help those who repent and He did. They succeeded in their battles with unimaginable victory. With Hashem's blessing, the dread of the Jews following their unpredictable triumphs, resulted in Hellenists wanting to jump on their bandwagon.

> Esther 8:17, "Many of the peoples of the land were becoming Jewish because the fear of the Jew came upon them."

Converts aren't accepted in one day as it takes a whole year of education and purification before a they are accepted into the Jewish nation. At the time of Esther, these "peoples of the land" were the Israelites who left their idol worship in order to save their lives from the Persian decree that anyone of the nation of Israel who did not keep the Torah would be killed.

The Israelites of the ten tribes did not have to convert; they were already the Children of Israel, but they became Jewish, meaning they accepted the religion of the Jews, who came from the exile of Judah and kept the Torah in the spirit of Daniel.

The Jews and the Israelites were returning to the Land of Israel and to Hashem by will or from fear. That's why Purim is even greater than Yom Kippur, the Day of Atonement. On this day, hundreds of thousands of the Children of Israel returned to their Father in heaven. This is certainly a reason to celebrate. The vast majority of Israel left idol worship and joined to be one nation under God. Hashem forgave even those who were seemingly too far gone to forgive. On the holiday of Purim, not only do we have cause to celebrate military victories, we can rejoice in how fortunate we are that God forgives even the seemingly unforgivable. There is never reason to give up hope.

The Ten Lost Tribes

Purim should also be the commemoration of the return of the Ten Lost Tribes to God and to Israel. Even members of those tribes who didn't return to Israel to build the Holy Temple left their idolatry. The Jews of lost tribes that we find today do not worship idols, and most of them have some ancient biblical customs. That wouldn't be the case had they not repented during the time of Esther and Mordechai.

> Esther 10:3, "Mordechai is loved by most of his brothers."

Why most? Most of his brothers were loyal but some of the Ten Tribes that did not return were lost and assimilated with the nations of the world. Some Israelites became Christian or Moslem. Today we have found many remnants of the lost tribes who were exiled after the destruction of the First Temple and did not return to Israel when the Second Temple was built. Religious Israeli leaders as well as the state itself have been slowly bringing them back to the Jewish faith and to the Land of Israel. Nevertheless, the majority of the Ten Tribes have already been within our midst since the days of Purim.

In Israel today there are many Jews who claim that they were in their countries of origin since the destruction of the

First Temple. For example, Yemenite Jews were not from the lost tribes. They were from the kingdom of Judea, but they did not return for the Second Temple period because their prophets told them that the Second Temple would also be destroyed.

On the other hand, we have Jews from Northern India who have a very strong heritage of being the children of the tribe of Reuben. These Reubenites may have been part of the wars of Purim because the Scroll of Esther says that the kingdom included all the countries from India until Ethiopia. These Reubenites must have abandoned their idolatry because of the decrees of Artaxerxes but they did not all come to Israel. Today the Reubenites have finally returned. The ingathering of different Jews from many different lands is indeed the fruition of the prophecies of old.

> Jeremiah 23:3-4
> "I myself will gather the remnant of my flock out of all the countries where I have driven them and will bring them back to their pasture, where they will be fruitful and increase in number. I will place shepherds over them who will tend them, and they will no longer be afraid or terrified, nor will any be missing," declares the LORD.

Ethiopian Jews

The Ethiopian Jews are said to be descendants from the tribe of Dan, one of the lost tribes. We met an Ethiopian refugee in Israel who said that her family kept traditions for centuries. She told us that the day of Purim was a day of mourning because they thought that the Israelites of the other tribes were killed, and they were the only ones left of the Children of Israel in the Diaspora. When the Israeli government came into Ethiopia to rescue them, they were so happy that there were other Jews, but they were surprised that the Second Temple was gone. When they came to Israel and saw that Western Wall, a remnant of the Holy Temple, some of their elders cried bitterly that the Holy Temple had been destroyed.

It's interesting that the Ethiopian Jews thought that the Jews of Israel were alive and the temple was flourishing, but that the Jews of the Diaspora had been killed by Artaxerxes's decree. That's because the decree was only on those who did not keep the Torah.

An Ethiopian Holiday

The following is a news article describing a holiday that Ethiopian Jews celebrate in commemoration of the return of Jews from the Babylonian exile:

The Ethiopian Jews had a special holiday for the return of the Jews from the first exile! They call this holiday Sigd. The festival is based upon the events related in the Book of Nehemiah chapter 8 and 9 in which the Biblical prophets Ezra and Nehemiah led the Jewish people out of Babylonian exile and back into the Land of Israel. They celebrate with a ceremony of fasting and praying on a mountain top.

This means that they were around at the time and were in touch with the Jewish homeland. The runners of Esther and Mordechai made it all the way to Ethiopia to teach their brethren to believe in one God and observe the Torah. In the 1980's when the Israeli government got in touch with them they were keeping the basic laws of the Torah; for example, Shabbat, Passover and Family Purity.

The trip to Israel from Ethiopia is through the Sudanese deserts. They had to walk for weeks until they reached the nearest airport. Many Ethiopians died on the way. It is no wonder that they were so secluded and out of touch with their brethren for almost two thousand years.

The Ethiopian Jews thought that Purim was a day of mourning. Apparently the runners succeeded in reaching them with the first message but not with the new messages of victory and celebration. This supports that the Israelites of the Assyrian exile were in contact with the Jews of the Babylonian exile and my version of the story rings true.

Customs

After the first Purim, there were many refugees in Israel and especially in Jerusalem. It was important to provide food for the new visitors so that they feel welcome to return to the faith of their ancestors. Mordechai established a custom to give food packages to each other and presents to the poor on the holiday of Purim. This custom became a law that every Jewish family keeps until today. We go from house to house in masquerade just like the gentiles do on Halloween, but we come to give treats and food packages to the homes and not to demand anything from them. We also sing and dance on this day and we have a festive meal after the services in the synagogue where the whole story of Esther is read aloud from parchment.

Shushan Purim

There are two days of Purim. Jerusalem celebrates Purim the day after the rest of the world observes this holiday. The rabbis say that the second day of Purim is to commemorate the second day of fighting in Shushan, Persia, and so it is called Shushan Purim.

What's the connection to Jerusalem? The Scroll of Esther says that every city that is not walled should celebrate Purim on the fourteenth of Adar.

> Esther 9:19, "That is why rural Jews—those living in villages—observe the fourteenth of the month of Adar as a day of joy and feasting, a day for giving presents to each other."

The Hebrew Bible doesn't say villages; it says "cities without walls." The walls of Jerusalem had just been rebuilt. The Scroll of Esther was hinting that the Jews in the cities outside of Jerusalem started celebrating on the fourteenth.

Shushan is called Susa in the NIV Bible. There are cities in Israel that celebrate two days because they aren't positive that those cities were walled since the times of Joshua. However, no city besides Jerusalem celebrates the Shushan Purim exclusively. So why is Jerusalem so important?

Historically, Jerusalem was a walled city from the times of David. Nehemiah rebuilt the wall that was destroyed by the king of Babylonia, Nebuchadnezzar. Jerusalem is included in the celebrations of the fifteenth of Adar because Esther and Mordechai were there. The whole battle of the fifteenth of Adar was in Jerusalem. Shushan was just a cover to hide where the real action was.

There was more fighting in Jerusalem because there were more Persian soldiers Jerusalem. The leaders of Israel didn't want anyone knowing that there was a lot of killing in Jerusalem because King Artaxerxes would not be happy about it if he knew. They didn't want him to know that there were any infidels in Jerusalem. Of course this means that the story of Esther must have occurred after Nehemiah completed the building of the wall of Jerusalem in 445 BCE.

Esther 9:20–22

Mordecai recorded these events, and he sent letters to all the Jews throughout the provinces of King Xerxes, near and far, to have them celebrate annually the fourteenth and fifteenth days of the month of Adar as the time when the Jews got relief from their enemies, and as the month when their sorrow was turned into joy and their mourning into a day of celebration.

The whole Jewish people celebrate Purim on the fourteenth of Adar, and the Jews of Jerusalem celebrate on the fifteenth. In some cities they celebrate two days because there is a doubt if the city had a wall in the times of Joshua. If you look closely at the text, it looks like originally everyone celebrated two days of Purim. Mordechai wanted everyone to celebrate for Jerusalem. Jerusalem is the heart and soul of the Jewish people; if Jerusalem rests, we all are at peace. Many ancient coins of other cities had Jerusalem as an emblem.

Today nobody knows that Jerusalem of old, the walled city rebuilt by Nehemiah was at war on the fourteenth of Adar. Those Israelites living outside of Jerusalem have Purim as an equally important holiday as Shushan Purim.

There is a gravesite building in Persia that is claimed to house the graves of Mordechai and Esther in Persia near the ancient palace. If Esther was a queen, she would be buried with the other royal figures, including the king so these alleged gravesites are not authentic. The real gravesites are in Israel in Northern Galilee. They are open to the public.

Comparison to the Book of Nehemiah

Nehemiah went to the city of Shushan. Nehemiah 1:1, "I was in Shushan the Capital." The Jews in Shushan were still crying over the loss of Jerusalem. They described the total destruction, and then Nehemiah was mourning bitterly over Jerusalem. He was the appointed cup bearer for King Artaxerxes.

> Nehemiah 2:1–6
> In the month of Nisan in the twentieth year of King Artaxerxes, when wine was brought for him, I took the wine and gave it to the King. I had not been sad in his presence before, so the King asked me, 'Why does your face look so sad when you are not ill? This can be nothing but sadness of heart.' I was very much afraid, but I said to the King, 'May the King live forever! Why should my face not look sad when the city where my ancestors are buried lies in ruins, and its gates have been destroyed by fire?' The King said to me, 'What is it you want?' Then I prayed to the God of heaven, and I answered the King, 'If it is good upon the King and if your servant has found favor in his eyes, let him send me to the city in Judah where my ancestors are buried so that I can rebuild it.' Then the King, with the Queen sitting beside him, asked me, 'How long will your journey take, and when will you get back?' It pleased the King to send me; so I set a time.

Nehemiah is at the king's table asking the king for a favor in very similar words that Esther asked for a favor from her king, as found in Esther 8:5, "If it is good upon the King and if I have found favor before him." Also, similar language is found in Esther 5:4; 5:8; 7:3; and 9:13. Is this the allegory set in the Scroll of Esther?

Why Is this Revelation So Important?

This book is all about how the Torah that was given on Mount Sinai was passed over to us without error. This story shows that the Torah was returned to the entire people of Israel, not only the nation of Judah. Another important discovery here is the story of the repentance of the Jewish people and of the Israelites. This holiday is truly bigger than Yom Kippur because millions of Israelites left their pagan practices and accepted upon themselves the One God of Israel.

Why Hide the Truth?

To conclude this story, I think that it would be safe to say that most of the Ten Lost Tribes are among us. Hashem did not allow all the Israelites of the Ten Tribes to vanish. I finally got the answer to the question that I asked Hashem twenty-eight years ago. Why hide the truth of this story? The answer in one word would be "prejudice."

> Ezra 4:1–5
> When the enemies of Judah and Benjamin heard that the exiles were building a temple for the LORD, the God of Israel, they came to Zerubbabel and to the heads of the families and said, "Let us help you build because, like you, we seek your God and have been sacrificing to him since the time of Esarhaddon king of Assyria, who brought us here." But Zerubbabel, Joshua and the rest of the heads of the families of Israel answered, "You have no part with us in building a temple to our God. We alone will build it for the LORD, the God of Israel, as King Cyrus, the king of Persia, commanded us." Then the peoples around them set out to discourage the people of Judah and make them afraid to go on building. They bribed officials to work against them and frustrate their plans during the entire reign of Cyrus king of Persia and down to the reign of Darius king of Persia.

The "enemies" of Judah and Benjamin were non-Jews from the Assyrian exile. They entered the land of Israel even before the Jews of Babylon. They are called "the exiles" because the Assyrians were in the habit of breaking up nations and spreading them out to different countries so they will lose their strength. They put a tribe of non-Jews in Israel and they wanted to serve the God of Israel. The displaced gentiles fought the Jews for no good reason. It was so disastrous that the building of the Holy Temple was postponed. Finally, two prophets, Haggai and Zechariah, helped make peace between them.

> Ezra 5:1-2
> Now Haggai the prophet and Zechariah the prophet, a descendant of Iddo, prophesied to the Jews in Judah and Jerusalem in the name of the God of Israel, who was over them. Then Zerubbabel son of Shealtiel and Joshua son of Jozadak set to work to rebuild the house of God in Jerusalem. And the prophets of God were with them, supporting them.

The Jewish prophets had to teach the Jews to accept anyone who wants to serve the God of Israel and they made peace between them. After the victory of the Jews over the heathens, Mordechai witnessed prejudice between the different tribes. That is why he commanded the Jews to give out presents on this holiday. The presents were for anyone, Israelites or not, who was willing to accept the belief in the one God of Israel. Ezra was afraid that there would be prejudice against the Ten Tribes that still did not learn Torah and were just beginning to leave their idolatrous ways. Therefore, he decided to abolish the tradition of division according to tribes.

Instead Ezra declared three divisions: (1) *Cohanim*, priests from the descendants of Aaron; (2) Levite descendants of the tribe of Levi; and (3) Israel, the rest of the nation.

Ezra 10:5, "So Ezra prayed arose and administered
an oath to the chiefs of the Cohens, the Levites and
all of Israel to carry out this matter, and they swore."

Every tribe included Levites, Cohens and Israelis so all three divisions of the chosen nation were represented in every tribe. The Levites and Cohens were the teachers and priests and they were spread out among all the tribes. The Israelis were simply all the rest of the people who were not Levites and Cohens. Ezra wanted to erase any memory of tribal divisiveness within the Jewish people. Until today, the custom of delegates of each of the three divisions of Jews constitute the congregants in synagogues. There isn't a separate synagogue for Cohens, another for Levites and a third for Israelis. They mix together to form congregations and they are called up to bless the Torah in synagogue on Shabbat; first is a Cohen, second is a Levi and third through seven is an Israeli. This custom is kept in synagogues worldwide.

Traditionally, many synagogues have pictures of the emblems of the twelve tribes on the walls in honor of their memory. The children of the generation after Ezra were told that the tribes were lost. That is the tradition until today.

Below is a picture of the emblems of the tribes of Israel. The emblems were chosen as symbols that relate to the blessings that Moses gave the tribes before his passing. It is unknown to the congregations that these symbols were instated as a memory of the tribes that were divisions that were abolished after the miracle of Purim.

Asher
Stitches: 6867
Size: 3.55 x 3.24 "

Benyamin
Stitches: 5148
Size: 3.55 x 3.26 "

Dan
Stitches: 5882
Size: 3.55 x 2.97 "

Gad
Stitches: 6216
Size: 3.55 x 3.09 "

Issachar
Stitches: 7784
Size: 3.55 x 3.61 "

Joseph
Stitches: 8443
Size: 3.55 x 3.15 "

Judah
Stitches: 8801
Size: 3.81 x 3.05 "

Levi
Stitches: 6842
Size: 3.55 x 2.87 "

Naftali
Stitches: 5744
Size: 3.55 x 3.57 "

Reuben
Stitches: 9145
Size: 3.55 x 2.65 "

Simeon
Stitches: 6371
Size: 3.55 x 3.27 "

Zebulun
Stitches: 6247
Size: 3.55 x 3.31 "

Reuben- water
Simeon- fortress
Levi- breastplate of the High Priest
Judah -lion
Zebulun -ship
Issachar- donkey
Dan-snake
Asher-tree
Gad- round tent
Naftali-fawn
Joseph-sheaves
Benjamin-wolf

The prophet Isaiah foresaw this phenomenon: the miracle of the union between the Northern Tribes and the nation of Judah as is described in the following passage. In the Bible, Ephraim symbolizes the Ten Tribes because their first leader, Jeroboam, was from the Tribe of Ephraim (1 Kings 11:26).

> Isaiah 11:12–13
>
> He will raise a banner for the nations and gather the exiles of Israel; he will assemble the scattered people of Judah from the four quarters of the earth. Ephraim's jealousy will vanish, and Judah's enemies will be destroyed; Ephraim will not be jealous of Judah, nor Judah hostile toward Ephraim.

Hold it right there! Is this the famous Isaiah 11? I thought that Isaiah 11 was a prophecy for the future redemption, the Messiah.

Let's take a look at Isaiah 11:11, "In that day the Lord will reach out his hand a second time to reclaim the surviving remnant of his people from Assyria, from

Lower Egypt, from Upper Egypt, from Cush, from Elam, from Babylonia, from Hamath and from the islands of the Mediterranean."

I did the research, and found that each of the above countries mentioned by Isaiah were all part of the hundred and twenty-seven lands of the kingdom of Darius. Cush is Ethiopia; Elam is Persia; Hamath was north of Israel in Lebanon of today. The prophet spoke of the gathering of exiles in the times of Ezra, the man who also made peace between Ephraim and Judah.

However, all this would not have been possible without the first branch of Jesse who was Daniel. He was from the tribe of Judah, the same tribe as Jesse. Daniel was the man who for the first time spread the belief in God to those who were exiled. Daniel was a large branch, the kind that is attached to the trunk of the tree. From that branch stemmed other branches, who continued to spread Torah throughout the nation of Israel and the world. Isaiah 11:1, "A shoot will come up from the stump of Jesse; from his roots a branch will bear fruit." The exact translation of the Hebrew is, "A branch with come out from the tree trunk of Jesse and a smaller branch will blossom from its roots." The first branch that comes from Jesse's lineage is Daniel, and the second branch will come out from the roots, which is Jacob, the root of all the Jews. The second branch is Ezra who was actually from the tribe of Levi. Hashem just said to me, "That is correct."

In Isaiah 11:11, the prophet says, "The Lord will reach his hand out a second time." The first time was in Egypt, and this was the second time. That isn't to say that there won't be a third time, but the third time will have to include a lot more countries!

The Torah knowledge and faith in God that began with Daniel still spreads out until today. In the history of the world, there have never been more Bible scholars with more belief and trust in God than there is today.

The Rose of Jacob

Every year the Scroll of Esther is read in the synagogue on the holiday of Purim in the month of Adar, which occurs in February or March. At the end of the reading there is a song that is customarily sung called "The Rose of Jacob." Ever since I was a little girl, I asked my father and my teachers what the rose of Jacob is. Nobody knew. The literal translation of the song is:

> The rose of Jacob is rejoicing and happy,
> When he sees them together.
> The light blue of Mordechai.
> Their redemption was forever,
> And their hope is from generation to generation.
> Blessed be Mordechai the Jew,
> Blessed be Esther for me.

***

After writing this chapter, I finally understood this song. The rose of Jacob is the unification of the tribes of Israel, the children of Jacob. Just like the petals of a rose separately don't seem so special, together their beauty is apparent.

What is the meaning of "The light blue of Mordechai." When Mordechai was wearing the clothes of the king, they were all different colors, but the first color mentioned is light blue. Light blue is the color of the uniform of the Children of Israel. In Numbers 15:38–40, Moses teaches the children of Israel to wear a light blue fringe on their garments. Until this day, religious Jews wear these fringes: eight fringes on each corner of a four-cornered garment and one of the eight fringes is light blue. Mordechai taught the Jews to wear the light blue garment. This unified all the children of Jacob, when seen together in uniform apparel.

In the recent Diaspora, the Jews of Europe didn't always have the blue dye, so the fringes they wore were all white. Today in Israel, many Jews went back to the old custom of a light blue fringe on a four-cornered garment.

The garment with a light blue fringe is called *tzitzit*. When Jews are living in places of anti-Semitism, they hide their *tzitzit* so no one will know that they're Jewish. In this song the children of Jacob are happy, and they are seen together wearing their *tzitzit* with pride.

"Their redemption is forever" refers to the Ten Tribes of Israel that are forever with us but "their hope is from generation to generation." This is the hope that those remnants of Israel that did not return will come back. In the Jewish prayer books, there are daily supplications for the return of all the remnants of Israel to the Promised Land.

"Blessed be Esther for me." There are a couple of words missing. Blessed be Esther who prayed for me.

This song is further proof that the true story of Esther was hidden from the nation but known to the leaders. The real history was hidden from the Jewish people so there wouldn't be a risk of another division among tribes as there was in the times of the First Temple, that split the Kingdom of Israel in two.

There were hints purposely put into the Scroll of Esther so that someone would figure it out in the future. The secret was known to some lawmakers who made their rulings accordingly but the secret was not written down and got lost along with many other secrets of our sages.

Let's Start from the Very Beginning

Let's retell the story with the true version in a way that children can understand:

The Story of Esther the Prophetess

A very long time ago when the People of Judea, which is the southern part of Israel today, had a Holy Temple in Jerusalem there was an evil king called Nebuchadnezzar. King Nebuchadnezzar was the king of Babylon which is the country of Iraq today. Hashem sent Nebuchadnezzar to destroy the Holy Temple because the Jews were very bad. They worshipped idols instead of serving Hashem. King Nebuchadnezzar seized all the holy books from the Temple and all the holy vessels that were made of gold. He even took the Torah that was written by Moses.

When the Jews were in Babylon many of them were crying because they missed Israel and they were sorry for the sins that they did, especially the mothers, but many of the men continued to worship idols.

Daniel in the Lions' Pit

King Nebuchadnezzar looked for wise people to help advise him. He found four very smart and talented Jewish boys named Daniel, Mishael, Hananiah and Azariah.

Nebuchadnezar loved these Jewish servants and treated them well. Even though they refused to eat the non-kosher food of the palace he gave them beans and seeds and they stayed strong and healthy. When Nebuchadnezzar died, the country called Media conquered Babylon and King Darius became the ruler of Babylon and Media. All the servants of Nebuchadnezzar became servants of King Darius.

When Daniel was a servant of King Darius, he found a treasure in the library of the king. This library contained all the books that were taken from the Holy Temple in Jerusalem. One of the scriptures that Daniel found was the holy book of Jeremiah. It was among the loot that King Nebuchadnezzar took from the Holy Temple when it was destroyed about fifty years earlier.

Daniel read the book of Jeremiah and learned how bad the Jewish people had been and how the Holy Temple in Jerusalem had been destroyed. He prayed to Hashem with all his heart to ask forgiveness for his people. The other servants saw Daniel praying, and they reported to the king that Daniel was praying to the God of Israel.

It was against the law in the land of Media to pray to Hashem. King Darius loved Daniel and did not want to punish him, so he told Daniel to bow down to his idols, and he would be absolved. Daniel refused, of course; he would rather die than bow down to other gods!

The advisers of the king forced Darius to punish Daniel and throw him into the lions' pit. The king couldn't sleep all night in sorrow for what he had done. He woke up in the morning, ran and lifted the stone covering the lions' pit expecting to see Daniel's bones, but lo and behold, he saw Daniel healthy and strong without a scratch.

The king was crying in amazement and shock, but he was relieved that Daniel was still alive. Daniel was lifted from the pit, and the king hugged him and cried.

King Darius thought to himself, "These are strange lions; maybe they aren't hungry. Let me throw the slanderers who reported Daniel into the pit and see what happens." King Darius commanded his servants to throw these men into the lions' pit together with their whole families to see if these lions were really man-eating lions. Before the slanderers hit the ground, they were devoured.

Daniel told the king that the God of Israel saved him because his faith was so strong. The king proclaimed the God of Daniel to be the One and only God. He commanded his runners to spread the word to the Kingdom of Babylon, Persia, and Media. "I decree that in my entire kingdom men and women are to fear and tremble before the God of Daniel; for He is the living God forever. God's kingdom will never be destroyed. He answers our prayers and rescues those who believe in Him. He performs signs, wonders and miracles in heaven and on earth. He is the One who has also delivered Daniel from the power of the lions." These are the words of the Bible:

> Daniel 6:25–28
> Then King Darius wrote to all the nations and peoples of every language in all the earth: "May you prosper greatly! I issue a decree that in every part of my kingdom people must fear and reverence the God of Daniel. For he is the living God and he endures forever; his kingdom will not be destroyed, his dominion will never end. He rescues and he saves; he performs signs and wonders in the heavens and on the earth. He has rescued Daniel from the power of the lions." So Daniel prospered during the reign of Darius and the reign of Cyrus the Persian.

The message was heard by the whole Kingdom of Persia, Babylon, and Media. In these countries the Jews that were exiled from the kingdom of Judah resided. They belonged to the tribes of Judah, Benjamin and Levi. Mordechai himself was from the tribe of Benjamin. The other Ten Tribes of Israel that were dispersed throughout the Persian Kingdom didn't learn about Daniel, and they didn't remember that there was only one God.

After Darius the Mede, there was a very special king named King Cyrus of Persia who conquered the Kingdom of Media. King Cyrus was one of the best kings in the whole world. He believed in peace and freedom. He freed all the slaves, and he allowed the Nation of Israel to return to their land and build the Holy Temple in Jerusalem. After King Cyrus died, his son Darius took over the kingdom. He had the same name as Darius from the days of Daniel but he was the King of Persia.

King Darius of Persia was a very wise and powerful King; he conquered a hundred and twenty-seven countries. He knew that his father wanted the Jews to return to Israel but he was too busy conquering land and forgot about his father's decree.

A New King

King Darius passed away and his son King Xerxes ruled. After Xerxes a new king sat on the throne, King Artaxerxes. At first King Artaxerxes didn't want the Jews to build the Holy Temple in Jerusalem. However, Ezra the scribe, a court Jew who was very good friends with King Cyrus, showed the king a letter written by the late King Cyrus saying, "I hereby give my blessings to the People of Israel to build the Holy Temple in Jerusalem as is written in their Torah."

Little Esther

Esther's parents were from the Nation of Israel from the tribe of Naftali; they lived in the kingdom of King Artaxerxes but far away from Israel. Esther and her family heard the proclamation of the King and wanted very much to return to the Holy Land, so Esther's parents, her aunt and her family, began the long journey to the Promised Land.

On the way the family stopped in Babylon in order to rest from their travels. They met a very nice man named Mordechai. Mordechai was a Bible scholar and very good friends with Zerubbabel, the Cohen. Zerubbabel wanted to go to Jerusalem and help build the Holy Temple.

Mordechai fell in love with Esther's cousin, and they got married. Soon after, they set off for the big journey to the Promised Land together with Esther and her family, and Zerubbabel and his whole entourage (Nehemiah 7:7 and Ezra 2:2).

A Very Sad Little Girl

The trip was very difficult. There was a large stretch of desert land to cross. All they had were camels and donkeys. It was very hot and dry. Esther's parents and her aunt got very sick and died on the way.

Esther was heartbroken. She wouldn't stop crying. Mordechai was also grieving. He had just lost his beloved new wife. Mordechai told Esther that now all they had was each other. "Don't cry, you are not alone in the world. Hashem, the God of Abraham, will always be with you, and I will be your father."

Mordechai adopted Esther and taught her all about Hashem and the history of the Jewish people. In those days, young girls didn't attend school, so Esther didn't know very much. She was so happy to learn more and more! Mordechai also gave her a Hebrew name, *Haddasah* (Esther 2:7). Hadassah means the leaves of the fragrant myrtle tree. It was a translation of her Persian name.

Finally, Esther and Mordechai arrived in the Holy Land. Esther was very emotional. She saw the places that Mordechai taught her about and she cried from happiness.

After a couple of years of learning with Mordechai, Esther grew up to be a scholar herself. She saw young girls on the street and asked them questions about Torah. Soon she decided to make a school for girls, the first Jewish school for Torah learning.

Esther was very devout in her loyalty to Hashem and to her students. Hashem loved Esther very much. He started talking to her and helped her understand the Torah better. Slowly the word spread. Esther was a prophetess.

The Kings Decree

The new king, King Artaxerxes allowed the Jews to return to Israel and he agreed to build the Holy Temple on one condition, "Every man or woman of the descendants of the Israelites that does not keep your Torah will be punished by death, or will be thrown out of the land and his belongings will be confiscated" (Ezra 7:26).

King Artaxerxes wasn't a bad King but he was suspicious. He didn't want the Jews to take money from him to build a beautiful Temple and then use it as a fortress to fight and rebel. Therefore, he wanted to make sure that the will of the people was purely a religious one, and the Temple would be a place of worship, not of government.

Mordechai heard the new decree, and he was distraught. "Oh my God!" he said. "There are hundreds of thousands of Israelites all over the kingdom who are still worshiping idols." The Jews that lived in Babylon were mostly God-fearing because they followed in the footsteps of Daniel.

Once There was a Wicked Man

Artaxerxes was the son of Xerxes, and the grandson of Darius. A wicked minister in his palace told the king that there were many Israelites who did not keep the Torah. He said, "According to the decree of your majesty the King, all the Israelites who are still worshiping idols should be hanged. Let's send out our army to hunt them down!"

A decree was proclaimed throughout the kingdom of a hundred and twenty-seven countries. Runners brought the proclamation to every county that they could reach. A date was set to start war against all the people of Israel who were worshiping idols. They would be killed and all their belongings taken. The date was set; the thirteenth of the month of Adar. (Esther 3:13).

Mordechai and Ezra

Ezra the scribe panicked. He knew that many idolaters would be killed. He quickly travelled north to teach the dispersed Ten Tribes about Hashem and have them throw out their idols. He didn't tell the king how disturbed he was. Ezra just asked the king with great respect to take some leaders that can have a good influence and travel north to the Ten Tribes of Israel.

> Ezra 7:27–28
> Praise be to the LORD, the God of our ancestors, who has put it into the king's heart to bring honor to the house of the LORD in Jerusalem in this way and who has extended his good favor to me before the king and his advisers and all the king's powerful officials. Because the hand of the LORD my God was on me, I took courage and gathered leaders from Israel to go up with me.

Mordechai was even more worried. How could he possibly reach a hundred and twenty-seven countries before the armies of the King arrived? Only Hashem can help! "I have an idea," he said to himself. "My niece Esther is a prophetess; maybe she can ask Hashem for His mercy."

Mordechai visited Esther's school for girls and women. He waited at the gate dressed in an outfit made of old sackcloth. This was the garb that mourners used to wear. Mordechai was screaming bitterly that the whole nation was in mourning (Esther 4:3). Esther heard that her uncle was lamenting, and she was very upset. "We are in such promising times. We returned to the Holy Land and the Second Temple is about to be built. Why are you mourning?" She forwarded this message to Mordechai and with it she sent respectable clothing for him to wear in order to enter her school, which was a holy institute of Torah.

Mordechai refused to change his rags (Esther 4:4). Esther came to greet him and he said to her, "The entire nation is at risk. The king decreed that anyone who doesn't heed the Torah will be hung." Esther said, "The people of our nation sinned against God and his Torah. It is the law of the king and the law of God that idolaters be killed. There is nothing that I can do about it. Besides, I haven't had any prophecy in thirty days."

Now Mordechai got angry. "Is this the education I gave you? You don't care if your brethren will die? If you are silent at this time, the Jews will be saved by other means, and you and the people of your father's tribe will perish."

Esther never ever saw her uncle so angry. "I'm sorry," she said. "Tell the Jews to fast for three days. My students and I will do the same. After three days of fasting and praying, maybe I will be blessed with a prophecy."

After three days, Hashem appeared to Esther. She felt the light touch of a golden ray, and Hashem spoke. "My

Torah says that every idolater must be put to death, but this law is only applicable if they are prosecuted in a court of law. Furthermore, the tribes of Israel have been captured by the heathens and their parents sinned, but they are innocent as babies. They never learned about Hashem!

"If someone comes to kill them, of course they must fight back. If there is a fight, I am the Lord your God and theirs, and I will help them. Just as I told Jeremiah, children shall not suffer for their father's sins."

> Jeremiah 31:29–30
> In those days, people will no longer say, "The parents have eaten sour grapes, and the children's teeth are set on edge." Instead, everyone will die for their own sin; whoever eats sour grapes—their own teeth will be set on edge.

Mordechai heard the good news and he released runners to a hundred and twenty-seven different countries to inform the Israelites that they are permitted to defend themselves. They could fight and Hashem, who would see that they really want to repent, would help. In order to protect the secrecy of his plan he sent the message in fairy tale form. The Israelites understood the hint and prepared for battle while the runners who were not Jewish had no clue.

The Israelites didn't succumb to the Persian soldiers; they battled back. Big miracles happened and they were all saved, while many of the Persian soldiers were slaughtered. Some of the Israelites ceased worshiping idols merely out of fear of the Persian army, but after the conclusion of the war, they accepted Hashem as their only King.

Mordechai proclaimed a great holiday, the festival of Purim. Purim means "lots," like a lottery ticket. Purim is named as a memory of the lots that were drawn to choose the day of attack. An extensive war erupted on that day, the thirteenth of Adar, and on the fourteenth of Adar, the victories were celebrated. The Israelites saw the miracles and believed in Hashem. They desired to become part of the Judean community, which was already observing God's commandments. It says in the Scroll of Esther that the nations of the land became Jews. The Israelites from the Kingdom of Israel joined the people of the former Kingdom of Judah, whose members were called Jews.

After the war, many people were tired and hungry. Mordechai made a decree that the Jews should send out food packages to everyone and charity for the needy. He wanted to teach the Israelites that the Torah way of life was benevolent and generous.

In Jerusalem the war lasted one more day because Jerusalem was the capital city, so there were more soldiers to battle. In Jerusalem the holiday of Purim is celebrated on the fifteenth day of Adar and in tribute to Jerusalem, every walled city in Israel from the times of Joshua rejoiced with Jerusalem. In the rest of the world, Purim is remembered on the fourteenth of Adar.

Mordechai made another proclamation. Purim would be an everlasting holiday. Adar occurs in March and children love this holiday. In current times on this day, Jews have currently adopted the custom to dress up in costumes and bring food packages to all their neighbors. The practice of masquerade commemorates equality. A costume provides everyone the opportunity for anyone to request charity without revealing his or her identity. On this day, the custom is to offer charity to anyone who asks without questioning or investigating the requester. We also extend food packages wrapped up in fancy ribbons to all—rich and poor—in order to recall that we are all brothers and that we should all love one another. Amen.

CHAPTER 8

Chanukah: The Truth Beyond the Legend

After the miracle of Purim, the population in Israel continued to augment. Israelites from each of the hundred and twenty-seven nations received messages that were delivered regularly from Jerusalem by Mordechai and his staff of Torah educators. The Israelites began to return to their God and their land. The Persian Empire, which was favorable to Torah observance, was subsequently conquered by the Greeks around the year 330 BCE. Eventually Israel became controlled by the Syrians who practiced a much different doctrine than the religious freedom extended by Cyrus and then the Greeks.

The Greek empire was under the rule of Alexander the Great. He defeated the Persian Empire and started teaching the Greek language and customs to the inhabitants of the Holy Land of Israel. They taught reading and writing in Greek as well as Greek philosophy and religion. Modernization of an ancient way of life was very appealing to the common Jew of the time. When the Greeks overthrew a nation, they allowed the vanquished countrymen to keep their own religious practices, values, and customs as long as they paid taxes and served in the military. Nevertheless, many of the Jews subsequently left the faith of the Torah for Greek Hellenism. Following the dissolution of the entire Greek empire after Alexander's death due to civil wars, the Ptolemaic Kingdom of Egyptians ruled Israel. They, like their predecessors, allowed the Israelites to observe their own religion. Their rule continued until the Syrian Seleucid rule overthrew the Egyptians around 198 BCE under Antiochus. Unlike the Ptolemaic Egyptians, the Syrian Seleucids or Syrian-Greeks forced conquered nations to follow their religious practices. The Jews that admired the ways of the gentiles were named Hellenistic Jews, or in Hebrew *Mityavnim*, literally "becoming Greek."

Many of the Hellenists were actually Israelites of the Ten Tribes that still resided in the Diaspora. If you recall, I explained that most of the Israelites were fond of Mordechai, but not all (Esther 10:3). Many of them who returned to Hashem still resided in the Diaspora. Some of their descendants became Hellenists.

The Prophecy of Daniel

Daniel, who lived over three hundred years before King Antiochus, had a vision that a leader would arise and betray the faith of the Holy Torah and defile the Holy Temple. This prophecy foretold the future war initiated by the Maccabees or Hasmoneans.

Daniel 11:28–32
The king of the North will return to his own country with great wealth, but his heart will be set against the holy covenant. He will take action against it and then return to his own country. At the appointed time he will invade the South again, but

this time the outcome will be different from what it was before. Ships of the western coastlands will oppose him, and he will lose heart. Then he will turn back and vent his fury against the holy covenant. He will return and show favor to those who forsake the holy covenant. His armed forces will rise up to desecrate the temple fortress and will abolish the daily sacrifice. Then they will set up the abomination that causes desolation. With flattery he will corrupt those who have violated the covenant, but the people who know their God will firmly resist him.

Two hundred years after the Holy Temple was rebuilt, the Greeks conquered the lands of ancient Persia, Babylonia, Egypt, and Syria. Many Israelites from the Ten Tribes were still living in those lands at the time. These Israelites arrived in Israel for the first time as Syrian-Greek soldiers. They came to fight against their brothers.

The Maccabees

The Maccabean or Hasmonean period marks the time of the story of Chanukah, about 167 to 165 BCE. The heroes of the story, the Maccabees, saw how badly the situation in Israel had deteriorated under Syrian Greek rule. They prohibited the belief in one God and the observing of other religious practices under penalty of death. The Maccabees cried out to their brethren just as Moses cried out to the Israelites on Sinai after the sin of the golden calf: "Whoever is for God, come with me!" They assembled about ten thousand soldiers and decided against all odds to combat the Syrian Greeks and Israeli Hellenists, who sided with the Greeks.

The Maccabees were a family of *Cohanim*, or Jewish priests. In Judaism, priesthood is determined genetically.

The priestly family members are descendants of Aaron, the brother of Moses. The father, Mattathias (Mattityahu in Hebrew), was the head of his family and served as the High Priest. He would have been worshiping in the Holy Temple but was expelled from the Temple by the Syrian Greek invaders.

The story of Chanukah originated in Modiin, a city outside of Jerusalem. In Israel today, you can visit the tombs of the Maccabees in Modiin. It is a forty-five-minute drive from the Old City of Jerusalem. Two thousand years ago travelling the same distance would take at least a full day on a donkey. It isn't logical that the Maccabee Mattathias, who was the High Priest, would have voluntarily chosen to reside in Modiin when his duties were to be performed in the Holy Temple in Jerusalem. However, when the Syrian Greeks took control of the Temple and refused Israelite autonomy there, Mattathias fled with his family to Modiin.

Maccabees, which is a name that they chose for themselves, is an acronym composed of the initials of a question: "Who is like You Hashem among the gods?" This motto demonstrates that the war of the Maccabees was a war for God. They were pure of heart in their intentions and held no ulterior motives. The Maccabees were facing vastly superior numbers and military equipment. They developed the strategy of the first guerilla warfare known in history and it was a religious war.

The Maccabees were also called Hasmoneans. Hasmonean was also a name that they gave themselves; it is the initials of five mitzvoth, or commandments, that the Syrian Greek government prohibited them for performing. These proscriptions included: (1) Marking and celebrating the appearance of the new moon which was the basis for establishing dates for all the Jewish holidays, (2) Observance of the Sabbath, (3) Performance of circumcision, (4) The keeping of the laws of family purity including the practice of ritual baths. (5) Belief in one God and public learning of Torah.

According to the Book of the Maccabees, Antiochus banned traditional Jewish and Samaritan religious practices. He decreed possession of the Torah a capital offense and burned the copies he could find. Sabbaths and festivals with their associated feasts were banned. Circumcision was outlawed. Mothers who circumcised their babies were ordered to be executed along with their families. Ritual sacrifice was forbidden. An idol of Zeus, the Greek supreme god, was placed with other Greek gods on the altar of the temple. Hellenist Israelites set up altars to Greek gods and sacrificed "unclean" animals on them. These laws and their enforcement show how strong Antiochus' rule was against the Israelites. Syrian Greek supremacy fostered support for the Hellenizing faction in Judaea, the name for the land of Israel at the time.

In reaction to the Syrian Greeks seizing the Holy Temple and summarily dismissing all Jewish ritual, the Maccabean family and its followers grew in numbers and in adamantly opposing the acceptance and compliance with their conquerors' actions. The Syrian Greek army introduced idols in the Holy Temple and even sacrificed a pig on the Holy Altar simply in spite. The attempt to sacrifice a pig on an altar in Modiin was so contemptable and vile for Mattathias that he commenced his rebellion there with his first followers. The details of this historical description is written in the Book of the Maccabees.

The Maccabees were brave to a point of insanity. How could the Maccabees even begin to think that they could challenge the repressive, cruel and overwhelming Syrian Greek dominance?

Their faith in God was so strong that they believed in the impossible. These brave soldiers decided to attack the enemy from within. During the war, they suddenly knew where to hide and where to shoot, in the first underground militia ever formed. Hashem saw their unrelenting devotion and told them, by prophecy or psychic revelation, exactly what to do at each and every step of the way in their battles.

As the war proceeded, the soldiers saw open miracles just as in the days of Mordechai and Esther. Some of these Israelite warriors were told the story of Esther when they were children. When they saw their own initial victories against unimaginable forces, they recalled the Purim story that their parents passed on to them. This touched them in their hearts, influenced them and reinforced their allegiance and commitment to their cause. Their Hellenistic Israelite enemies began to realize that they were brothers. Many of the Hellenists switched allegiances and joined the Hasmonean forces where they began to learn about their heritage. Subsequently, they sent letters describing the occurrences in Judaea and their newly acquired faith to their families in the Diaspora.

After the Maccabees won the war, the families of the realigned foreign soldiers, totaling thousands of Israelites, journeyed to the Holy Land from all over the Assyrian Greek Empire to join their husbands and fathers. They returned to the land and the faith of their forefathers.

What a Find!

About three years after the commencement of the war, around 165 BCE, Mattathias passed away. Mattathias' sons, led by Judah, entered the Holy Temple and cleaned the desecration. The blood of impure animals had been spilled, and the curtains of the Holy of Holies were stained. Lo and behold, the original Torah that Moses wrote in the Sinai Desert was trampled upon, broken and disassembled. The Maccabees found many scrolls and tablets written by prophets that Ezra had appropriated from the Babylonian palaces with permission from King Cyrus almost three hundred years prior, approximately 430 BCE. They also found dishes made from gold and silver with holy writings on them.

The Maccabees were so excited with what they discovered that they immediately began to clean up and try to assemble the shattered stones and copy every word. They decreed that no one would be allowed to ascend to the Holy Temple Mount. The Maccabean Priests closed the temple to others in order to allow themselves time to inscribe the Torah and holy writings they uncovered without interruption.

The story in the Talmud expounds that there wasn't enough pure olive oil to light the Menorah for more than a day until new oil could be produced. During the war there had been so much destruction that the Temple's small oil bottles were shattered or their seals were damaged, and only one small jar of pure oil was found. In order for the oil to be pure, the priests have to count seven days from after touching a dead body and then immerse in a ritual bath. Then add one more day to extract the oil, so there would have been a minimum of eight days before new oil could be used by the priests in the Temple.

The Talmud relates that the jar of oil that was meant to last for one day miraculously endured for eight days. In that time the priests prepared a new batch of pure oil. It's an account that sounds unrealistic and magical, but the true story that Hashem revealed to me is even more amazing.

What Really Happened?

When the war finally came to an end, the Maccabees gathered into the Holy Temple to start copying the Holy Torah onto scroll in Aramaic letters so that the Israelite Hellenists who returned to Hashem, but didn't know how to read ancient Hebrew lettering, would be able to read it. It wasn't translated it was just transliterated, because they still understood Hebrew they just were not able to read and write the Hebrew letters.

When the time approached to light the Holy Menorah (candelabra), they were certain that they would have to stop writing and "call it a night." But the Menorah stayed lit all night long. Not only was that candelabrum burning, but the light emanating from the flame was as robust as modern florescent lighting. People from a distance saw the glow through the windows of the temple. Astonishingly, the light's brightness didn't diminish until they finished their copying of the Torah in continuous shifts of *Cohanim* (priests) working around the clock. The *Cohanim* labored for eight consecutive days to write the Five Books of Moses. They then felt the urge to open the doors of the Holy Temple to celebrate the completion of their first Torah scroll with the public. People witnessed the wondrous lights of the menorah and generated an immense celebration. Nevertheless, the *Cohanim* didn't stop there. They continued to work for many more years in order to copy over the rest of their discoveries onto scrolls, thus saving the sacred works.

After the consecration of the Temple, the seven-branched Menorah was lit every day and the light that emanated from it was enough to be seen through the windows of the Temple in daylight. Today, Jews light an eight-branched Menorah on Chanukah, to preserve the story commemorating a miracle of a light that didn't extinguish.

In truth, the miracle of Chanukah was much more than just candlelight that didn't douse. It was light from Hashem. It didn't only last longer; it provided a much brighter radiance than ancient men had ever seen before from an oil light. While the priests wrote the Torah on scrolls during those eight days of Chanukah, they felt that they were enveloped with holiness and the light of Hashem.

A Miracle Foreseen

There is a hint in the Torah that this miracle would happen from the much earlier incident of the burning bush. When Moses went onto Mount Sinai for the first time, he saw a bush that was burning without being consumed (Exodus 3:2). Moses asked himself, "Why doesn't the bush burn to ashes?" Did he ever really receive the answer? Hashem tells Moses who He is, and what His name is, but He doesn't give a reason for the burning bush.

It is not mentioned in the Torah, but Hashem revealed to me that He told Moses that in the future He would make a miracle of fire burning without fuel becoming consumed. This miracle will save the Torah forever. Hashem told me that not even a drop from the oil in the Menorah was consumed for eight consecutive days and it stayed lit continuously.

When the Maccabees found only one little flask of oil, they didn't worry about tomorrow. They ignited what they had. Hashem gives light and gives life. If He wills it, a fire can burn without fuel, and a man can live without eating or drinking, just like Moses for forty days on Mount Sinai.

During the original eight days of Chanukah, time stopped. The *Cohanim* were so engulfed in their mission to copy the Torah that they didn't feel the passage of time. The oil wasn't consumed at all. Neither did their strength or vision wane. Like Moses on Mount Sinai, they didn't eat or drink because they didn't feel that any time had passed. They were in a dimension above time. When the Maccabees finished their task of writing the Torah, the oil started to burn and extinguished by nightfall just like any other day.

The walls of Jerusalem were constructed in a concave style so that archers could shoot at their invaders through large window sills on the insides of the walls that diminished into smaller openings on the outsides to provide more protection against external attacks. In the photograph below, see the slits in the wall from the outside. It was too small for arrows to pass through when shot from a distance.

You can see how the inside looked in the next picture. The deep concave windows were designed for archers to shoot while protected by the wall.

The midrash, an anthology of oral tradition, says that the Holy Temple's windows, as opposed to the walls of Jerusalem, were narrower on the inside and wider on the outside. The light of the Holy Temple was so bright that it gave light to outdoors. The temple had so much spiritual light that it didn't need external sunlight to enter through its windows to provide light inside.

Let's take a closer look at this midrash. Scholars at the end of the Second Temple Period and the first two centuries afterward wrote the midrash stories. They didn't know how the Temple appeared before the Maccabean era. However, many of them were witness to the last fifty years of the Second Temple period. Archeologists use the Midrash and the Talmud to learn about historical findings. When the Maccabees renovated the Holy Temple the windows were fixed so that the light would shine outwardly.

At the end of the Second Temple period, there was a special light emanating from the Holy Temple in Jerusalem. The light that burned from the Holy Menorah continued to provide a powerfully holy radiance, so much so that that brightness emanated across the whole Temple Mount.

The nation of Israel rose to a heightened level of faith they never had since the giving of the Torah on Mount Sinai. They were so excited to learn Torah and perform the mitzvoth that they felt it in their bodies and souls.

> Isaiah 12:1–3
> In that day you will say: "I will praise you, LORD. Although you were angry with me, your anger has turned away and you have comforted me. Surely God is my salvation; I will trust and not be afraid. The LORD, the LORD himself, is my strength and my defense; he has become my salvation. With joy you will draw water from the wells of salvation."

Water is an allegory for Torah. The tribes of Israel began to learn from the well of the Torah and the whole Bible. The Hellenists were not afraid of their Syrian Greek superiors, they switched over to the side of the Lord. This was the salvation of the entire nation.

Synagogues

Some copies of the Torah were placed in synagogues in Jerusalem from the time of Ezra. In the beginning of his book, Ezra mentioned that many Jews were not willing to return to the Holy Land from the Persian Empire and share in the building of the Holy Temple. Only forty-two thousand Jews came with Ezra on his voyage to the Holy Land.

After the miracle of Chanukah, the Maccabees copied the Torah many times over and distributed it throughout the country. Many Israelites from the Ten Tribes were part of the Assyrian-Greek army. When they were defeated, they stayed in Israel and started learning Torah with their brethren. This augmented the population in Israel, and new towns were established. Every town that was found by archeologists had a synagogue, and most had a *mikvah*, a ritual bathhouse. The men's *mikvah* was used for immersing in holy water before writing scriptures. The women's mikvah was for family purity. Married women customarily immerse themselves in a mikvah seven days after their monthly cycle, in accordance with Torah law.

This mitzvah of the women is kept until today. There is a mikvah in every Jewish orthodox neighborhood worldwide. The ritual baths are constructed by digging a well in the ground and then building a bathhouse around it. Running water is added to the well water that arises so there is always fresh clean water. In the event that there is no *mikvah*, any natural body of water that is deep enough to cover the whole body by slightly crouching down is a kosher mikvah according to Jewish Law. Visiting the beach and entering the water with a loose robe so that every part of the body is immersed works fine. Some men and women do it just to feel pure, especially after personal repentance or on the eve of the Day of Repentance, Yom Kippur.

Holy Vessels

The holy scriptures of the entire Bible were found in the Holy Temple. Some were written on stone, some on scrolls, and some on receptacles of gold and silver. The book of

Ezra mentions the numerous vessels that were taken out of the palaces of Nebuchadnezzar in Babylon.

> Ezra 1:7–11
>
> Moreover, King Cyrus brought out the articles belonging to the temple of the Lord, which Nebuchadnezzar had carried away from Jerusalem and had placed in the temple of his god. Cyrus king of Persia had them brought by Mithredath the treasurer, who counted them out to Sheshbazzar the prince of Judah. This was the inventory:

gold dishes	30
silver dishes	1,000
silver pans	29
gold bowls	30
matching silver bowls	410
other articles	1,000

> In all, there were 5,400 articles of gold and of silver. Sheshbazzar brought all these along with the exiles when they came up from Babylon to Jerusalem.

These couldn't have been vessels for meals because there were very few *Cohanim* on call at any given time. Twelve loaves of bread were baked in the temple every day. That would be enough for up to twenty-four Priests. What would be the use for thousands of bowls and dishes? In the detailed descriptions of the receptacles of the tabernacle, there was no mention that silver and gold bowls must be produced.

It was customary in ancient times to write books on bowls. The prophets gave so much importance to their writings that sometimes they wrote them on gold, silver, and copper. The Greeks did not destroy these vessels because they had esthetic value. After the Maccabees transcribed the Torah from stone to scroll, they continued their mission to copy all the writings of the holy vessels, which were later compiled into our Holy Bible, the Old Testament.

Since every copy would be handwritten on leather scrolls, they would be very costly. Hundreds of years earlier, Ezra the scribe established a custom of building a place of study, with one Torah scroll to be shared with the whole town. The Israelites that were under Hellenistic rule did not continue this custom because of the religious persecution.

The Israelites that insisted on keeping their faith joined the Maccabees in the Hasmonean revolt. After the war, the Hellenistic Jews that fought them made a total turn-around and wanted to be close to God and learn His Torah. They sent for their wives and children to join them in the Holy Land. The Maccabees built many synagogues and made sure that every town in Israel had a copy of the Torah. They also began to copy other holy books of the prophets and publicize them. The Jews and Lost Tribes of Israel that were almost totally Hellenized began learning the Bible and observing the precepts of their heritage. They encouraged learning all the holy books by heart so that in the event of another tragedy, the Torah would be written on their hearts and in their minds. This is the secret of the survival of the Jewish people. They never forgot their Torah, or their Old Testament Bible, in the original language word for word as they passed it down throughout the generations.

The Bible scribes counted the letters of their work after copying a holy book. They wanted to make sure that there were no errors, not even one letter. The Hasmoneans also transcribed copies of the Holy writings from ancient Hebrew into Aramaic letters in order that the Israelites of the Assyrian Greek armies would be able to read them. The

Aramaic letters were the letters of the Assyrian language. This helped the Hellenistic Jews that wanted to learn the Torah. These letters are fashioned for writing on parchment and slowly the rest of the Jews adopted them for their writings.

In the Dead Sea scrolls different types of parchments were found. The secular contracts were written in ancient Hebrew and the Holy writings are in Aramaic letters. The Bible scrolls are written with Aramaic letters aside from God's name which is in ancient Hebrew. I always wondered about this fact, but now I understand. The scribes wrote all of the Holy writings in Aramaic lettering so everyone will understand. The Jews of Babylon spoke Akkadian, an ancient dialect of Aramaic which used cuneiform lettering. The Talmud was written in Aramaic mixed with Hebrew but all in Aramaic letters which are the Hebrew letters we use today. These letters are called Ktav Ashuri which means Assyrian lettering. Ancient Hebrew is called Ktav Ivri which means Hebrew lettering.

Eventually the entire Jewish people adopted Aramaic, the dialect of the Hellenists as the language of the land and as the official alphabet because it was extremely popular all over the world just like English is today. They also knew Greek; however, the Greek language was discouraged by the Jewish leaders because it was associated with Greek mythology and philosophy which is antithetical to Jewish beliefs.

It is interesting to note that most of the Bible was not translated into Aramaic, it was transliterated. This shows that the emphasis on the education was on the memorization of God's words. The educational system was different then. In a society with few books, you memorize before you understand. After memorizing the whole Bible, they had a text in their brains and they could start learning, understanding and debating.

The stories of the Bible were learned by all of Israel as a result of King Artaxerxes' decree to observe the Torah. The Israelites of the entire Persian Kingdom had been brought up learning Bible stories orally for over two hundred years since the story of Purim. They didn't have books but they had great memories. The Assyrian Greek soldiers and their families that returned to Hashem were educated in Greek and Aramaic and were interested in learning Torah from the text. They wanted to know the exact words of God. They knew some Hebrew and were happy to learn the Hebrew words even without understanding it perfectly. The stories of Daniel, Ezra and Nehemiah were translated into Aramaic because they were totally unknown to the Hellenists and it was important that they understand exactly what happened. The proof of this is that the Scroll of Esther is written in Hebrew. This story occurred after Daniel which is written in Aramaic, during the times of Ezra and Nehemiah which are also Bible volumes that are written mainly in Aramaic, yet there is not a word of Aramaic in the whole Scroll of Esther. There was no need to translate the scroll of Esther because its story was famous all over the hundred and twenty-seven nations of the Empire.

The Dead Sea Scrolls

In Israel near the northern part of the Dead Sea, remnants remain of a town that was built for the purpose of copying over the whole Bible. There are stone tables and benches in this town called Qumran that were made for inscription, as well as special lettering rooms and ritual baths. The writers dipped their bodies in the baths in order to be clean and pure before the holy writing.

On the Dead Sea Scrolls only Hashem's name was written in ancient Hebrew script while the rest was inscribed in Aramaic letters. The books of the Bible were copied separately in no special order. Only generations later, in the year 200 CE, Yochanan Ben Zakkai and his students canonized the Bible and put it in the order that we have today.

Light and Darkness

The people that lived in Qumran were part of a Jewish sect called Essenes that flourished from the second century BCE to the first century CE. In the notes of the Essenes, there is mention of the Children of Light opposed to the Children of Darkness. The idea that light is good and dark is bad started after the miracle of Chanukah. Until this day, light is considered positive, and darkness is negative. To illuminate or to shed light on something is positive. The Dark Ages were called dark because there was ignorance, poverty, disease, and suffering. The story of Chanukah changed our way of thinking. It is so ingrained in us that light is a sign of wisdom and goodness and that dark symbolizes sadness and evil, that the associations go unnoticed.

The word Chanukah means the dedication or inauguration of a building. The Maccabees rededicated not only the Holy Temple and the Holy of Holies, they rededicated themselves to the Torah. As a result of the holiday of Chanukah, also called The Holiday of Lights, the wisdom of the Torah is called the light of Torah. The Maccabees brought the light of Torah to the Jewish people, who until then limited their religious observances to Temple services only.

Prophecy of a High Priest

When the Second Temple was just beginning to be rebuilt, the services began outdoors on the Temple Mount. The high priest was named Joshua and he had a prophecy:

> Zachariah 4:1–6
> Then the angel who talked with me returned and woke me up, like someone awakened from sleep. He asked me, "What do you see?" I answered, "I see a solid gold lampstand with a bowl at the top and seven lamps on it, with seven channels to the lamps. Also, there are two olive trees by it, one on the right of the bowl and the other on its left." I asked the angel who talked with me, "What are these, my lord?" He answered, "Do you not know what these are?" "No, my lord," I replied. So he said to me, "This is the word of the LORD to Zerubbabel: 'Not by might nor by power, but by my Spirit,' says the LORD Almighty."

The above passage is a prophecy of the miracle of Chanukah. The description of the golden lamp is the lamp of the Holy Temple. The olive trees symbolize the miracle of the olive oil. An olive branch also symbolizes peace because of the dove that brought back an olive branch to Noah. Hashem's spirit would appear through the olive oil for lighting the Menorah in the Holy Temple. The two olive trees symbolize peace between brothers. The Hellenist Israelites made peace with their Jewish brothers. Until this day, the Temple Mount and the Western Wall have many doves flying overhead. Below is a photograph of a dove sitting inside a crevice of the Western Wall of the Temple Mount in Jerusalem.

The most important miracle of Chanukah is not the victory of the war. The miracle is that the nation felt Hashem's spirit and saw His miracles in the victorious war against overwhelming numbers and firepower. They were filled with awe and returned to their country, their nation, and their God.

The following is a poem summarizing the true story of Chanukah that has been unknown until today. In synagogues today on Shabbat, the Holy Ark is opened and a hand written Torah scroll is removed. The cantor walks around the congregation with an open scroll to allow the congregants to kiss the Holy Parchment before someone reads a portion of the Torah from the center stage. That's why I wrote in the following poem, "Now we can kiss you."

Torah

Once upon a time in history,
More than three thousand years ago,
God called out to us from a mountain,
Ten statements or commandments to know.

He taught our teacher Moses directives,
How to be honest and go the straight way.
How to keep the *mitzvoth* in Israel,
To stay close to Hashem and not stray.

Hashem gave two tablets to Moses,
He told him how to build an ark.
A golden ark inside a Temple,
Never to depart.

In the Holiest of Holies,
At the side of that ark was their site,
Five holy books, that Moses came to write.

Torah, Torah, how much did we miss you?
Then there was no way to kiss you.
You were hidden for the while.

We now have you, Torah,
We're very happy to read you.
Now we know how much we need you.
You can stay in style.

There was a scribe whose name was Ezra,

More than two thousand years ago.
He found the Torah and holy vessels
That were captured by our foe.

When Ezra read to the Jewish people,
They didn't hesitate or think of other things,
They believed those were the words of the King of Kings.

Torah, how much did we miss you?
Then there was no way to kiss you.
You were hidden for the while.

We have you, Torah.
We're very happy to read you.
Now we know how much we need you,
You can stay in style.

Once upon a time in history,
Greeks entered into our schools,
Wanting to change our allegiance,
Making us forget we were Jews.

Then came Mattathias the Cohen,
And his children, five in all.
They came out to rescue and save us.
Restoring the Torah was their call.

They came into the Holy Temple
To do their job as holy priests.
They found the Torah desecrated,
And picked up every piece.

They arranged all the fragments.
"Now we have a job to do."
"We have to copy every word too."

There was a tiny flask of oil
That would emit a holy light,
Illuminating until they finished,
What they had to write.

And then they made a celebration,
Chanukah for eight days.
From then on Torah would guide our ways.

Torah, how much did we miss you?
When we open the scroll, we can kiss you.
You are in our heart.

We have you, Torah
We're very happy to read you.
Now we know how much we need you
Never to depart.

....

Purim and Chanukah

The Talmud says that in the future, the only holidays that we will celebrate will be Purim and Chanukah. This quote always bothered me. How can we ever abolish holidays like Passover that are written in the Torah?

Now I understand these words. What would be the point of Passover or any other Jewish holiday if we had lost our people to idolatry?

The Talmud was saying that one day, someone will reveal the true stories of Purim and Chanukah, and the Jewish people will understand that these two holidays are the landmarks for saving the Jewish Tradition and the Bible.

Why Hide the Truth?

Why wasn't this story passed down as the true miracle of Chanukah?

To answer this question, we must jump ahead from 140 BCE to 103 BCE, when the Hasmonean king named Alexander Janneus reigned over Judea. This isn't Alexander the Great, who conquered major empires and came to the throne in 336 BCE. Alexander Janneus, or *Yanai* in Hebrew, was a third-generation Maccabee, then called Hasmonean, who lived in the time that the Pharisees began to emerge. The Pharisees had new and different ideas about Judaism. Alexander Yanai was afraid that they would take control. He started ordering their deaths one by one. He killed hundreds of Pharisees for no reason until he died an early death.

Alexander Yanai had a wonderful wife named Salome Alexandra or Shlomtzion in Hebrew. After Alexander's death Shlomtzion became queen. Queen Shlomtzion made peace with the Pharisees and even allowed them to conduct the services in the Holy Temple. The information that is written in the Talmud about sacrifices and service in the Holy Temple came from these fifty years of peace and brotherhood in Jerusalem.

After the destruction of the Second Temple, the Pharisees created Rabbinical Judaism, a religion that could exist in the absence of the Holy Temple. The Pharisees wrote the Talmud and instituted Jewish Law. Chanukah was celebrated as a beloved holiday for young and old, but they played down the real miracle of Chanukah for a few of reasons:

1. The Pharisees didn't want to give so much honor to the Hasmoneans or Maccabees because of their wicked descendants, who actually murdered Pharisees. For that same reason the books of the Maccabees were not included in the holy books of the Bible.

2. The Pharissees worked very hard on instilling the belief in a Messiah that would come from the House of David and not from the Maccabees, who were from the descendants of Aaron. Aside from killing rabbis, the Hasmonean kingdom also became corrupt in the practice of the holy services in the temple. The people wanted to look forward to a different kingdom—the true kingdom of the Bible, the Kingdom of David.

3. From the Hasmonean House arose a new cult called the Sadducees, who were at odds with the Pharisees during the period of the destruction of the Second Temple. The Sadducees rejected the teachings of the Pharisees and the rabbis.

4. The idea that Torah learning was strengthened by the Maccabees was not to be publicized. The rabbis preached that the Torah was never forgotten since it was given on Mount Sinai. They wanted the Jews to be attached to Moses and not to the Hasmonean rulers. Moses is even nicknamed Moses our Rabbi, or, in Hebrew, *Moshe Rabeinu.*

The Men of the Great Assembly

The rabbis mention a group of people called the Men of the Great Assembly. They were responsible for handing over the Torah to the next generation. The opening statement of famous early writings called *Ethics of the Fathers* reads:

> "Moses received Torah from Sinai. He handed it over to Joshua. Joshua handed it over to the elders. The elders handed over to the prophets. The prophets handed the Torah over to the Men of the Great Assembly."

They also called the synagogue, a House of Assembly or *Beit Knesset*. The men of the great Assembly were the Maccabees, who saved the greatest synagogue of all, the Holy Temple in Jerusalem. The Talmud gave them a nickname in order to give them credit for what they did without stating their genealogy.

Many customs were instated by the Men of the Great Assembly. They include the lighting of the Chanukah candles, the Sabbath candles, and all the laws of the holiday of Purim. The Maccabees didn't want us to wait for Chanukah to remember the great holy light, so they told the nation to light candles every week before the Sabbath begins. The *Shabbat* (Sabbath) candles are known to bring peace to the home and the family. Every Jewish woman who lights these candles can feel their holiness and the energy that they give. On Friday night our homes become Holy Sanctuaries.

The customs that were initiated after the Maccabean revolt have real value. The miracles that occurred at the time of the Hasmonean period were so profound that they had to be very holy to receive such divine protection and inspiration. They had the merit to bring back Torah to the Jewish people. The whole goal of the Maccabees was so holy that Hashem gave them success beyond the realms of nature.

The Pharisees are the original founders of rabbinical Judaism. Seven Jewish laws are considered rabbinical. Some of them were started by the Maccabees. These include Sabbath candle lighting, Hanukah candles, reading the Scroll of Esther on the holiday of Purim, and washing hands with a cup as was done in the Holy Temple before eating bread. The Maccabees started these customs in order to remember the great miracles of their generation. The Pharisees wrote prayers to say before and after these Mitzvoth and gave them great importance. When we were in school, we learned that washing hands before bread was a law initiated by the scribes. We asked our teacher who the scribes were, and she said King Solomon! Little did we know that the profession called scribes didn't begin until the return of Israel to Zion, centuries after Solomon lived.

The nation loved these mitzvoth and kept them diligently. The rabbis created blessings before performing religious rituals even though they are not commandments from the Torah. For example, "Blessed are you Hashem our God the creator of the world that sanctified us with His mitzvoth and commanded us to light the candles of the Sabbath."

The mere fact that the rabbis made it a law to recite such blessings would imply that they believed that these laws were God-given. Otherwise, prayer recital over rabbinical laws would constitute taking God's name in vain. The rabbis were very strict not to use God's name in vain.

The Maccabees were so revered at the time that the customs they established were unanimously observed. The people felt that the words of the Maccabees were the words of prophets. There is a Talmudic passage that says that after the destruction of the Second Temple, prophecy ceased. The only prophets that we know of in the Second Temple period were Zachariah, Malachi, and Chagai and other prophets that helped build the Second Temple. So why didn't the rabbis say that since the building of the Second Temple, there was no prophecy?

They said that since the destruction there was no more prophecy because they believed that the Hasmoneans were also prophets. If they instated customs, the rabbis felt that they came for Hashem.

There was a short but beautiful period during and after the Hasmonean war and the miracle of Chanukah, when the holiness of the Temple was felt in the atmosphere. Then, Jews as well as gentiles flocked to the Temple to give thanks to their Creator as it says in the Prophet Isaiah, 56:7, "For my house is a house of prayer it will be called upon for all the nations."

CHAPTER 9

Reading and Writing

As I explained many times throughout this book, Hashem created this world as a home for people that can be proficient enough to communicate on a high level and be literate enough to learn the Bible. In order to succeed in educating an entire nation to be fully literate they must have motivation. Motivation comes with the realization of the importance of reading and writing.

My friend's six-year-old daughter was having trouble learning to read. She seemed very precocious, so I asked her why it's important to learn how to read. She said that she doesn't have to know how to read because her mother can read for her. I asked her, "Would you like to be able to read the signs on the streets? Do you want to read a story?" She had no interest. She had no insight into the need to be independent and had no clue of the importance of reading and writing, and no will to learn. She had the intelligence, but without the will and motivation to learn, she could not succeed.

Ancient Greek philosophy preached literacy for the masses. Once the Israelites learned to read and write Greek, learning Hebrew was not a problem. After the victory of the Maccabees, the Jewish people, who already knew to read and write in Greek were motivated to learn to read Hebrew scriptures. This was what Hashem anticipated. He waited for the time that the Bible could be studied and chanted in Hebrew, the language of Abraham, Isaac, and Jacob. Hashem did not want the religion to be ruled by a hierarchy. He wanted every man, woman and child to be able to learn the Torah independently. When you can learn by yourself, you can develop insight. Insight is a key to success in life. The Jews of the First Temple lacked insight; they just followed the actions of others.

The First Schools of Israel

During and after the Hasmonean Dynasty the Land of Israel was called Judea up until the destruction of the Second Temple. After the war of Chanukah some schools were opened in Judea for boys and girls, as well as Torah centers for men. The education demanded oral repetition, memory and comprehension. Girls were required to learn the laws and customs of women, how to educate the young children under the age of seven, as well as home maintenance.

Despite the Torah's mandate to study and become educated, most children of the time after the Second Temple did not learn to read and write. At least 90 percent of the Jewish population of Roman Palestine in the first century CE could merely write their own name or not write and read at all. The literacy rate was about three percent among non-Jewish populations and five percent among the Jews.

In a world where there were not enough books, education meant learning everything by heart. For many generations, the Jews memorized the Bible in its entirety.

The Hidden Torah

In the last chapters of Deuteronomy, Moses told Israelites that their descendants would stray, forsake the Torah, and be severely punished. As a remedy for this, he tells the Levites to hide the Torah that he has written.

> Deuteronomy 31:26–29
>
> Take this book of the Torah and place it at the side of the Ark of the Covenant of Hashem, your God, and it shall be there for you as a witness. For I know your rebelliousness and your stiff neck, behold! While I am still alive with you today, you have been rebels against Hashem—and surely after my death. Gather to me all the elders of your tribes and your officers, and I shall speak these words into their ears, and call heaven and earth to bear witness against them. For I know that after my death you will surely act corruptly, and you will stray from the path that I have commanded you, and evil will befall you at the end of days, if you do what is evil in the eyes of Hashem, to anger Him through your handiwork.

Hashem protected the Torah in the Holy Temple until the very beginning of education and literacy of the masses. As generations passed we became more and more literate until the point where people of all ages could read and write, work on the computer, and even learn Bible through the Internet. The importance of detail is understood, and we can go deeper and deeper in our understanding of the meaning of the words in the Torah and in the whole Bible. The Torah was written, more than anything else, for those who are living today. With every generation since the Maccabees, we have become wiser and more erudite.

Until the printing press was invented, most learning was done by heart just by chanting and memorizing. In our present generation, we have the privilege of being able to have access to a tremendous amount of knowledge through books and the Internet. We can research anything on any subject in the Bible and achieve greater and greater understanding and appreciation.

Learning about science, nature, and natural medicine also helps us approach Hashem as we embrace the world that He created for us. That is why the Torah starts from the story of creation. The beginning of the Bible including the whole book of Genesis is meant to be taught to very young children; that's why there are almost no laws in the first book of the Bible. Entertain the young ones with stories; when they get older, they will feel like they know their forefathers personally and they'll be happy to learn from their actions.

The more you expand a child's mind, the smarter he or she will become. If you teach children Bible in a fun and enjoyable way, you are also teaching them to love Hashem "with all their hearts, all their souls and all their might" (Deuteronomy 6:5).

During the First Temple period the Torah was not studied from a written source. Any prophets or scholars that knew Torah knew it by heart. When Ezra showed the Torah to the Jewish people around 400 BCE they didn't recognize it but they were eager to learn. Still, with the lack of a printing press and a very small population that returned to Zion, learning was limited.

Studying and writing the Torah became more widespread during the Hasmonean Era. They had the incentive to copy the Torah because of the shock they experienced when they saw the Torah shattered into pieces. Everything Hashem does is for the best. He allowed the Assyrian Greeks to enter the Holy Temple and destroy the Torah in order to fulfil the prophecy of Jeremiah.

Jeremiah 24:6-7

> My eyes will watch over them for their good, and I will bring them back to this land. I will build them up and not tear them down; I will plant them and not uproot them. I will give them a heart to know me, that I am the LORD. They will be my people, and I will be their God, for they will return to me with all their heart.

The path to return to God with all your heart is through learning Torah and the Old Testament. The Bible teaches us who God is. The more we learn, the more we get to know Hashem, return to Him and observe His Torah with love.

Teach Your Children

The world is different today. Children learn to read and write from a very young age. This is a relatively new advancement. School systems to educate children to read and write, developed over the past four centuries. In some countries, schools to educate children originated only in the last fifty years.

The Torah commands us to read, learn, teach, and write the words of Moses. Hashem says that the whole Bible is included in this mitzvah. The most important part of this mitzvah is to teach your children. The following explanation of a famous Bible quote will demonstrate the importance of reading and writing for Hashem.

Exodus 13:8–10

> On that day tell your son, "I do this because of what the LORD did for me when I came out of Egypt." This observance will be for you like a sign on your hand and a reminder on your forehead that this law of the LORD is to be on your lips. For the LORD brought

you out of Egypt with his mighty hand. You must keep this ordinance at the appointed time year after year.

Are We Really Smarter?

At first glance, archeologists believe that increases in intelligence is an evolutionary process. Aside from the fact that I don't believe in evolution, the level of intellect in the world is not equal on all planes. There are pictures found in caves that are works of art from thousands of years ago and are quite superior to primitive drawings from the Byzantine era around 200 CE.

In the same generation, Moses and Joshua were genius scholars and scribes while the common Israelite couldn't read at all. It's not only that they didn't know how to read, they didn't have the intelligence to learn how to read.

One of the reasons this is so is because if you wait too long to teach a child a new language, they lose their ability to acquire it. If a child is not spoken to at all until age eleven, he or she will have very limited ability to even speak one language. If the Israelites were slaves, it's possible that the children were not taught anything; they were enslaved and just had to work. Child labor was a part of history and family life up until as recent as only a hundred years ago.

The other reason that we are so much smarter today is because by now we have the experience of many reincarnations. Every lifetime we become brighter. Today there are children who can play piano for a concert at age seven. I myself helped many women breastfeed their babies before I had a child of my own. I had no special training and I read one book about it. Some of these mothers had three or more children that they did not succeed to breastfeed even though they really tried. This was years before I had any psychic abilities. I acted as if I had years of knowledge and experience and a nursing counselor; maybe I did.

If you meet young people that act like they have many years of experience, treat them accordingly. Give them the respect that their knowledge and demeanor portrays. They may be older than you are in total life time experiences.

We are living in a generation where some children are more intelligent than their parents; on the other hand, some very educated parents have children with learning disabilities. Those children might be here for reasons that are unknown to us but are known to the *neshama* of the child.

Nevertheless, we must give our children the highest exposure to knowledge that we can. Don't discourage them from pursuing seemingly unrealistic goals. If your child wants to play violin, do everything in your power to make it happen. She might miss her violin from a past lifetime.

Thirty-five hundred years ago, people obviously had less experience from past lifetimes. The world of intelligent humankind was relatively new. Slowly we acquired more experience and we became better teachers to our children and students. In my book *Who Is God*, I wrote a whole chapter about reincarnation entitled *Life after Life*.

The *Mezuzah*

Mezuzah is first mentioned in the Torah in Exodus 12:7 when the Israelites were commanded to place the blood of a lamb or kid on their two doorposts before they left Egypt. There is a commandment in the Torah to write the words of the Torah on your doorpost. When the new leaders, the Maccabees, learned that it says in the Torah to keep this commandment, they began to think of practical ways that this commandment could be kept. This is another sign that the Torah was intended for a later generation. Hashem wouldn't command us to write if we didn't know how to write.

> Deuteronomy 11:19-20 says, "Teach them to your children, talking about them when you sit at home and when you walk along the road, when you lie down and when you get up. Write them on the doorframes of your houses and on your gates."

When Moses taught the Israelites, he taught them everything by heart whether they understood it or not. Only in the future would the whole nation be educated enough to understand the Torah. Today there is close to 100% literacy of the Hebrew language among healthy Jewish school children in Israel.

The Jews have many prayer articles: a prayer shawl or *Tzizit* in Hebrew, Phylacteries or *Tefillin* in Hebrew and a *mezuzah*. A *mezuzah* is a tiny scroll with words of Torah written on it. It is placed in a rectangular box and nailed or taped to the door post. This is an example of a *mezuzah* on a doorpost in Jerusalem.

Today, the commandment of *mezuzah* is observed by producing rectangular containers with a scroll within that contains the words of Deuteronomy 6:4–9 and 11:13–21. This scroll within a case is attached to the right side of the doorpost. Today every traditional Jewish home has a *mezuzah* on its doorpost to entrances to the house as well as on doors inside the house. Excavations of the Second Temple period find carved-out crevices in doorposts in the shape of a *mezuzah*. Apparently the custom was to put the holy scroll of writings inside these crevices. *Mezuzot*, the plural of *mezuzah*, literally means door frames but it has come to mean this special religious article that is posted on the doorframe. The commandment is to "write them on the doorframes of your houses and on your gates" (Deuteronomy 6:9).

When the people of Israel were in Egypt, even though the Pharaohs might have had some parchment for royal documents, the Israelites did not have leather parchment for the common person. The commandment to write on parchment could not be observed by ancient man. Hashem had in mind that many of the mitzvoth would not be observed for thousands of years. Putting a *mezuzah* on the doorpost is one example. He commanded with our generation in mind. Deuteronomy 6:9, "And you shall write it on the door posts of your house and on your gates."

Here is a photograph of the parchment that will go into a *mezuzah* on the doorpost. They are the words of Deuteronomy 6:4-9 and Deuteronomy 11:13-21.

שְׁמַע יִשְׂרָאֵל יְהוָה אֱלֹהֵינוּ יְהוָה אֶחָד וְאָהַבְתָּ אֵת
יְהוָה אֱלֹהֶיךָ בְּכָל לְבָבְךָ וּבְכָל נַפְשְׁךָ וּבְכָל מְאֹדֶךָ וְהָיוּ
הַדְּבָרִים הָאֵלֶּה אֲשֶׁר אָנֹכִי מְצַוְּךָ הַיּוֹם עַל לְבָבֶךָ וְשִׁנַּנְתָּם
לְבָנֶיךָ וְדִבַּרְתָּ בָּם בְּשִׁבְתְּךָ בְּבֵיתֶךָ וּבְלֶכְתְּךָ בַדֶּרֶךְ
וּבְשָׁכְבְּךָ וּבְקוּמֶךָ וּקְשַׁרְתָּם לְאוֹת עַל יָדֶךָ וְהָיוּ לְטֹטָפֹת
בֵּין עֵינֶיךָ וּכְתַבְתָּם עַל מְזוּזֹת בֵּיתֶךָ וּבִשְׁעָרֶיךָ
וְהָיָה אִם שָׁמֹעַ תִּשְׁמְעוּ אֶל מִצְוֹתַי אֲשֶׁר אָנֹכִי
מְצַוֶּה אֶתְכֶם הַיּוֹם לְאַהֲבָה אֶת יְהוָה אֱלֹהֵיכֶם וּלְעָבְדוֹ
בְּכָל לְבַבְכֶם וּבְכָל נַפְשְׁכֶם וְנָתַתִּי מְטַר אַרְצְכֶם בְּעִתּוֹ
יוֹרֶה וּמַלְקוֹשׁ וְאָסַפְתָּ דְגָנֶךָ וְתִירֹשְׁךָ וְיִצְהָרֶךָ וְנָתַתִּי
עֵשֶׂב בְּשָׂדְךָ לִבְהֶמְתֶּךָ וְאָכַלְתָּ וְשָׂבָעְתָּ הִשָּׁמְרוּ לָכֶם
פֶּן יִפְתֶּה לְבַבְכֶם וְסַרְתֶּם וַעֲבַדְתֶּם אֱלֹהִים אֲחֵרִים
וְהִשְׁתַּחֲוִיתֶם לָהֶם וְחָרָה אַף יְהוָה בָּכֶם וְעָצַר אֶת
הַשָּׁמַיִם וְלֹא יִהְיֶה מָטָר וְהָאֲדָמָה לֹא תִתֵּן אֶת יְבוּלָהּ
וַאֲבַדְתֶּם מְהֵרָה מֵעַל הָאָרֶץ הַטֹּבָה אֲשֶׁר יְהוָה נֹתֵן לָכֶם
וְשַׂמְתֶּם אֶת דְּבָרַי אֵלֶּה עַל לְבַבְכֶם וְעַל נַפְשְׁכֶם וּקְשַׁרְתֶּם
אֹתָם לְאוֹת עַל יֶדְכֶם וְהָיוּ לְטוֹטָפֹת בֵּין עֵינֵיכֶם וְלִמַּדְתֶּם
אֹתָם אֶת בְּנֵיכֶם לְדַבֵּר בָּם בְּשִׁבְתְּךָ בְּבֵיתֶךָ וּבְלֶכְתְּךָ
בַדֶּרֶךְ וּבְשָׁכְבְּךָ וּבְקוּמֶךָ וּכְתַבְתָּם עַל מְזוּזוֹת בֵּיתֶךָ
וּבִשְׁעָרֶיךָ לְמַעַן יִרְבּוּ יְמֵיכֶם וִימֵי בְנֵיכֶם עַל הָאֲדָמָה
אֲשֶׁר נִשְׁבַּע יְהוָה לַאֲבֹתֵיכֶם לָתֵת לָהֶם כִּימֵי הַשָּׁמַיִם
עַל הָאָרֶץ

There is a sect of Shomronites living in Israel today that write words of the Torah directly on the doorpost. They are carved into the stone wall. This may be the literal translation of this mitzvah but it desecrates God's holy name. Writing the words with God's name on a doorway that is exposed to the elements may cause the words to be erased or destroyed. Jews are very careful with God's name. We don't even leave a holy book open in the house let alone leave it exposed continuously.

The Ten Commandments are the axioms in which to understand the rest of the Torah. If a mitzvah desecrates the third commandment Exodus 20:7, "You shall not misuse the name of the LORD your God, for the LORD will not hold anyone guiltless who misuses his name." we must find a way to do it differently. The way the Jews perform this mitzvah protects the holy words while letting their energy enter the home and sanctify it. We also put a *mezuzah* on every single doorway in the entire house aside from the bathroom.

Phylacteries?

The rabbis tried hard to understand what the Torah meant and came up with a physical holy object for prayer. The oldest phylacteries that were found were in the Kumran village where the Essenes lived. They were made of silver and contained a parchment inside with the Ten Commandments. The evidence shows that the mezuzah is a much more ancient custom than *tefillin*, or phylacteries in English. The Torah scholars in the years before and after the destruction of the Holy Temple wore phylacteries while studying and praying.

Today's phylacteries or tefillin are two leather boxes with parchments inside that have holy writings from the Torah. The people who make them are genuinely trying to please Hashem and to love Him, "with all their hearts and all their might."

Boys begin the custom of wearing tefillin for the morning prayers from thirteen years old. They usually start a month before their Bar Mitzvah. The following illustration is the photogragh of a Bar Mitzvah boy wearing tefillin and a prayer shall while praying at the Western Wall. Jewish girls are not obligated to not wear tefillin.

Deuteronomy 6:6–9
    These commandments that I give you today are
to be on your hearts. Impress them on your children.
Talk about them when you sit at home and when you
walk along the road, when you lie down and when
you get up. Tie them as symbols on your hands and
bind them on your foreheads. Write them on the
doorframes of your houses and on your gates.

The next paragraph is the exact translation of these
words. These verses are part of the prayers that religious
Jews say twice a day:

Deuteronomy 6:6–9
    "And the words that I command you today should
be remembered by heart. And you should teach the
words of the Torah to your children over and over
again, and you shall talk about them, when you are
sitting in your home, when you are walking on the
path, when you are lying down and when you wake
up. And you shall tie it as a sign on your hand, and

it should be for 'totafot' between your eyes. And you shall write it on the door posts of your house and on your gates."

A Word with a Secret for the Future

The word *totafot* is one of a kind. There is no other word in the entire Bible that even has the same root. Rashi says that it comes from two words from other languages that both mean two. Two and two are four, therefore; he concludes, four passages should be written in the phylacteries or what we call *tefillin*. This is not consistent with any Torah rules. We don't know of any foreign words in the first Five Books of Moses.

This word *totafot* is mentioned in two other sites in the Torah, all in the context of placing the words of Torah between your eyes. In Exodus 13:9, there is an identical verse except instead of *totafot* it says, "as a reminder." Thus there are some modern commentators who suggest to translate totafot as a reminder. That doesn't make sense to me. If *totafot* meant reminder, then why would the Torah use a different and unknown word?

It must have another meaning.

Let's take a closer look at that verse where the word "reminder" is used: Exodus 13:8–10:

> On that day tell your son, "I do this because of what the LORD did for me when I came out of Egypt." This observance will be for you like a sign on your hand and a reminder on your forehead that this law of the LORD is to be on your lips. For the LORD brought you out of Egypt with his mighty hand. You must keep this ordinance at the appointed time year after year.

If you look at all the details in the above passage, the "reminder" is an ordinance at the appointed time; in other words, on the holiday of Passover. So now we have another clue for the word totafot. Every day you do X, but once a year you will have a reminder. We don't wear phylacteries on Passover or on any holidays, so it makes sense that the celebration of the exodus from Egypt will serve as a reminder.

One more important point, the NIV translation says "a reminder on your forehead," while the literal translation is "a memory between your eyes." The NIV translates "between the eyes" as forehead because the translators are influenced by the rabbinical interpretation that this is a commandment to wear phylacteries, which are worn on the forehead.

Hashem intentionally put an unknown word in the Torah because it contained a secret that is only applicable in our times. It took me years of pondering on this one word, *totafot*, to finally, with the grace of God, get an insight and deeper understanding.

Exodus 13:9, "And you shall tie it as a sign on your hand." The phylacteries are traditionally tied on the left arm with a leather band down to the middle finger of the left hand. The box itself is tied onto the arm. The Torah surely knows the difference between a hand and an arm. It says that God took us out of Egypt, "with a strong hand and an outstretched arm" (Deuteronomy 4:34). Read on to discover more intriguing clues of the meaning of *totafot*.

Writing Script

"And it should be a sign by your hand" (Deuteronomy 6:8).
It's not enough just to read; Hashem also wants us to write. Hashem was waiting for the day when we will write

with our hands—when we will make signs on paper. When we write any language in script, we are making connections of letters and words with our hands. When we take notes in class, we make signs with our hands to remember what the teacher said, just as Exodus 13:9 reads,

> "This observance will be for you like a sign on your hand and a reminder on your forehead that this law of the LORD is to be on your lips. For the LORD brought you out of Egypt with his mighty hand."

Interestingly enough, the word for sign, *ot* in modern Hebrew, means letter—not a letter that you write to a friend but a letter in the alphabet. When you write script, you tie the letters into words with your hand. Those words are a sign to help you remember. In other words, your notes are a reminder. Even if you know a song by heart you may want to have the words in front of you while you sing, as a reminder.

Therefore, I would like to mention, that this mitzvah to write the words of Torah is not a replacement for learning them by heart. On Passover, we don't write, but we can read our notes in order to remind us what to say at the holiday table when we tell our guests and children about the Exodus from Egypt.

A Compound Word

The word *totafot* must be Hebrew. There are no foreign languages in the Hebrew Bible as Rashi claims. There is a possibility that it is a combination of two or three Hebrew words.

Jehovah, God's name, is a composition of three words: "was," "is," and "will be," or past, present, and future. This means that the ancient Hebrew language can accept a compound word.

Hebrew grammar regularly compounds words with pronouns; "your seed" in Exodus 32:13 is one word and "their sin" in Exodus 32:34 in one word. Also, small words such as *and*, *in*, *to* and *like* are usually compounded with another word in the biblical text and in modern Hebrew.

The word *taf* in the Bible means children. Exodus 12:37, "Six hundred thousand men on foot besides the (*taf*) children." The second part of the word *totafot* is from the root "tavot," meaning to weave. In Hebrew grammar, the letter "vav" that is a "V" sound is sometimes sounded like the letter "O".

The words that Moses is commanding will be woven with our eyes as we read back and forth, up and down. Even our small children will be literate enough to weave the words of the Torah with their eyes. When ancient men or women did read, they read slowly and had very poor reading comprehension. The Torah is commanding us to learn how to read and teach our children to read fluently. Evidently, the real meaning of the phrase is: "And you shall write signs (or letters) by the easy flow of your hand. You and your children shall read the words of the Torah easily, weaving through words with your eyes."

There is a third word in this word, *pat*, which means bread. (The letter "*pay*" of *totafot* can sometimes make a P sound.) In the future redemption, the nation will have hunger and thirst for Torah. The words of Torah will be your bread, your sustenance for life.

Amos 8:11, "The days are coming," declares the Sovereign Lord, "when I will send a famine through the land— not a famine of food or a thirst for water, but a famine of hearing the words of the Lord.

The above study does not mean that I discourage wearing tefillin. The opposite is true. A mitzvah that has been performed for over two thousand years by righteous God-fearing Jews cannot be simply thrown away. Wearing the tefillin for just half an hour a day gives the person a spiritual feeling that Hashem is near. However, I conclude from the explanations that I received from God, that the higher purpose of tefillin is to be a reminder to learn Torah to have it printed and available for all.

It is also a mitzvah to write your own commentaries and insights and share them with to others. Only by giving God-fearing people freedom to use their own intuition to explain the infinite wisdom of the Torah can we keep the Torah alive. When you translate the word *totafot*, this way, it is incumbent on the women as well as they are the educators of the children.

Summary

The widespread learning of the Bible began with the Maccabees. Ezra brought the Torah to the Jewish people, but until after the Maccabean victory, they could not read and write Hebrew well enough to study and learn Torah and the Bible. God foresaw this already from the time of Moses at the burning bush. He gave Moses the Torah with the clear knowledge that it would take many centuries until it would be learned word for word by the masses. The Torah and the whole Bible are even more widespread today than ever before.

In this generation, we are not only book literate but computer literate as well. Our children can read and write fluently. They make signs with their pens, which are in their hands, and they read quickly, weaving the words with their eyes. Tying all the pieces together, I would like to translate our most famous Torah passage in a new way. These are the words that Moses said to the children of Israel on the last day of his life. We chant these words in our prayers twice a day, in the morning and before going to bed. It is considered the most important prayer in the Bible and is taught to young children as early as possible.

> Deuteronomy 6:4–9
> Listen Israel the Hashem is our God Hashem is one. And you must love Hashem your God with all heart, all your soul and all your strength. And the words that I am commanding you today will be memorized by heart. You should recite them with your children repeatedly, and speak about these words, when you are sitting in your home, when you are walking on the street. When you lay down and when you wake up. And you should write them with your hand and read them with your eyes. And you should write them on your doorpost and your gates.

I would like to explain that the words the Bible is referring to are the words of the entire book of Deuteronomy which is the last speech that Moses gave to the Israelites before his death.

My Right Hand

> Psalm 137:1–6

> By the rivers of Babylon we sat and wept when we remembered Zion. There on the poplars we hung our harps. For there our captors asked us for songs. Our tormentors demanded songs of joy. They said, "Sing us one of the songs of Zion." How can we sing the songs of the Lord while in a foreign land? If I forget you, Jerusalem, may my right hand forget its skill. May my tongue cling to the roof of my mouth if I do

not remember you. If I do not consider Jerusalem, my highest joy.

In the above Psalm are the famous words "May my right hand forget its skill." The Bible is referring to the skill of writing. The few people who could read were not always able to write. Writing was a skilled worker's profession, almost like the ability to be an artist.

Today a man who writes the Torah on scroll is called a scribe or a *sofer* in Hebrew. He must have artistic talent, study the laws, and practice for almost a year before he can master this skill.

This Psalm was written by the Maccabees, who lived around 163 BCE. Many of them were skilled scribes. It was written in memory of the Jews who were exiled to Babylon a few hundred years earlier. The Maccabees swore that if there was another exile, they would never forget how to write the words of the Torah. They will continue to make copies forever wherever the Israelites live and they will tell their descendants about the beauty and holiness of Jerusalem.

"How can we sing the songs of Hashem in a foreign land?" We had to, because in the diaspora before this one, in the Babylonian Diaspora, the Jews hung their harps and forgot everything. The Maccabees foresaw the future destruction and made a decree: we will not sing anything, "Let our tongues stick to our mouths," if we don't remember Jerusalem.

There is a tradition to say this Psalm at every wedding and break a glass. At every gathering of joy and celebration, we must remember that we cannot be totally happy because the Holy Temple of Jerusalem isn't built.

Even more important than mentioning Jerusalem is "singing songs of the Lord." Music and song are the best ways to teach faith to the next generation. Music enters the memory and the heart like nothing else. Even the mentally challenged can learn scores of songs by heart. In my book *Who Is God?* I wrote a whole chapter about music.

When we sing to Hashem with all our hearts, it makes Him happier than just prayer alone. Hashem gets so much pleasure to hear our voices sing to Him. Do you think He gets pleasure from animal sacrifices, from killing one of His creatures?

Of course not. Hashem just instituted animal sacrifices so the Israelites wouldn't kill animals in a vicious way. Even today, animals in non-kosher slaughterhouses really suffer. In my next book called *Choose Life* I will go into more details. If you don't want to support cruelty to animals use only kosher meat and poultry for your health and for your conscience. This is my suggestion to Jews and non-Jews alike.

Tzitzit

The NIV calls *tzitzit* tassels. The tassels are tied onto a four-cornered garment, and a prayer is said before wearing it. It is usually worn on top of an undershirt or as a prayer shawl, which is called a *tallit*.

Numbers 15:37–41

The LORD said to Moses, "Speak to the Israelites and say to them: 'Throughout the generations to come you are to make tassels on the corners of your garments, with a blue cord on each tassel. You will have these tassels to look at and so you will remember all the commands of the LORD, that you may obey them and not prostitute yourselves by chasing after the lusts of your own heart and eyes. Then you will remember to obey all my commands and will be consecrated to your God. I am the LORD your God, who brought you out of Egypt to be your God. I am the LORD your God.'"

Below is a picture of the fringes with a light blue cord. The dye is traditionally made from a type of snail called a Murex trunchular. The prayer shawl has these fringes on all four corners. You can look up *tzitzit* on line to find a full color photograph. Many Jews wear *tzitzit* that are all white because in the diaspora the dye was not available.

Hashem gave the Israelites a mitzvah to wear this garment as a sign that Hashem is watching. The light blue color is the color of the sky and of the sea—a sign that God is everywhere. It is also the color of the Israeli flag, which mimics the familiar stripes of a prayer shawl.

This paragraph comes right after a story of a man who collected wood on the Sabbath. The man was stoned to death. Hashem saw that the children of Israel were still sinning even after being punished severely for the sin of the spies in Numbers chapters 13 and 14. This is the first sign of Hashem realizing that He has to go a little softer. He didn't want to start stoning people regularly. "If punishment doesn't work, let's think of another idea! A uniform! Not something difficult that will take away people's free choice as to what to wear every day, but something small that will be a sign." The Israelites couldn't read, so an emblem would have little meaning. A colored tassel would be the sign that is not too haughty but is clearly seen. The color is a beautiful turquoise called *tekhelet* in the Bible.

There is evidence that these tassels were worn by ancient Jews. This dye was discovered on a piece of fabric found near the Dead Sea in the 1950's in a cave at Wadi Murba'at, where Jewish fighters hid during the Bar Kokhba revolt in the second century. In December of 2013 Dr. Na'ama Sukenik tested the color found in the fabric and was able to determine that it was derived from the Murex trunchular, a mollusk widely believed to be the marine animal known as the *khilazon* in the Talmud—the source of the rare blue dye.

Along the northern coast of Israel and up into Lebanon, dyeing houses took in harvests of the sea snail and cooked them for many days in salted water with fenugreek. Near Tyre, archaeologists have found large mounds of snail shell remains, indicating where local dyeing industries flourished in Biblical times. Remains of the techelet snail have also been found on Mt. Zion, Jerusalem, indicating an ancient dyeing industry there.

Most impressive to me about these discoveries is that we are actually performing this same mitzvah today. The Jews were so scrupulous with their education that the tradition was passed down from father to son with no error. Even the Torah scrolls themselves are identical all over the world and are also identical to the Dead Sea Scrolls. There might be a few tiny difference of spelling, but not one changes the meaning in any way.

This alone is a sign that God had a hand in this. Who can make a perfect copy of even one book when copying by hand, let alone hundreds of thousands throughout the centuries? Only God could assure such perfection. Not only that, but the unwritten message of the exact color and the source of the dye for the tzitit was not changed for 2000 years.

CHAPTER 10

The Book of Psalms

Of all the Books of the Bible, Psalms has been the most popular to Jews and Christians. When you read Psalms you can feel that every word is your personal prayer as if it was written for you. Our sages have praised Psalms as an almost magical book. Reading a few paragraphs a day, with your mind and soul attentive to the words, will make you feel better and give you more faith.

How did Psalms get so popular? Well one reason is because it is that good. Its high level of literature and depth of ideology is really one of a kind. You can learn Psalms your whole life and never stop learning new things and getting new inspirations.

It is important to note the Psalms was written for the purpose of prayer and it was to be kept for future generations. Many of the chapters are written with a syntax that is very general and can be used on a daily basis for each person's individual needs. Psalms is the oldest prayer book that is still in use today. In Israel, there are books of Psalms for public use at every holy site and cemetery. Many of the chapters are incorporated in the Jewish songs and in the Jewish school curriculum.

Who Wrote Psalms?

The author of Psalms referred to a Torah that was easily accessible to all. Psalms 119 openly praises the study of the Torah.

> Psalms 119:72 "The Torah words that you utter are better for me than thousands of pieces of gold and silver."

King David lived about nine hundred years before the Maccabees. There was no parchment during the times of David. If David wrote anything he would have had to chisel it on stone or just recite the poetry by heart. As I mentioned earlier, the first evidence of any parchment was at the end of the First Temple period.

Even the most orthodox Jewish authorities say that the first seventy-two Psalms were written by David and the rest are from anonymous writers because of the following verse:

> Psalms 72:20, "The prayers of David the son of Jesse have been completed."

The famous "On the Rivers of Babylon" Psalms 137 is one example of a Psalm that could not have been written by King David. This chapter talks about the Babylonian diaspora of the Jews after the destruction of the First Temple, hundreds of years after King David's death.

Another example of chapters that could not have been written by David are the fifteen passages of the songs of the ascents. These songs, chapters 120-134, were sung on the fifteen steps leading up to the Temple. King David didn't live to see the Temple built and First Temple didn't even have fifteen steps to sing on. It was the Second Temple that had fifteen large semi-circular steps between the woman's court and the court of the altar.

The beginning chapters of Psalms reveal an ideology of fighting for what you believe in, killing your enemies, enduring the pain and suffering at the hands of your enemies and celebrating the victory of the righteous. These chapters were obviously written at a time of war.

Psalms 22:16 is a verse of proof that the Psalm could not have been talking about David. "Dogs surrounded me a group of evil men have encircled me, like the prey of a lion are my hands and my feet."

There were no dogs in Israel in David's time. However, the Greeks in the wars of the Hashmonean Era used dogs in their warfare. They also began to use pictures of lions as a sign of strength. It is also not possible that the war in Psalms is referring to the war with the Romans, because the wars in Psalms are all victorious for the Israelites. In Roman times, Israelite defeat and bloodshed were the rule.

The entire Book of Psalms is written in similar language from the same time period. It is not possible that some chapters were written by King David and others written 500 years later. The style of writing is unique to any other books of the Bible and is similar to other Second Temple literature that has been found in archeological digs.

You may argue that it is possible that King David wrote some passages and they were edited later. I agree that this is possible, but the editors would have to be the same ones who wrote the latter chapters. The style of writing in Psalms is very unique to the rest of the Bible but it is the same style as Second Temple poetry that was found in excavations. Biblical critics agree that Psalms was written in the Second Temple period.

A Newborn Nation

Psalms 22:27-31

All the ends of the earth
  will remember and turn to the LORD,
and all the families of the nations
  will bow down before him,
for dominion belongs to the LORD
  and he rules over the nations.

All the rich of the earth will feast and worship;
  all who go down to the dust will kneel before him—
  those who cannot keep themselves alive.
Posterity will serve him;
  future generations will be told about the Lord.
They will proclaim his righteousness,
  declaring to a people yet unborn:
  He has done it!

The Christian translations say an unborn nation because the Christian nation was yet to be born. However, the literal translation is to a newborn nation. The true intention of this Psalm is the rebirth of the Jewish people that had for the most part, been lost to Hellenism.

The Maccabees and their comrades, are the first writers of Psalms. Other Psalms were written by former Hellenists who were exited to return to God and his people. Every single chapter can be explained if you incorporate my explanation of the Holiday of Chanukah. There are many chapters that describe the victory of right over wrong and the exalted feeling it brings.

The Maccabees united the nation and taught them Torah. Many of the chapters just celebrate different Torah stories because they were so excited to learn stories that they never knew. For example, Psalm 114, "When Israel came out of Egypt, Jacob from a people of foreign tongue"

The new nation of Israel was a United Israel after a civil war. Psalm 3, "I will not fear the myriads of the nation that surrounded me in ambush." The nation is singular and "myriads" is tens of thousands. The tens of thousands of our own nation who rose up against the Maccabees, Hashem "smacked the cheeks of my enemy and broke the teeth of the evil ones." The enemies are not killed but rather get a 'smack in the face'. The allegory to cheeks and teeth shows that after seeing God's miracles, they were speechless. All of their Hellenistic values did not hold up and they changed their ways.

One of the biggest goals of the Maccabees was to get to the Holy Temple to purify it in order to continue to serve Hashem for the rest of their lives. Psalms 27: 4, "One thing I ask of Hashem, 'May I sit in the house of Hashem all the days of my life."

This prayer could not have been written by King David. The only ones who are allowed to sit in the Holy Temple or the House of God are the Cohanim, the priests. Even a king cannot enter the Holy Temple if he is not from priestly ancestors. The sacrifices that were performed were sacrifices in the front court of the Holy Temple, outdoors.

The Maccabees were Cohanim (priests), they prayed to return to the Holy Temple because the Greeks exiled them and defiled the Temple. Hashem blessed the Maccabees with success.

Psalms 27: 6 "Now my head is raised above my enemies around me and I will slaughter offerings in His tent accompanied by joyous song."

Utopia

The period after the victory of Chanukah was a period of utopia. Peace inside the country and peace with the nations of the world. In the times of the last surviving Maccabee, Simon, the Nation of Israel was just beginning to learn the Torah. They were so excited about what they learned that they wrote songs about it. Some of the Psalms reflect on different parts of the Torah. Psalm 114 describes the miracle of the splitting of the Red Sea. Chapter 29 describes the Revelation at Mount Sinai. Many other Psalms describe the ideology of the Torah as depicted in Deuteronomy. Chapter 115 is an example of a chapter that impugns idol worship and promotes trust in one God.

After the war of Chanukah was over the only Maccabee that survived was Simon. Together with Joshua Ben Perachia he established Torah learning centers in the whole land of Judea. The Jews at this time became more and more devout and loyal to Hashem. Hashem says that the singing in the Holy Temple at this time was on a very high spiritual level. The whole nation was on a high as they celebrated their newly discovered ability to learn Torah. Psalms 119: 66, "Teach me good taste and knowledge because I believe in your Mitzvoth."

The writers of Psalms are anonymous. Their names are not mentioned. They lived in the times of the miracle of Chanukah, survived the war and were healthy enough to come to the Temple to give thanks to the Lord. Some of the writers were Cohanim and worked in the Holy Temple. They were the five sons of Matthias, their colleagues, soldiers and their children. There is no mention of the destruction of the Second Temple in Psalms so it must have been completed before the trouble started.

The scholars of the Second Temple period wrote down everything that they learned. They learned lots of wisdom and stories from their ancestors but it was not in writing yet. Another book that reflects the wisdom of that generation is Ethics of the Fathers. This is a book of wise sayings that was taught orally at this time but was written down a few generations later. A lot of the wisdom of the New Testament was taken from the ideas taught in Ethics of the Fathers. "The fathers" here refers to the earliest Pharisees, the fathers of rabbinical Judaism. A copy of Ethics of the Fathers is available on line for free.

The Introductory Titles

How can I say that the Psalms were not written by David if so many titles say so? Many chapters begin with "A song for David" and "For David." All Bible critics say that the titles were added later. How much later? The Dead Sea Scrolls Psalms have the titles so it had to have been added before the Dead Sea Scrolls. The Bible was canonized in 200 CE. The canonization was a long process that began with the Pharisees a generation after the miracle of Chanukah, and continued with the first Rabbis called Tannaim in the first century CE. Rabbi Yochanan Ben Zakai was one of the first rabbis to edit the Bible. He lived between 30 C.E. and 90 C.E.

After the Maccabees died there were lots of different sects within the Jewish people. When the first Pharisees segregated themselves from the Sadducees, another sect, the first book that they edited was Psalms. The key edition was the addition of titles to every Psalm. They also divided the verses and chapters and decided on the order in which they would appear in the final canon.

Psalms was a prayer book already in use in the Second Holy Temple. It was beloved by the people. By assigning authorship of Psalms to King David, the people thought of him when they recited the Psalms. The nation began to become emotionally attached to King David for writing such profound prayers. The Pharisees also assigned Ecclesiastes, Proverbs and Song of Songs, three other books of the Bible, to King Solomon, the son of King David. They especially threaded Solomon's name into these three works. These early rabbis sought to strengthen the idea that David's line of descent is the bloodline of royalty and the Psalms illustrate just how great this man was to write such profoundly divine writings.

Hashem revealed to me that Proverbs, Song of Songs and Ecclesiastes were written after the return of Ezra the Scribe to Zion by different prophets and scholars of that era. The language of these books predates the syntax used in Psalms.

Many people question the holiness of Song of Songs even though no one can question its beauty. The Song of Songs is a celebration of the divine connection between man and wife. I expounded on this idea in my book called, *God Meets the World* in the chapter entitled, "Do not Commit Adultery." Surely the goal of peace and love in the home is a virtue worth being included in the Bible. This is especially so in a generation where men were commanded to leave their pagan wives and get Jewish wives in their stead. There are words in Song of Songs that were Babylonian words like *Pardes* which means orchard. That would prove that King Solomon did not write it. All Bible critics agree that these books were written later than King Solomon's time.

Ecclesiastes is written at a time where people had to make big changes. The Jews in Ezra's day didn't want to leave the diaspora and start anew. The author wanted to say to them that worldly things don't matter, material belongings are nothing. There was a time for death and despair during the destruction of the Temple, but now it's time to forget everything and build Jerusalem.

Ecclesiastes 1:10-11

Is there anything of which one can say, "Look! This
is something new"?
It was here already, long ago;
    it was here before our time.
No one remembers the former generations,
    and even those yet to come
will not be remembered
    by those who follow them.

The new generation had no Torah knowledge they did not even know what holidays to celebrate. That's why the prophet says, "No one remembers the former generations."

Proverbs

Proverbs was apparently written by many authors. It is an anthology of ancient wisdom. Proverbs accentuates the importance of wisdom, especially Torah wisdom, The Tree of Life. The new generation is so weak and innocent that they must learn not only Torah, The Tree of Life, but also wisdom of the world. The Torah is a feminine word and that's why it is referred to as *she*.

Proverbs 3:18-20

"She is a tree of life to those who take hold of her;
    those who hold her fast will be blessed.
By wisdom the LORD laid the earth's foundations,
    by understanding he set the heavens in place;

by his knowledge the watery depths were divided,
and the clouds let drop the dew."

Truly Divine

Psalms is a book that is far more modern than the period in which it was written. The writers of Psalms were blessed with divine intuition even beyond their own ability to understand the words that they wrote. This is true of all prophets. The prophecy is divine, not the prophet.

Psalms is a collection of prayers to replace the need for sacrifice. Psalms 40:6, "Sacrifice and meal-offering You have no delight in; mine ears you have opened, burnt-offering and sin-offering you have not required."

Psalms 50 even ridicules those who think that God needs sacrifice. It explains that Hashem desires your prayer and appreciation. What He detests is pride, slander, theft and promiscuity.

Psalms 50:8-15
I bring no charges against you concerning your sacrifices
    or concerning your burnt offerings, which are ever before me.
I have no need of a bull from your stall
    or of goats from your pens
for every animal of the forest is mine,
    and the cattle on a thousand hills.
I know every bird in the mountains,
    and the insects in the fields are mine.
If I were hungry I would not tell you,
    for the world is mine, and all that is in it.
Do I eat the flesh of bulls
    or drink the blood of goats?

"Sacrifice your thankfulness to God,
    fulfill your vows to the Most High,

and call on me in the day of trouble;
    I will deliver you, and you will honor me."

The Maccabees were very attached to the written words of the prophets and they learned that Hashem was not happy with the sacrifices of the Jewish people. They cleaned up the Holy Temple from the animal blood of the Greeks and proposed a new way of worship, worship through prayer. Isaiah 1:11-17 proposes this new way of worship:

Isaiah 1:11-17
    The multitude of your sacrifices-- what are they to me?" says Hashem. "I have more than enough of burnt offerings, of rams and the fat of fattened animals; I have no pleasure in the blood of bulls and lambs and goats. When you come to appear before me, who has asked this of you, this trampling of my courts? Stop bringing meaningless offerings! Your incense is detestable to me. New Moons, Sabbaths and convocations-- I cannot bear your evil assemblies. Your New Moon festivals and your appointed feasts my soul hates. They have become a burden to me; I am weary of bearing them. When you spread out your hands in prayer, I will hide my eyes from you; even if you offer many prayers, I will not listen. Your hands are full of blood; wash and make yourselves clean. Take your evil deeds out of my sight! Stop doing wrong, learn to do right! Seek justice, encourage the oppressed. Defend the cause of the fatherless, plead the case of the widow.

Psalms 40:6-7
Sacrifice and offering you did not desire—
    but my ears you have opened
    burnt offerings and sin offerings you did not require.
Then I said, "Here I am, I have come—

it is written about me in the scroll.

In this chapter not only says that God doesn't need any offerings but there is evidence here that the writer is a famous person that is written about in a scroll. If you just say the scroll in Hebrew it denotes the scroll of Esther. The writer says that in the scroll of Esther it writes about him. This means that writer was from the Ten Tribes who was proud that he arrived in Israel and returned to his father in Heaven.

Imagine how unbelievable his devotion to God was! This man was an idol worshipper and now all he wants is God's love and closeness. He believes that all the wealth of the wicked will do them no good because their soul will die:

> Psalms 49:13-15
> This is the fate of those who trust in themselves,
> and of their followers, who approve their sayings:
>
> They are like sheep and are destined to die;
> death will be their shepherd
> (but the upright will prevail over them in the morning).
> Their forms will decay in the grave,
> far from their princely mansions.
> But God will redeem me from the realm of the dead;
> he will surely take me to himself.
>
> Psalms 141: 1-2
> I call to you, LORD, come quickly to me;
> hear me when I call to you.
> May my prayer be set before you like incense;
> may the lifting up of my hands be like the grain
> offering.

Some verses mention no need of any offerings but Psalm 96:7-8 says, "Ascribe to the Hashem, all you families of nations, ascribe to the Hashem glory and strength. Ascribe to the Hashem honor His name. Bring a grain offering and come into his courts."

The above Psalm was written after the Maccabees were able to enter the Holy Temple. From studying the Bible, they learned that God doesn't want sacrifices anymore. At the start of the return of Israel to Zion the prophet Malachi told the Jews that Hashem does not want animal sacrifices He will be happiest with a grain offering. In Malachi 2:3 he describes animal sacrifices very negatively.

"Because of you I will rebuke your descendants; I will smear on your faces the dung from your festival sacrifices, and you will be carried off with it."
In the next chapter Malachi writes,

Malachi 3:3-4
"Then the LORD will have men who will bring offerings in righteousness, and the offerings of Judah and Jerusalem will be acceptable to the LORD, as in days gone by, as in former years.

This is not a contradiction. If you look at the Hebrew, the word "offerings" is a translation from the word *minchat* which means a grain offering.

When the Maccabees were victorious they wanted to perform at a higher level of worship through song and prayer as depicted in Psalms. They did not use animal sacrifices until a few generations later when the people decided to sell sacrificial animals at the gates of Jerusalem in order to profit.

The Highest Level of Faith

The highest level of faith is to be trusting even when things are difficult. When Hashem sees this He puts you up to the next level.

Psalm 23:1-3
The LORD is my shepherd, I lack nothing
    He makes me lie down in green pastures
he leads me beside quiet waters,
    he refreshes my soul.
He guides me along the right paths
    for his name's sake.

When God gives you enough intuition to know what to do and feel His presence, He is like your shepherd. Sheep don't have worries; they trust their shepherd. The Maccabees won the war because Hashem was their shepherd. He guided their moves.

Psalm 23:4
Even though I walk
    through the valley of death
I will fear no evil,
    for you are with me;
your rod and your staff,
    they comfort me.

Hashem's rod and staff are his gift of prophecy and intuition. We all go through a lot of very tough things in our life. If you trust that Hashem does everything for your own good, then you will be happy even with the punishments. "Your rod" is the rod of reprimand as it says in Proverbs "The one who spares the rod hates his child." Here in Psalm 23 the rod of God as well as His staff (literally; the supporter) are a comfort to me.

The Maccabees were very afraid; they were few and the Greeks had many soldiers and horses. But they believed in the righteousness of their cause and prevailed. Psalm 33 describes how the soldiers celebrated Hashem's justice over the vast armies of the enemies:

> Psalms 33:16-19
> No king is saved by the size of his army;
> no warrior escapes by his great strength.
> A horse is a vain hope for deliverance;
>   despite all its great strength it cannot save.
> But the eyes of the LORD are on those who fear him,
>   on those whose hope is in his unfailing love,
> to deliver them from death
>   and keep them alive in famine.

Let's Have Some Actions

Many people complain that they pray and God doesn't answer. If He doesn't answer, then you have to check your actions and see what you could be doing wrong. If you can't figure it out, the best way is to do good deeds. Good deeds can erase our sins. Psalms 34 says that the most important good deed is to watch what you say. Use your lips to say words of truth and of peace.

> Psalms 34:12-14
> Come, my children, listen to me;
>   I will teach you the fear of the LORD.
> Whoever of you loves life
>   and desires to see many good days
> keep your tongue from evil
>   and your lips from telling lies.
> Turn from evil and do good;
>   seek peace and pursue it.

This is a very new concept for ancient people. Remember this is approximately 150 B.C. No one ever heard of being careful with their words. The writers of Psalms learned this from the Torah. Some Jews were learning Torah for the first time and they were very excited about it. The prohibitions of slander and false witnessing were very appealing to them because they suffered so much from the biased courts of the Greeks. The Hellenistic Israelites just returned from the Greek Empire with all its philosophy. They were educated people. They wanted to learn and they were used to philosophy, art and literature so they enjoyed Psalms very much as a book that combines all three.

Psalms is an artistic way of presenting Biblical ideas to the people. It contains the full spectrum of emotions and ideas; joy, sadness, persecution, suffering, loss and victory, truth and falsehood, reward and punishment, and even more.

Psalms describes the essence of Jewish philosophy. If you want to pour your heart out to God, Psalms is your book of prayer. If you just feel sad and need to feel strengthened and consoled, Psalms is the best remedy for you. The writers of this book of prayers were surely blessed with the ability to use holy words that are God's gift for our soul.

CHAPTER 11

Oral Law

As I explained in the chapter called *Tree of Knowledge*, the story of Adam and Eve is a parable. It ends with angels protecting the Tree of Life. The Tree of life, the Torah, was in need of protection from the Israelites who worshipped idols. If they would have seen the Holy Torah that Moses wrote in its original form, they would have felt the holiness and, because they didn't know how to read, the Israelites would have immediately turned the Torah into an idol. The false prophets who did know how to read would be free to tell the masses what was written in the Torah, and they would believe it. Therefore, the Torah, our Tree of Life, was hidden in the Holy of Holies until the temple was destroyed.

Even after the Torah was revealed to a population that had many true scholars and scribes, the leaders told the people any interpretations they liked because the majority of the masses were illiterate. This caused the rise of different sects and religions.

Orthodox Judaism teaches that the Torah was never forgotten since Moses gave it in the Sinai desert. Jewish rabbinical curriculum teaches that lengthy details explaining the Torah were taught by Moses to the Israelites and were passed down orally from generation to generation with no exception until today. This oral tradition is the foundation of Jewish law.

Moses Taught the Israelites

There is no doubt that Moses had a lot to explain, and he had almost forty years to do so. Numbers was written in the second year of the Exodus, and Deuteronomy was written in the fortieth year. We do not know what precisely Moses taught to the Israelite people in all those thirty-eight years.

What we do know is that during the First Temple Period, the Kingdom of Judah sinned and forgot the Torah. By the time of the destruction of the First Temple, idol worship was so bad that the Jews were sacrificing their children to an idol called Molech.

As early as the times of Joshua, the Israelites worshipped idols. Joshua 24:23, "And now remove the strange gods that are in your midst and turn your heart to Hashem the God of Israel."

The Jewish people at the time of the destruction of the First Temple were so drenched in idol worship that they didn't even know who Hashem was. Isaiah tried to teach the people that there is a God who created the world:

> Isaiah 40:28, "Didn't you know? Didn't you hear?
> Hashem is the God of the World. He created the ends
> of the land and doesn't tire nor become weary."

If Moses taught any Oral Law, there were not many people who could have passed it down. During the years of the First Holy Temple the sacrifices in the temple were kept properly, so we know how to slaughter animals in a kosher way. That was handed down through the Cohanim.

Circumcision is another law that was never forgotten, but most other laws of the Torah were not kept at all, including the Sabbath.

> Ezekiel 20:21, "But the children rebelled against me: They did not follow my decrees, they were not careful to keep my laws, of which I said, 'The person who obeys them will live by them,' and they desecrated my Sabbaths."

When Daniel repented he brought the whole nation with him. The Babylonian Jews started to observe the Torah because the Torah law became the law of the land. King Cyrus wanted the Jews to keep the whole Torah including the mitzvah to build the Holy Temple.

When Ezra returned to Israel to build the Second Temple, the Jews had no memory of ever keeping the holiday of *Succoth* (Tabernacles).

> Nehemiah 8:17, "And they sat in the Tabernacles as they did not do so since Joshua the son of Nun."

Even basic laws of the written Torah were forgotten; how much more so for anything that was orally transmitted. All the books of the First Temple prophets are mainly occupied with teaching the people to stop idol worship, especially sacrifices to idols, and to worship one God. That was the main focus of their concerns. There are verses that preach Sabbath observance, truth and justice, protection of widows and orphans, and there is a one-time mention about the treatment of slaves. There are only a few verses in the prophets that mention any other Torah laws.

From the prophets' writings, it is not clear if they even had a copy of the Old Testament. There were no books or classrooms yet. Many Israelites of the First Temple Period knew about their forefathers, but they still turned to their idols.

The prophets learned the Torah from their parents. There were always some righteous Jews who kept the Torah alive. The original Torah was written without vowels or punctuation. Ezra knew how to read the Torah because he came from a righteous family of Cohanim.

Around two hundred years later the victory of the Hasmonean revolt brought many Israelites back to their land and their heritage. The Maccabees were very holy and with pure intentions commenced the building of a country based on Torah.

In only three generations the Jews started to separate into different sects: the Pharisees, the Essenes, the Zealots and the Christians. A religious sect by nature does not want too many scholars. They want their congregation to be ignorant so they can be ruled. The Pharisees first and foremost goal was Torah education. They taught the Jewish people to read and write Hebrew and to memorize the Bible. They practiced laws that were written in the Bible and wrote down details in order to build an internal justice system.

When Did Rabbinical Judaism Begin?

During the rule of the last surviving son of Mattathias, Simon the Maccabee, from 142-134 BCE and especially after his reign, the leaders of the Sanhedrin, Rabbi Joshua ben Perachiah and Nitai Ha'Arbeli—who served the people first under Simon and then Yochanan Hyrcanus—instituted universal Jewish education, strengthened the Torah schools, raised many disciples and encouraged Jewish identity. They urged the creation of a society based upon respected teachers, loyal friends, charitable judgment of others, condemnation of evil and evildoers, and a tenaciously optimistic view of life.

They also compiled a book called *Ethics of the Fathers* as I mentioned earlier. In Israel we call it Pirkei Avot. The quotes that are mentioned in *Ethics of the Fathers* were taught in bits and pieces from the time of Joshua ben Perachia 167 BCE and it was compiled and organized into its current version in the second century CE by Rabbi Judah the Prince 135-220 CE. This is a book of wisdom and proverbs of the first rabbis. They are speaking at a time when the Second Holy Temple was still standing. Even though this book is ancient, its wisdom is still applicable and it is a pleasure to read. It was recently translated into Korean and sold by the thousands to non-Jews in Korea. Check it out online. The following site has all the chapters translated into English free of charge: http://www.chabad.org/library/article_cdo/aid/680274/jewish/Ethics-of-the-Fathers-Pirkei-Avot.htm

The first verse of Pirkei Avot says: "Moses received the Torah from Sinai and gave it over to Joshua. Joshua gave it over to the Elders, the Elders to the Prophets, and the Prophets gave it over to the Men of the Great Assembly. They would always say these three things: Be cautious in judgement. Establish many pupils. And make a safety fence around the Torah."

Here we learn that the Torah, the written law, was passed down through the prophets. The Torah was passed down orally until the Men of the Great Assembly made sure to distribute written copies. The Oral Law that was not written down was mostly forgotten. That is why the sages wrote the Talmud which was written with extreme insight and even Holy Spirit. If they said things that were handed down to them through their forefathers, it was the forefathers from the recent past of a few hundred years, but not from Sinai.

The Talmud was written in the year 500 CE. By then The rabbis already had a rich heritage of close to a thousand years of observing the Torah, since Daniel. Even if their heritage only began from the Pharisees in 167 BCE it is still 667 years of knowledge!

Learning Torah in Caves

The Talmud writes about how Rabbi Shimon Bar Yochai and his son, Elazar, were learning Torah in caves while they ran away from the Romans around 150 CE. When we look at the archeology, it becomes apparent that they were dwelling in the caves in the Dead Sea area. Hundreds of caves were found in the Judean Desert with archeological findings. They have carved-out ceilings in order that the Biblical scholars could light fires in order to cook and for warmth. They could also run from cave to cave. Therefore, they could hide and never be found. Many skeletons were found in these caves because the Jews died of starvation during the war of Bar Kokhba in the second century CE. Documents and letters in Greek and in Hebrew describing the Bar Kokhba revolt and the predicament of the Jews were also discovered. In Israel, we celebrate the holiday of Lag BaOmer in commemoration of Bar Kokhba by lighting bonfires, campfires, and barbecues because Bar Kokhba lit fires in the caves for light and warmth.

What were these cave dwellers actually learning? Most Orthodox Jews would say that they were learning the secrets of the Oral Torah, which were later written down in the Talmud and in the Zohar, the first book of the Kabbalah.

In truth the holy rabbis of the second and third centuries CE were learning the Bible, not the Talmud, as there was no Talmud from which to learn. The rabbis worked very hard, to memorize, understand, and maybe discuss laws that are mentioned in the Bible. They learned not only in the caves but also in their homes and synagogues. In the caves, the

Jews were learning only the Old Testament, repeating every word in order that the Torah never would be forgotten. If there had been any Talmudic writings in that period, something would have been found amongst thousands of secular letters and documents that were retrieved.

The Talmud also speaks of large assemblies of men learning in large institutions for a whole month twice a year while the agriculture could take a break for the crop to grow. All of these gatherings were devoted to learning the Old Testament. Only at the end of the day the rabbis may have told a story or a few words of insight and a way to end the learning. These stories were told and retold orally. They were written down 500 years later.

The Talmud has sixty-three volumes. Today there are groups that study two sides of a page every day in the evening after work. The group is called *Daf Yomi* which means "a daily page." At the rate of one page a day, it takes seven years to complete the review of the whole Talmud.

If the scholars would have been discussing the Talmudic discourse all day long and writing it down, it might have taken more than seven years to write sixty-three volumes because it is easier to read than to write, but they sure would have completed their mission in the course of one lifetime. What I want to say is that even though the Talmud seems to be a very large project, it was an anthology of a very minor part of the day of learning for centuries.

The most important of the rabbis' endeavors was to canonize the Bible: to edit it, divide it into verses and sections and to decide which books would be included in the Bible and which wouldn't. The actual division into chapters was done by the Christian scholars. The Old Testament was canonized in the year 200 CE. The New Testament was canonized in the year 400 CE with numbered chapters on the entire Bible. They did not change the Old Testament at all. The first translation of the Bible was in translated by Jews into Greek for the Israelites who wanted to return to their faith to understand. It is estimated to have been translated between the third and first century BCE. This translation is called the Septuagint. The date coincides with the Hashmonean period. My story fits in!

The entire Bible is essentially the word of God. None of the editions changed the meanings in any way. The first Five Books of the Bible were written by Moses in the same exact words that we have today. There was no possible way of editing it because thousands of Jews already knew it by heart.

As previously mentioned, when the Talmud praises others for learning Torah and encourages them to learn more, they meant the whole Bible. The Talmud mentions Rabbi Chia, of the late second century, who went around to villages giving little boys portions of the Bible on scrolls. He told each child to study his own portion and then teach it to the other children. Books were very scarce, so it was important to learn Torah by heart. The children would chant it out loud daily; explanations and interpretations were a prize.

The most important religious book to learn is the Bible. It should be your daily bread. It is more important than any other learning. Unfortunately, this is not the case in Jewish orthodox schools today.

The Talmud

The biggest source of Oral Law is the Talmud. It is the most widely studied Jewish work in orthodox schools for boys and men. Women traditionally don't study Talmud at all. Their expertise is Bible as I will explain later.

The Talmud is a compilation of stories and discussions of rabbis from different time periods ranging from the first century CE, when the Second Temple was standing, until 500 CE. The Talmud mandates that some laws that are not specifically written in text, were given on Mount Sinai. However, most of the Talmud does not teach actual law, only different possibilities and ideas. The details of the laws and how to perform them were decided by different rabbis, hundreds of years after the Talmud was completed. Laws are still instated by rabbis today on individual cases. They base their decisions on the discussions in the Talmud. This is why modern Judaism is called Rabbinical Judaism. It is nice to have individual attention and understanding from your local rabbi, but is what he says really the word of God?

Intuition

Most of what Moses taught the Israelites and was not written down has been lost. As we mentioned earlier, there are a few oral laws, commandments and teachings that were remembered and passed down from father to son by the prophets and the Priests of Israel. These are some examples:

1) The way to slaughter an animal painlessly.
2) The way to circumcise a baby boy.
3) The pronunciation and definitions of the words of the Torah. The vowel design and punctuation of the Bible was instated from the seventh century until the tenth century CE by a group of Jews known as the Masoretes. The final product was developed by the Ben Asher family in a written codex according to the tradition of his family that was passed down for generations. We still have this codex today in the Israel Museum in Jerusalem. The Ben Asher family was part of a movement called the Masoretes who

created vowels with dots and dashes below, above or inside the Hebrew lettering.

4) The expertise on the sighting of the moon which is the foundation to making the Hebrew calendar in order to celebrate the holidays of the Torah.

5) What constitutes work that is forbidden on Shabbat

The other laws that the Talmud writes as originating from Moses might have been given from Moses, but they were not remembered. The rabbis who discussed these laws in the Talmud were blessed with intuition, interpolation and insight that were a Godly gift. Sometimes they learned Jewish law from the women, who did not abandon the customs of their mothers. For example, in order to the codify the laws of kosher eating, the rabbis observed the women who learned how to keep kosher from their mothers and decided accordingly how to unify the different practices.

Some of the laws of the Talmud are admittedly rabbinical in origin but they are extremely important. For example, we need rules for marriage and divorce, as does any civilized nation. Hashem wants us to make rules and regulations. As long as it is explaining the Torah and the practical implementation of the commandments, it is interesting. If it changes the Torah, it is wrong.

There are many stories in the Talmud; some are true and many are not even possible, like the story of Choni, a rabbi who slept for seventy years. They should be read as parables or fables. Even if they are fairy tales, they can teach great lessons.

In the year 500 CE, men with no claims to prophesy wrote down the collection of stories, laws, commentary of the Bible, and ideology that were found in letters written by rabbis and teachers that corresponded to each other for many years. Many of these rabbis were seers and holy men aside from being astronomers, philosophers and mathematicians; great men of their times.

I've visited some of the graves of these Talmudic scholars in Safed, Israel, and I could feel their greatness in the air. These were powerful men that worked very hard to spread the Bible to the Jewish people and to the world. The rabbis of this era of the Talmud are called Amoraim. The scholars of the generation prior to that were called Tanaim. The Tanaim were interested in canonizing the Bible and teaching the Jews how to observe it. They were also the authors of the Mishnah which is the most ancient part of the Talmud. The Amoraim were the ones who began formal learning and discussions. They wrote some things down on personal notes. In later generations the notes and correspondences of the Amoraim were gathered and used in order to begin compiling the Talmud in the year 500 CE.

Why Not Claim Prophecy or Vision?

The Talmud was written in the Dark Ages. At this period of time, anything supernatural got you into a lot of trouble. Even during the Renaissance, Joan of Arc was burned at the stake. The witch hunts of Salem of the seventeenth century were only a bit of history repeating itself. In the Middle Ages, so-called witches and warlocks were executed for any excuse.

In the land of Palestine in the midst of the Crusaders, no one wanted to have any claim to fame. You were either a simple person or you made believe that everything you knew was knowledge that you learned from others. You could not claim prophecy or any divine interaction, especially if you were Jewish. The Jews were always considered children of the devil. All the Catholic hierarchy needed was some allegations of receiving heavenly messages as an excuse to hang a Jew on the gallows. This is the true reason that the legend was born that everything was passed down from Sinai. They said it for protection.

It was very important for the Catholic hierarchy to forbid any type of prophecy that negated the precepts of their faith. However, if someone was a visionary that was not in opposition to the Christian religion, he was accepted and even respected. There were a few nuns like Hildegard of Bingen that were considered illuminators.

Why is the Talmud Such a Big Part of Jewish Learning?

In the Dark Ages of Europe there were many anti-Semitic laws. One of the most arduous was the prohibition on learning Torah from the Hebrew text. The Christians insisted that only the Greek translation could be used. At first the Jews decided to read different parts of the Bible on the Sabbath that reminded the congregants of the Torah portions that were traditionally read. We still read these Bible portions today after the regular Torah portion every Saturday in synagogue. They are called the *Haftarah*.

The Christian hierarchy wanted to persecute the Jews even more, so they eventually prohibited any Bible learning whatsoever. This is when the Talmud became more popular. The Talmud was written in ancient Aramaic so it was easier to hide the Hebrew Bible verses within its pages. Still there was fear of Christian censorship when they found out that the Talmud spoke against Christianity. Many pages were blackened out so that the Jews could still study. This lasted until the 13th century when the Talmud was confiscated and burned in the center of Paris. Copies of the Talmud were also burned in 16th century Rome. The Jews continued to suffer severe persecution for centuries all over Europe. You can learn all about this topic and more online at JewishVirtualLibrary.org

In the distant country of Yemen, even though Jews were persecuted they were allowed total freedom of religion. They are a tribe of Jews who escaped the Kingdom of Judah during the destruction of the First Temple but never returned to build Jerusalem during the return to Zion with Ezra. The Yemenite children memorized the entire Bible for centuries. They had many other Jewish books, but the Bible was their main focus of study. After many years of lack in communication with the rest of the Jewish people the Yemenite Jews wrote to Rabbi Moses Maimonides and he corresponded with them. He acknowledged their claim of Judaism and sent monetary help along with his books of law and wisdom. The Yemenite Jews follow his religious precepts to date.

Moses Maimonides

The Rambam, Moses Maimonides' nickname, was a very righteous man and a physician for the king of Egypt. He lived in the days of the Renaissance 1125-1204 CE. He wrote many books on Jewish ideology.

The Rambam was the first rabbi to emphasize belief in one God as well as the mitzvah to love God and trust Him. The Rambam believed that the Oral Law was God given and he worked hard to make the Talmud easier to learn. He simplified Jewish law enough to be understood by the common Jew. His most famous work is called *Yad HaChazakah*, fourteen volumes of Jewish law and ideology. He wrote them when he was young, and his brother supported him and his family. When the Rambam was thirty years old, his brother died, and he began working as a physician for the king of Egypt. He wrote many books on health and medicine. It is quite amazing that one man could have written all that he wrote in a lifetime.

The Karaites are a group who do not believe in Oral Law and only abide by the words of the written Old Testament Bible. During the times of Maimonides (Moses Ben Maimon), in the twelfth century CE, there were more Karaites in Egypt and in Iraq than Rabbinical Jews. Maimonides taught many Karaites Jewish law and brought many of them back to mainstream Orthodox Judaism.

The Karaites said that they were following the written Torah, but they really ignored the parts of the Torah that emphasize faith and feelings. They also made fun of the Rabbinical Jews' obsession with divine intervention.

The Rambam emphasized blind faith and taught his students to see that everything that happens is from God's providence. He taught the Jews to look into their deeds if something goes wrong. In his book *Guide for the Perplexed*, he explained the meanings for the laws and the esoteric concept of an invisible God. This made Hashem very happy, and He blessed the work of the Rambam, a prominent Rabbinical Jew.

A Religion Founded on Love

As I mentioned earlier Rabbinical Judaism began with the last surviving Maccabee, Simon ben Mattathias who got together with Yehoshua ben Perachia and Nitai Haarbeli who began schools for children. They emphasized awareness of Hashem's presence and also the commandments in the Torah that teach us to love God and to love our friends as ourselves. Orthodox Jews, the followers of the Pharisees, are very helpful to each other to date. They have organizations all over world Jewry that assist other Jews with medical, financial and emotional problems. Hashem blessed this way of Judaism because it was so much better than the Karaites, who kept every word of the Torah perfunctorily but did not emphasize the most important points; the constant awareness of God's presence, the importance to love God and to help other people in need.

This is very surprising to me. How did the Karaites overlook such basic principles of faith? It says in the Torah again and again to know Hashem and to realize that everything is from Him. For example,

> Deuteronomy 4:35, "You were shown these things so that you might know that the LORD is God; besides him there is no other."

> Psalms 63:6-8
> On my bed I remember you;
>   I think of you through the watches of the night.
> Because you are my help,
>   I sing in the shadow of your wings. I cling to you;
>   your right hand upholds me.

The laws of loving and caring for people are very clear in the Torah, for example:

> Deuteronomy 15:7-8, "And if there will be a poor man from one of your brothers in the land that I have given you, do not harden your heart and do not tighten your fist from your poor brother. Open your hand and lend him enough to supply for his needs."

Hashem told me that the Karaites were not sensitive to these laws because the ancient societies in which they lived were insensitive to human rights and feelings.

The Christian religions all preach love. Nevertheless, the vicious wars of the Crusades and the public slaughter of innocent people by Catholic hierarchy prove that preaching love is not enough to create a religion of love.

The Rambam was blessed with wisdom and intuition above his time. He had the willpower and the charisma to restore deep faith to many of our brethren and expand the awareness of one God to the Jews and to the world at large. He was the first to explain and promote the concept of an incorporeal God. Maimonides worked for the King of Egypt on a daily basis and he was willing to debate Catholic priests and other hierarchy. That is why his work affected the history of the world. The world is still very far from perfect but the Rambam began a new era that opened the minds of a people living in a primitive world and taught them how to love God and how to love each other.

Although the Rambam had many adversaries when he was alive, he stood firmly in his beliefs. One of his opponents' main arguments was that he wanted people to learn his book *Yad HaChazakah* instead of studying the Talmud. He felt the Talmud was too difficult for the masses. Even after many hours of study and learning, the Talmud does not come to a conclusion as to what are the definitive laws to follow. He wanted people to know how to perform the commandments of the Torah and not just to learn for the sake of learning. The rabbis of his time opposed him with a passion.

Today all Jews respect Maimonides's teachings. They study his works in addition to the Talmud and not instead of it. Not all Jews follow his interpretations of Torah law to the letter, but they all revere the Rambam and all of his literature.

The Rambam believed strongly in the holiness of the Land of Israel, but in his day the land was stricken with wars and famine so after he visited the Temple Mount in Jerusalem, he returned to Egypt. The Rambam asked to be buried in Israel in his last will and testament. With great difficulty, he was brought to his tomb in Tiberias, a city in Northern Israel. We visited the site and found a small museum near his tomb and the tombstones of other famous Rabbis.

The Rambam's work is considered part of the rabbinical tradition. He didn't write discourses that were conveyed to him from Mount Sinai. He was a great scholar, very intuitive and he even was a visionary. Hashem revealed to me that the Rambam got messages from Him directly and indirectly through study.

In those days, all doctors were psychic. He was considered one of the leading doctors in history. He could observe a person and detect what was wrong with him physically. In his memoirs, he wrote that when he came home from a day's work in the palace for the Egyptian royal family, he had a queue of people waiting for him outside his residence to await his diagnosis and medical advice.

His psychic abilities were what gave him the strength and insight to write his earlier books. He received a gift from God and not a legacy that was handed down from Mount Sinai.

On the tomb of Moses Maimonides, the Rambam, a famous statement is inscribed. It reads, "From Moses until Moses there was no one like Moses." Hashem agrees with this statement. He feels that the principles of faith that reign in the world today are as a result of this great rabbi's work.

Do Not Add and Do Not Subtract

Deuteronomy 4:1–4
Now, Israel, hear the decrees and laws I am about to teach you. Follow them so that you may live and may go in and take possession of the land the LORD, the God of your ancestors, is giving you. Do not add to what I command you and do not subtract from it,

but keep the commands of the Lord your God that I give you. You saw with your own eyes what the Lord did at Baal Peor. The Lord your God destroyed from among you everyone who followed the Baal of Peor, but all of you who held fast to the Lord your God are still alive today.

In Deuteronomy 4:2, the Torah specifically states a prohibition on adding or subtracting any laws. Baal Peor is the name of an idol that the Israelites worshiped in the desert. Deuteronomy 4:4 continues and reads, "You that held fast to God, are all alive today." How can we hold fast to Hashem? The previous verse, Deuteronomy 4:2, explains:

> "Do not add to what I command you and do not take away from it to keep the commandment of Hashem your God that I am commanding you today."

The Torah is like a very advanced formula for attachment to Hashem. If we change the formula in any way, we risk the success of our ability to be connected to our Creator.

There is a widespread notion in the Orthodox Jewish world that more is better. But the Torah tells us that this isn't so. You are not allowed to add anything to what the Torah commands. Hashem knew exactly what to write, and He asks us to trust Him and obey the Torah law as it is written. If so, how were the rabbis allowed to add anything?

The answer of the rabbis of today and of the past ten centuries to the above question is that they are not adding anything; they are just putting a fence around the Torah to protect it from being violated. I disagree; the amount of laws that have been added is much more than just a fence. It's a whole way of life.

Several verses in the Bible prohibit from adding anything to the Torah. Besides Deuteronomy 4:2, Deuteronomy 5:32, Deuteronomy 28:14, and Joshua 23:6 all say, "Do not sway from anything right or left."

It is forbidden to add anything and make it a law. The wisdom of the Torah can be flexible to interpretation because Hashem could have had different meanings in mind at the same time. However, when it comes to the Ten Commandments, they are our Constitution. They cannot be changed at all even for gentiles. For example, it says, "Thou shall not have other gods before me." You cannot make an interpretation that you can have two gods that combine into one, just as you can't make an excusable way to lie in a court of law. I expounded on this topic in my book *God Meets the World*.

Can We Add Customs?

Hashem says that you can add customs as long as they are not laws. Even if additions are known to be rabbinical and are enforced for everyone in the community it is OK, as long as no one says that they come from God. Hashem enjoys our customs when they are not mandatory and everyone is free to use their imagination as, for example, special foods and songs for the festivals. Mandatory laws are vital in order to build a community that is moral and safe like laws of justice, marriage and divorce. If everyone knows that these are man's laws everything is copasetic.

A multitude of questions that you might imagine regarding Jewish law have been asked and answered in the Talmud or in Jewish literature. How conclusions are reached are also explained. It is better than any other civil laws of modern countries, which may have no rhyme or reason.

It's important to have laws, but we can't claim that they are from Sinai when they are not. Even if a law was written from psychic insight, it still doesn't give it the status of Torah. Even a prophet cannot add a mitzvah or commandment to the Torah. He or she may add something for a year as an emergency measure, but not as an eternal commandment.

Laws of Prophecy

"If a prophet tells you to worship idols the prophet must be killed" (Deuteronomy 13:5). The same thing goes for any of the Ten Commandments. You cannot listen to your own prophecy if it tells you to go against one of the Ten Commandments or to change the meaning of the words of the Torah. This simple law prevents us from listening to any false prophets or cult leaders. It can also prevent a schizophrenic from doing outrageous things. Crazy people won't accept that they aren't hearing what they're hearing, but they can understand that the law is that you are not allowed to adhere to any prophecy, even your own, if it is against any one of the Ten Commandments.

Rabbinical Judaism claims that what the rabbi says is what God demands. The phrase that they base their belief on is in Deuteronomy 17:11, "Do not turn aside from what they tell you, to the right or to the left." However, if you look carefully at the scripture, you will find that this verse is really referring to a judge's decision, a verdict of a court, not on a Torah Law.

> Deuteronomy 17:8–11
>
> If cases come before your courts that are too difficult for you to judge—whether bloodshed, lawsuits or assaults—take them to the place the LORD your God will choose. Go to the Levitical priests and

to the judge who is in office at that time. Inquire of them and they will give you the verdict. You must act according to the decisions they give you at the place the LORD will choose. Be careful to do everything they instruct you to do. Act according to whatever they teach you and the decisions they give you. Do not turn aside from what they tell you, to the right or to the left.

Anyone who shows contempt for the judge or for the priest who stands ministering there to the LORD your God is to be put to death.

The above verse accentuates the permanence of the Laws of the Bible. When directed by Hashem, a prophet may change a law temporarily that is not part of the Ten Commandments.

One very important law is to choose life over death (Deuteronomy 30:19). For emergencies we are permitted to break laws even the Ten commandments. We desecrate the Sabbath in order to bring a patient to the hospital. You are allowed to kill someone who is trying to kill you and you can take medicine that is not kosher if you must. My next book will be called Choose Life and it will teach many wonderful secrets for good health.

This is a different approach than other religions. Jehovah Witnesses for example would chose to die rather than get a blood transfusion. Devout Christians would endanger a pregnant teenager's life rather than allow for abortion.

Why Do We Need So Many Explanations?

The Torah is written in a way that it is not self-explanatory. It is open to interpretation. Why didn't Hashem write the Torah in a way that it wouldn't need so much commentary and discussion?

The Torah leaves room for us to look into our own hearts for understanding. Only in this way can the Torah be applicable forever and in every generation. A book that is made to last forever has to be infinitely complex. This is the main reason that Hashem waited for so many years to allow the Torah to be learned. He didn't want us to have blind faith in our leaders. He wants us to learn for ourselves.

We enjoy learning Torah with commentaries that were written by rabbis and we gain from their insight. That doesn't mean that what they say was given over to us from Moses and is absolutely obligatory to accept. It's the other way around. A forced interpretation leaves people unwilling to comply and maybe even arouse rebelliousness.

In our modern times, we can still have new insights that were never mentioned before. It is important to realize that the Torah is divine and therefore has endless depth. Just as the rabbis of old wanted to learn and write their views, we have a right to do the same, whether it is from divine inspiration or just from scientific, scholarly and biblical research or deductive reasoning. This way we can find solutions to modern problems and situations. The Talmud is full of these examples which make it very unique and enjoyable to study.

This is the beauty of the Bible and, even more so, the beauty of Judaism. You are always allowed to ask questions and offer new ideas. This kind of learning gives room for Hashem to bestow intuition on people. I have many friends who feel that they are blessed with ideas when they speak or teach. This is all beautiful as long as their advice is not considered mandatory and their way is not considered the only way. Our Sages have taught us that that there are seventy different ways of interpreting to the Torah. I might add to that. I believe that the Torah is infinite.

The above is true as far as the stories, wisdom and syntax of the Torah is concerned, but not actual mandatory laws. The prohibitions of the Torah are never to be changed because of an interpretation, God Forbid.

The Compilation of the Talmud

During the first centuries after the destruction of the Second Temple, the main learning was the study of the Bible. At the end of the day, the rabbi would teach his students a story or a law. This lesson may have been written down on an odd piece of parchment by a scribe who was listening to the class or lecture. In the course of hundreds of years, the notes accumulated. In the beginning of the fourth century, the *Amoraim*, or "spokesmen," in Babylonia realized that the notes were not organized, so they started compiling what was penned.

The Talmud was written in the Land of Israel. All scholars agree that the Jerusalem Talmud was written in Tiberias. I believe that the Babylonian Talmud was written in Safed, a holy city where Jewish scholars lived and studied for centuries. The reason I say this is because there are many graves of Amoraim in Safed and in the surrounding areas.

Babylonia as an empire was long gone when the Talmud was written. A tablet dated 275 BCE states that the inhabitants of the city of Babylon were transported to Seleucia, a city in ancient Greece, where a palace and a temple were built. With this deportation, Babylon became insignificant.

The Talmud speaks a lot about Christianity because the Christians ruled in the Land of Israel, then called Palestine. The Talmudic scholars were terrified that if they were found they would be executed by the Catholic hierarchy for writing any religious works. Therefore, they called the Talmud the Babylonian Talmud to say that it was transcribed long ago in a faraway land, a country that didn't exist anymore and they were just learning it. In later generations, the rabbis of Europe took many verses out of the Talmud or painted over them in black ink because of fear of Christian retaliation.

The Talmud Arrives in Europe

The Talmud was first brought to Europe in the eleventh century, when Rabbi Shlomo Yitchaki, nicknamed Rashi, started his commentary in France. The Talmud was on a very high level compared to other books of that era.

Between the writing of the Talmud and its distribution, hundreds of years had passed.

Rashi was born in France in 1040 and died in 1105. He wrote a commentary on the Bible and on the Talmud. Some of his writings are based on his own knowledge and intuition; some are based on the Midrash and Talmud. Even after Rashi started teaching the Talmud, no one had a copy of that Talmud. The most that one owned was a single page. The Jews learned Rashi's commentary, and because he quoted the words that he explains, students were able to learn the original words of the Bible and the Talmud without the original text in front of them. His commentary on the Bible is from the same Bible we have today with no exceptions, but there is evidence that the Talmud on which he commented was not entirely identical to the Talmud that we retain today.

In order to understand the Bible, we rely on the commentaries. Most of the interpretations are based on the Talmud or on the intuition of our sages. The Talmud doesn't actually make new laws. The Talmud's protagonists discuss the possibilities and present different and novel ways of discerning. The Talmud also includes many educational stories and discusses ancient Jewish values and perspectives.

A Great Work

We can look at the Oral Law as a great piece of work, but not without flaw. There are undoubtedly countless pages of real wisdom from which to learn. However, it cannot be accepted with blind faith the way that we accept the Torah. When the Talmud was written, it was acceptable to tell a story that had a moral from which to learn, even though the story was just a fable. Many people today get upset to read ridiculous stories in the Talmud that could not have happened. In those days, it was normal to tell a fable or a fairy tale. Nobody gave a thought to the validity of the story, or if it really happened. They just enjoyed it and taught it for its moral value just like we can enjoy Aesop's fables.

These imaginary stories and scenarios give a basis for different modern day situations. For example, there is a question in the Talmud about a pregnant cow. If we remove the embryo from the cow and put it into another cow, who is the mother? The discussion seemed to have no purpose at the time; however, this Talmudic discussion provides the basis of the laws of fertility and birth through surrogacy today.

Women and the Talmud

The learning of Talmud and other books of the Oral Law should not replace the learning of the Bible. Many boys' schools of young Jewish scholars do not learn the written Bible more than once a week after eighth grade.

The girls' schools teach Torah and prophets daily from age seven until twenty-one. In my opinion, the girls are fortunate. They have an opportunity to learn from the source. They study about three hours a day of Bible daily, in addition to Jewish ideology, history, and secular subjects. They also sing, dance and have much more extracurricular activities than the boys do.

From ninth grade, the boys' curriculum has about five hours a day of Talmud, and that's in the modern schools. The ultra-orthodox learn Talmud from morning till ten at night. The girls don't learn Talmud at all.

Teaching the Daughters

It says in the Talmud, "If you teach your daughters the Torah, it is as if you are teaching them obscenity." This comes from the book of the Talmud called *Sotah*, page 20, and is quoted in the name of *Rabbi Eliezer Ben Hurkenus*. All the rabbis have a problem understanding these words of Rabbi Eliezer in the Talmud. There is an opinion that Rabbi Eliezer was referring to the Talmud, not the written Torah, and that girls should be prohibited from learning Talmud, the Oral Law.

Rabbi Eliezer ben Hurkenus was the student of Rabbi Yochanan Ben Zakai and a teacher of Rabbi Akiva. He lived between 80 CE and 118 CE. If it was really he who said that girls shouldn't learn Torah, he didn't mean that girls shouldn't learn Talmud, because the Talmud wasn't written yet. It could be that it was someone else who said this and didn't want to be known to the authorities, so he used the name of an ancient rabbi.

Whoever did write the above statement said that you shouldn't teach your daughter Torah. It didn't say that you can't teach your wife! The statement was meant that fathers should avoid teaching Torah to their young, innocent, unmarried girls.

Girls were very protected in those days. They didn't know anything about sexuality until a few weeks before their wedding day. If the girls would learn Talmud or even Torah, they would find out information that they weren't supposed to know, because the Torah is very open about sexual laws. They were so afraid for their little girls that they didn't want them to get any information about sex from a man. It doesn't say that a mother is prohibited from teaching Torah to her daughter. The job of teaching the daughters was the mother's responsibility because there are so many sexual details in the Bible that it was considered an obscenity to learn from a man.

Education of Jewish Girls

There was a famous female scholar, two generations after Rabbi Eliezer, named Bruria. She was married to Rabbi Meir, a disciple of Rabbi Akiva. If it were common knowledge that a woman shouldn't study Torah, she would have never been accepted as a scholar. She wouldn't have even had the opportunity to start studying, let alone reach high levels and teach male students. She presented classes of Bible to large groups of men. Her opinion is often quoted in the Talmud.

Rabbi Eliezer did not assert that what he stated was law or prophecy. He didn't write it down anyplace. It was just hearsay, and it was hearsay of hearsay because Rabbi Eliezer lived centuries before the Talmud was written. If he did proclaim that one shouldn't teach his daughter Torah, he was just expressing his feelings about the education of little girls. It was a legitimate opinion for a man living in the beginning of the second century CE. As a matter of fact, there is a book that Rabbi Eliezer did write called the Chapters of Rabbi Eliezer and it mentions nothing about girls' education.

This misunderstanding caused future families not to teach women to read and write Hebrew for centuries. In Europe, the vast majority of non-Jewish families were not literate at all, until the Renaissance, but Jewish men and boys always knew how to read and write Hebrew so that they could study Torah and pray. The girls did not learn in schools like the boys did.

This is an example of how times have changed. The words of Rabbi Eliezer were totally misconstrued, and they were taken much too seriously. It may have been proper for his time and place, but it isn't right for today, and it wasn't even suitable five hundred years ago. We should not think of the Talmud as perfect. It's an anthology of the words of medieval scholars doing their best.

Meam Loaz

For centuries, many Jewish women didn't learn Torah from the text. In Turkey in the eighteenth century, there arose a genius named *Rabbi Yaakov Culi*, who compiled an anthology of Torah stories and laws called *Meam Loaz*. This multivolume work was composed in Ladino, a Spanish Jewish dialect, made especially for women because they weren't supposed to learn from the written Bible. Ladino was a Spanish dialect with Hebrew lettering and represented the language of Turkish Jews as well as other Sephardic Jews, who escaped the Spanish Inquisition.

My own great-grandmother knew the original volumes of this encyclopedia of Jewish folklore and literature by heart. This anthology has since been translated into many languages and can be purchased today in English and other languages on the Internet.

Although the *Meam Loaz* collection was compiled in the year 1760, the stories and insights are still fascinating and a pleasure to read. This anthology has stories and commentaries that we never learned in school.

While *Meam Loaz* was being studied by Jewish women and girls in Turkey, the maidens in Eastern Europe weren't so well versed. In the early twentieth century, when public education became obligatory, Eastern European girls attended public school and many Jewish girls became irreligious. A very great woman named Sarah Schenirer opened up the first Jewish school for girls in Krakow, Poland and in 1915 began teaching them a little Torah. When the rabbis saw how well the girls learned and how urgent it was for them to study Torah, they decided to follow the opinion in the Talmud that the prohibition for females against learning Torah meant to forbid them learning the Talmud. They allowed the girls to learn the whole Bible, just not the Talmud. Sarah Schenirer had a lot of patience to interest the girls in Bible studies and Jewish ideology. She arranged social activities and the girls really enjoyed themselves.

In the same spirit today, Jewish girls' schools are very advanced scholastically as well as socially. The girls study the whole Bible, Torah, prophets and writings, while the boys learn Torah when they are young and then mostly Talmud from eleven years old. Even though some rabbis have a difference of opinion, most Orthodox schools do not teach Talmud to girls or even to married women.

The Torah commands us to learn and relearn its words. Deuteronomy 6:7 states, "And you shall teach your children these words by heart and speak about them when you are sitting in your house, when you are walking on your path, when you go to sleep and when you wake up."

The literal translation is to teach your sons, so the Talmud pronounces that it means to teach your sons and not your daughters. However, in Hebrew the word for sons is the same as the word for sons and daughters combined. Hashem says that the Torah here is talking about your children; it is a mitzvah to learn and teach the entire Bible. Even learning about history is a mitzvah, as it says in Deuteronomy 32:7, "Remember the days of old, understand the years of every generation."

The Printing Press

The printing press was invented in 1440. The first Hebrew Pentateuch, meaning the Five Books of Moses, was printed in 1482 and the first Hebrew Bible was printed in 1488. For centuries, everything in the Talmud was learned by heart. There were no books, but there were notes and letters of correspondence between rabbis. A lot of those notes were added to the Talmud up until the first completed edition of the Talmud was printed in 1520.

Of the many different versions of the Talmud only two were picked randomly to be printed and distributed. One was for the Babylonian Talmud and the other was for the Jerusalem Talmud. Today the Babylonian version is the basic textbook for study. The Jerusalem Talmud is studied by the more ambitious scholars.

Before the printing press, there were many versions of the Talmud. One adaptation was chosen to be printed in the sixteenth century to the greater exclusion of other versions. Even that transcription has since been heavily censored because of fear of Christian persecution. The Talmud that is commonly studied today includes less than half of the content of the original.

In every generation before the printing press was invented, Jewish men and boys knew the Torah by heart and some even knew the whole Bible. It is common opinion that the Talmud was finished and finalized in the year 500 CE. In reality, that's just when the first draft emerged. It was edited many times and censored as I mentioned earlier. The Munich Talmud is the oldest full manuscript of the Talmud that has survived till today. It was written in 1343. It was an uncensored copy and is used as a source of historical findings. The Talmud has gone through many changes since that time.

The Invention of Mathematics

There are mathematical equations in the Talmud that could not have been even thought of before the year 780 CE, when the number zero, a new invention, was first brought to Iraq from India, and with it fractions and decimals. In Rome, the city of the exile of the Jews of the Second Temple, they were using roman numerals for many years after the introduction of the number zero in Iraq. Arabic numerals were introduced to Europe only in the eleventh century and gradually dominated within the next couple of hundred years.

The whole way of thinking of the Talmud was far superior to the level of thought in life of the early Dark Ages. The Talmud offers complicated computations of astronomy and geometry. The sages that are mentioned in the Talmud did exist but they didn't know that the Talmud would endure and their names would appear in it. As a matter of fact, many of the discussions in the Talmud are between people that lived more than a hundred years apart from each other. The sages of old were quoted but they had no intention of being written in the Talmud, they only wanted to learn the Torah and teach others how to observe. Many of the names quoted in the Talmud were used to hide the true identity of the writer lest he be executed for writing a religious book that does not support the belief in Jesus.

Modern Jewish Law

For many generations, Jews would go to their rabbi with any questions. The rabbi used his intelligence, intuition, and his background in scrutinizing Talmud in order to give an educated answer and to help the person who came with the question.

The system of Torah law counseling gave the local rabbi prominence. If he were a good man, he kept his congregation in sound emotional and spiritual health. The custom of consulting a rabbi to ask what the law is still stands to this day. However, today's rabbis are well versed in Jewish Law and make their rulings accordingly. When new questions arise, different rabbis have different opinions. Sometimes rabbis convene to make rulings on subjects like politics, modern medicine and other issues that may affect the general public.

I would like to tell you about an interesting example of how rabbis assembled and changed their ruling. In the past, Orthodox Jewish women were instructed not to use contraception of any form unless their doctor said that they have a medical problem. In the year 1990 a mother of nine, let's call her Sarah, told her husband that she needed a break and she couldn't get pregnant again as she felt too tired. Sarah's doctor said that she was fine. There was nothing wrong with her. Therefore, Sarah's rabbi prohibited her from using contraception. Sarah conceived and died in childbirth. There was a major uproar in the community and the Rabbis of Jerusalem convened and decided to permanently change their ruling. The woman's personal feelings became the deciding factor on whether she should use contraceptives or not and the decision to become pregnant is hers.

The Tower of Babel

The country Babylon is first mentioned in the Bible in Genesis 11:1-9 in the story of the Tower of Babel. The name Babel is identical to the Hebrew word for Babylon. Babylon is in English, but in the Torah it says *Bavel* just like the name of the country and the name of the Talmud.

It isn't possible that this story of the Tower of Babel is accurate. There were no architectural capabilities to build towers in such ancient times. The Egyptian architecture, with its palaces and pyramids which were constructed in a much later era, was a phenomenon that was never seen before. Hashem told me that this Babel story is a parable.

This parable had two fold meanings. One is on the ability of man to rule other men as I described in the chapter called, *In the Beginning.* The other parable is about the Jews who created Rabbinical Judaism.

After the story of Adam and Eve, a parable of the First Temple's destruction, comes this allegory about the Second Temple Period. Before the destruction of the Second Temple, the Jewish rabbis started building a tower of words. "They built them so that they will have a big name for themselves lest they spread out over the whole world" (Genesis 11:4). God saw this, and He scattered the Jews all over the world, speaking different languages and observing diverse customs. Genesis 11:9 says, "The city was called Babel because God confounded the people." Babel means confusion. Hashem foresaw the problem that people would want to write more and more additions to the laws of Moses. He weakened their plan by spreading them throughout the Diaspora.

When I was growing up with Ashkenazic Jews in America I felt stifled by their stubbornness to accept our family's different customs. In Israel today the exiles of the Diaspora have gathered together and they have many different ways of observing Judaism. People respectfully accept each other and their differences.

Why Add?

I asked Hashem a question: "Why did the Jews want to add to Torah law?" Orthodox Jews are so devoted to Hashem. Why would they want to do more than what Hashem asks from them, specifically against what it says in the Torah?

The answer is that there is a problem with their whole outlook on the purpose of Torah. First we have to understand the basic difference between what people think Hashem wants, and what He really wants. In Deuteronomy 30:19 it says, "Life and death I put before you, the blessing and the curse and you should choose life in order that you and your children shall live."

The purpose of the *mitzvoth* or commandments is to give you a better life. We can only succeed if we obey His laws. If we don't, our life won't be so good. If we add or subtract from the formula, it won't work. It's like baking a cake. Adding an extra ingredient could frequently detract from the tastiest outcome.

People think that they want Hashem to be happy with them, so they do extra as if they are giving Him more. I asked a woman why she was so obsessive about all kinds of laws. She said that she wanted to be good. Eventually her will to be good cost her a trip to the psychiatrist to treat her obsessiveness. Others think performing additional mitzvoth will compensate for their "sins."

The truth is that Hashem doesn't want us to suffer or pay for our sins as it says in Ezekiel 33:11:

> "I, the living God say to you, 'Do I want the death of the wicked?' Rather the wicked would return from his way and live. Return, return from your bad ways and why should the house of Israel die?"

We correct our sins by repenting, which includes praying to Hashem, praising Hashem, asking Him to forgive us and planning a better future. We must make changes in our lives for the better.

God's Law

We began this chapter saying that we do not know what Moses taught the Jewish people after the Torah was given. Was there really an Oral Law? It is possible that Moses taught the Israelites how to practice the law and how to understand what the Torah meant on every level. He absolutely did not add laws, nor did he make any allowance for laws to be added.

Hashem told me that the Israelites were reciting the Torah as they camped in the desert. They learned the words by heart and that is how it was remembered from father to son. When the Israelites sinned, there still always were some scholars and prophets that continued reciting the Torah and teaching it to their children. That is why *Ethics of the Fathers* says that the Torah was passed down from the elders, who were the wise men of the first and second generation that left Egypt, on through the prophets, who were some of the very few that kept the tradition. It was through this tradition that we still know how to pronounce the words of the Torah, and we know what the Hebrew words mean. The Jewish people never forgot the language of the Hebrew Bible.

A New Bible?

There is a story about a man who went to his rabbi to ask him if he is allowed to say *Kiddush,* the benediction for the Sabbath, on milk if he doesn't have wine. The rabbi told the man that he would have to think about it. After a few days, the man came back to the rabbi. It was already Friday, so he needed an answer to his question. The rabbi said, "After looking through the works of our sages, I came to the conclusion that it would be okay to recite Kiddush over a glass of milk. However, I understood that if you wanted to bless over milk, you obviously don't have meat for the Sabbath, because you are not allowed to drink milk with meat. You also don't have bread for *Shabbos* (Sabbath in Yiddish), because it is known you are allowed to recite *Kiddush* over bread. I took the time to get the funds from the community to buy you meat and bread and wine so that you can have a good *Shabbos.*"

This little anecdote describes how people used to ask a rabbi for advice on Jewish Law. It took the rabbi time to look up the answer in the Talmud, which is the size of a very large encyclopedia of sixty-three volumes, without a table of contents or index. He used his own judgement and intuition to make decisions and give counsel.

In the year 1555, Rabbi Joseph Caro wrote down the *Shulchan Aruch*, "The Code of Jewish Law." It was written in Turkey and by 1570, the *Shulchan Aruch* was brought to Poland, where it was adapted and fixed for Ashkenazic customs by Rabbi Moshe Isserles. Today, if a rabbi would be asked if you were allowed to say Kiddush on milk, he would just say, "No, in the *Shulchan Aruch* it says that you are allowed to make Kiddush Friday night on wine or grape juice or on bread."

As a result of this book the Orthodox Jews of today are swamped with laws. They eat, dress and pray a certain way. Uncounted embellishments have been made to God's original laws. This is not what Hashem wanted for his Torah. He wanted us to be free as long as we know how to choose to be good in the way that the Bible teaches us. As we stated above, the Bible does not permit us to add new laws. However, all those additions are not nearly as bad as the biggest addition of all.

Adding books to the Bible itself and calling them the New Testament is a direct prohibition of the Torah. Furthermore, many religions teach the Bible but they add and take away from its basic laws and concepts, and do not demand the observance of the law as it was given on Mount Sinai.

After all is said and done, the Jews are the only group that really observes the Torah. We still keep the language of the Bible and most of the laws that are written in it. We also study the entire Old Testament Bible in its original language. We even sing and pray in that language. The revival of the Hebrew language was successful because so many Jews worldwide still spoke Hebrew and even wrote books in Hebrew. The doors to Palestine opened in 1917 with the Balfour Declaration. The addition of words with modern applications to a language that was already in use was not that difficult or complicated.

Hashem knows that the Jews added too many laws to His original commandments; however, they are closer to fulfilling Hashem's will than any other group. There are many Orthodox Jews today who realize that Rabbinical Judaism has too many add-ons, yet they still love Hashem and want to be religious. This book will be an eye-opener for them. It will help them understand the answers to questions they have had their whole lives.

Hashem wanted to give humankind a set of laws to help people create a better world. He didn't mean for us to be obsessive about it. There are so many laws for Jews to keep that many live in fear that they might do something wrong. I also lived with that fear for years. God is the creator of all nature, including human nature. If a law causes you to be physically or emotionally ill, by definition it cannot be God's law. God doesn't want us to be tied down or limited in our ambitions because of rituals. God's laws are the laws of the Five Books of Moses, no more no less.

Conclusion

The world at large is having a hard time keeping the Law of Moses. Different cultures exist with multitudes of religious practices. Others, like the nations of Communistic countries, made science and logic their religion. Even Judaism with its many denominations and divisions has added and subtracted from the basic laws of Moses. What Hashem wants is for all the people in the world to keep the Ten Commandments. I wrote a whole book explaining the Ten Commandments called *God Meets the World*. It's a book with great insight on every one of these Ten Commandments and the relevant verses in the Bible that explain them.

Modern society has reached a level of understanding and knowledge that is incomparable to any previous generation. Still, only a divine intelligence can write a book that never gets old or out of style. The Talmud was a source of very fascinating learning for many years, but just like with all ancient literature, some parts have become outdated. Look how beautiful the Old Testament is. It remains as new and exciting as the day it was written, and more is yet to be discovered and understood.

The purpose of this book is to impress upon my readers that the Torah that we have today is the Torah that was given to Moses. Not only that, the Torah was written for our generation and for the future generations with full knowledge that it would not be observed initially. The Torah is geared for a generation of scribes and scholars young and old. Hashem had faith in us, His chosen people, that we would persevere. Hashem knew there would always be a remnant of Jews that would keep the Torah and revive it for the biggest comeback that history has ever seen.

GLOSSARY

Adar: A Hebrew month that usually corresponds to the month of March. It is the last of a series of months that originated in the Babylonian Diaspora and are still in use today in Israel and on every Jewish calendar.

Amoraim: The plural of Amora. A rabbi in the Dark Ages from 200 to 800 CE. The Amoraim are known to be the writers of the Talmud.

Ashkenazic: Descendants of Jews who formed communities in central and eastern Europe, traditionally speaking Yiddish.

Canonization: The sealing of a religious book or set of books. After canonization the book cannot be revised or edited. The Old Testament was canonized in 200 CE. The New Testament was canonized in 400 CE.

Chanukah: Also spelled Hanukkah. It is an eight-day Jewish holiday also known as the Festival of Lights. Chanukah begins on the 25th day of Kislev of the lunar Hebrew calendar, which occurs from late November to late December in the solar calendar. Chanukah memorializes the rededication of the Holy Temple in Jerusalem at the time of the Maccabean Revolt around 165 BCE. Traditionally, foods made of oil are consumed to recall the legendary miracle of one small can of oil fit to light the Menorah, the seven branched candelabra, for eight days instead of an expected single day. Special prayers and songs are recited and sung in honor of the festival and a celebratory mood is kept for the entire eight days. In Israel, schools are closed for the eight days of Chanukah.

Cherubim: The two golden winged figures that adorned the cover of the Golden Ark. The Golden Ark contained the tablets of the Ten Commandments. The Golden Ark was located in the Holy of Holies, a room in the Holy Temple that was off bounds for everyone except for the High Priest who entered it once a year on *Yom Kippur*, the day of Atonement, in order to beg forgiveness for the sins of the people of Israel.

Cohanim: Israelite or Jewish priests.

Cohen (singular for Cohanim): Priest (plural: priests).

Dead Sea Scrolls: Scrolls from over two thousand years ago found from 1946 to 1956 that were preserved in caves near the shore of the Dead Sea. The texts include the earliest known surviving manuscripts of works later included in the Hebrew Bible. All the books of the Bible were found there with the exception of the Scroll of Esther. Otherwise, the holy writings are identical to the Bible that we have today. This is true evidence that the Bible hasn't changed for two thousand years.

Diaspora: The dispersion or scattering of a nation from its homeland.

Essenes: A Jewish cult of the first century BCE to the first century CE. The Essenes lived in the area of the Dead Sea called Qumran. They were a group of celibate men who worked all day copying the Bible and preserving it. The Dead Sea Scrolls were found in caves near the Dead Sea between 1946 and 1956. Their writings also include their rules and customs. The Holy writings are identical to the Bible that we have today. All the books of the Bible were found there with the exception of the Scroll of Esther. This is true evidence that the Bible hasn't changed for 2000 years.

Ethics of the Fathers: See *Pirkei Avoth*.

Gematria: A Jewish system of numerology that assigns a numerical value for each Hebrew letter. The numerical value of a Hebrew word or phrase and the identical numerical value of those words and phrases suggests a relationship between them.

Gentile: Anyone who isn't Jewish.

Geonim: These men were the generally accepted spiritual leaders of the Jewish community worldwide from 609 CE until 1040 CE. They were involved in dissemination of the ideas in the Talmud and the construction of the first prayer book. Gaon means "pride" or "splendor" in Biblical Hebrew and in modern Hebrew means genius.

Hashem: Literally "The Name." A nickname for God. This word is the most common name that Orthodox Jews use for God, even when they are speaking in other languages.

Hasmonean: See Maccabees.

High priest: There were many priests in the Holy Temple to do the work of the sacrifices, but just one high priest who led the ceremonies. He entered the Holy of Holies, where the Tablets of the Ten Commandments were kept along with the Torah, once a year on Yom Kippur, the Day of Atonement.

Israelites: The descendants of Jacob, who was also called Israel. He acquired that name from an angel who fought with him all night until Jacob won. Israel in Hebrew is *Yisrael*, a combination of the two words *Yashar*, meaning straight or honest, and *El*, meaning God. Thus, *Yisrael* is the Hebrew word for Israel. It means straight to God and nothing or no one intervenes between man and God. The faith of the Israelite must be honest with no sacrilegious motives.

Karaites: A Jewish sect that believes only in the written Torah with no rabbinical interpretations.

Kabbalah: A body of mystical teachings of rabbinical origin, often based on an esoteric interpretation of the Hebrew Scriptures.

Kabbalist: An expert who is highly skilled in obscure, difficult or esoteric matters as a student of the Jewish Kabbalah.

Kiddush: A prayer said over wine on Friday night in honor of the Sabbath.

Kumran: An ancient city near the Dead Sea. Today it is an archeological site of the Essenes' culture.

Levite: A man who belongs to the tribe of Levi, the third son of Jacob. The Levites served in the Holy Temple singing and playing musical instruments. They washed the hands and feet of the priests and assisted in the maintenance of the temple and the tabernacle in the wilderness. They were responsible for teaching Torah to the Jewish people. They did not receive an inheritance of land, so they could spread out in the land to instruct the people in the laws of the Torah.

Levites: Plural of Levite.

Maccabees: In 167 BCE, Matthias and his five sons formed a small army to fight the Assyrians and the Hellenists. They called themselves Maccabees for the initials of their motto, "Who is like you, Hashem among the gods?" They conquered the Temple Mount, purified the temple and restored the temple service. They were also known as the Hasmoneans. The Hasmonean Dynasty held rule in Israel from 142 BCE to 63 BCE.

Megilla: A scroll constructed from animal skin intended for writing.

Mezuzah: Literally means doorpost. Today's Jewish practice involves the placement of hand written Biblical verses on a piece of parchment which is rolled up, placed in a container, and affixed to the upper right doorjamb on all doors entering and within the home except the bathroom. The verses from Deuteronomy 6:4-9 and 11:13-21 are inscribed on the parchment. The quotes include "Hear, O Israel, the LORD our God, the LORD is One." and "Write them on the doorframes of your houses and on your gates."

Midrash: A story that helps in the understanding of Biblical contents. Midrashim (plural of midrash) were originally passed on orally and began to be written down starting in the second century common era.

Mikvah: Also spelled mikveh. A ritual bath connected to a direct source of rain or well water. A mikveh must have enough water to cover the entire body of an average-sized person. A mikveh must hold a minimum of approximately 575 liters. Immersion purifies ritual impurity. A natural source of water such as a pond, lake, river, sea, or ocean may also serve as a *mikvah*.

Mitzvah: Literally and biblically a commandment from God. In modern colloquial Hebrew the word *mitzvah* is used as a merit that one receives for keeping one of the Commandments. For example, "You'll get a big *mitzvah* if you help me get a loan." *Mitzvah* is also used as a way of defining an act as being a favorable deed to do according to the Bible. For example, "It's a *mitzvah* to help that girl."

Mitzvot or *mitzvoth*: The plural of *mitzvah*.

Molech: A pagan god to which the Israelites of the First Temple worshipped and sacrificed their children.

Nefesh: The part of the soul that gives life.

Neshama: The part of the soul that gives human understanding and especially speech.

Pekuach nefesh: Life-threatening emergency.

Pentateuch: The first five books of the Bible, also known as the Torah.

Pirkei Avoth: Hebrew term meaning *Ethics of the Fathers*. This is a book of sayings and morals of rabbis that lived before the destruction of the Second Temple. Pirkei Avoth taught faith and moral behavior by heart until the second century common era when it was written down.

Rambam: A nickname for Rabbi Moses Maimonides made from his initials.

Rashi: Rabbi Shlomo Yitzchaki. He was the first rabbi to write a clear word for word commentary on the entire Bible and Talmud. Rashi lived in the eleventh century common era but his commentaries are still the most popular and the most widely studied within the Orthodox community.

Reincarnation: The rebirth of a soul in a new body. Life after life cycles where in every lifetime the soul has new challenges in order to further grow and develop.

Righteous: Morally good. Someone who excels in goodness and who acts in good ways for God, not for his own pride.

Safed: A city in Northern Israel situated on high mountains. In Hebrew it is called Tzfat. The city has ancient history and is still a vibrant town full of historical sites and tourist interest.

Sefer: Hebrew word for a book.

Seminary: A post-high-school institute for religious studies. In Jewish girls' seminaries, there are also secular studies for career options, mostly careers in education.

Sephardic: Descendants of Jews who lived in the Iberian Peninsula, predominantly from Spain and a minority from Portugal before the late fifteenth century. The Spanish and Portuguese Inquisitions forced many Sephardic Jews to convert to Christianity or maintain their Jewish faith in secret as Crypto-Jews. Sephardic Jews under persecution emigrated then and even in later centuries to South and North America, North Africa, Asia Minor, the Middle East, and elsewhere around the world. Sephardic Jews also descend from Crypto-Jews who remained in Iberia. Sephardic Jews are unified in their prayer book and traditional customs, which differ from the Ashkenazic Jewish customs and liturgy.

Shabbat: Sabbath in Hebrew with Israeli pronunciation.

Shabbos: Sabbath in Yiddish, or in Hebrew with Ashkenazic pronunciation.

Shulchan Aruch: Literally, a set table in Hebrew. This is the name of the book of Jewish Law for Sephardic Jews. It was written by Joseph Caro in Turkey in the year 1550. This book unites the Jewish law for the whole Jewish people. There are comments on the foot notes for differences in the laws Ashkenazic Jews observe.

Sukkoth: (Also spelled Succot) Plural of Sukkah. Known in English as the Feast of Booths or Tabernacles. It is a holiday to recall the exodus of the Israelites from Egypt and the wandering for forty years in the Sinai wilderness, dwelling in huts. Meals are eaten inside the sukkah, and some people sleep there as well.

Tabernacles: See Succoth.

Tallit: See *tzitzit*.

Talmud: The central book of Rabbinic Judaism, written in the year 500 CE and revised many times until the invention of the printing press.

Tanaim: The rabbis living in Israel from the year 70 CE until 200 CE.

Tefillin: Also called phylacteries. They are a set of small black leather boxes containing scrolls of parchment inscribed with hand written verses from the Torah. They are worn by male religious Jews on the arm and head during weekday morning prayers.

Tekhelet: See Tzizit

Ten Lost Tribes: The tribes of the Kingdom of Israel that were exiled after they were conquered during the First Temple Period.

Torah: The first five books of the Bible known as the Pentateuch. Literally means teaching or instruction. In Jewish jargon, the word Torah includes the entire Old Testament and even the Oral Law. In this book, I sometimes call the Old Testament of the Bible Torah, but I do not include the Oral Law.

Tractate: A portion of the Talmud. There are sixty-three tractates in the Talmud.

Tribes of Israel: The Israelites were divided into tribes according to their ancestors, the twelve sons of Jacob.

Tzitzit: A four-cornered garment with eight fringes on each corner, in accordance with the biblical *mitzvah* (Numbers 15:38–39). One of the cords of the fringe is light blue or turquoise, called *tekhelet*. These fringes are also tied to the corners of the Jewish prayer shawl called a *tallit*.

Yeshiva: A school for religious studies, usually for boys over eighteen years old. The girls attend seminary, while the boys and men study in a yeshiva.

Yiddish: A language that Jews spoke in Eastern Europe and Russia. It is a German dialect laced with Hebrew words and written in Hebrew letters. Today the language remains alive in some parts of New York and of course, Jerusalem

Yad Hachazakah: A fourteen-volume book of Jewish law and ideology written by the Rambam. Literally it means the "strong hand." The numerical value of the word *yad*, which means hand, is fourteen, and that's where the book got its name.

Yom Kippur: The Day of Atonement. The single most important day of the Hebrew calendar. Yom Kippur is a fast day and also a day of prayer for repentance. In Israel, all businesses are closed, even the television stations. The roads and beaches are empty; 95 percent of Israelis do not eat or drink anything, even water, for twenty-five hours. Many Jews spend the day in the synagogue praying for a good new year and asking for forgiveness from God. In the days before the fast, it is customary to ask forgiveness from family and friends.

Index

A

Aaron (Moses's brother), 72, 93-95, 194, 214, 235

abominations, 80, 118-19, 213

Abraham (Hebrew patriarch), 20, 70, 73-74, 109-10, 117, 205, 240

Achashverosh (king), 166-70, 172-76, 182

Adam (first man), 34, 36-43, 45-48, 50-51, 53-55, 57-62, 64, 67, 69-70, 74, 76-77, 130, 151, 155, 159, 161, 278, 310

Ahasuerus (king), 174-75

Akiva (rabbi), 303-4

Alexander III (king), 234

America, 15, 17, 37, 81-82

animal sacrifices, 123, 258, 274

Antiochus (king), 212, 215

Aramaic letters, 218, 225-28

Ark of the Covenant, 63-64, 91, 98, 241

Artaxerxes (king), 174-76, 182-83, 187, 190, 192, 204, 206-7, 227

Azariah (Levite), 103, 174, 201

Azria (Darius's servant), 180

B

Babylon, 99, 101-2, 108, 174, 176-77, 179, 181-82, 201, 203, 205-6, 224, 256-57, 263, 300, 310

king of, 86, 101, 201

Babylonian exile, 102, 177, 188-89

Ben Hurkenus, Eliezer, 303-5

words of, 303, 305

Benjamin (Jacob's son), 111-13, 167, 193, 203

Ben Perachiah, Joshua, 281

Bible, vii-xiii, 2, 4, 10-11, 18, 44-45, 50, 71, 74, 81-84, 86-87, 124-25, 142-43, 165-66, 172, 190, 222-23, 225-28, 234-35, 239-43, 253-57, 264, 268-69, 281, 283-91, 298-308, 313-15, 318-19, 321-22, 324

C

calf, golden, 63, 73, 92-97, 120, 129, 213

Chagai (prophet), 238

Chanania (Darius's servant), 180

M

Maccabees, 212-20, 222-23, 225, 228, 234-38, 240-41, 245, 255, 257, 263, 265-68, 272, 274-76, 281
Mahoney, Timothy, 98
Maimonides, Moses "Rambam," 290-91, 293-94, 322, 325
Malachi (prophet), 48, 238, 274
Mattathias (high priest), 214-16, 232, 281, 291
Meam Loaz, 305-6
mezuzah, 245-47, 249
mikvah, 139, 223, 321
miracles, 10, 56, 60, 92, 95, 150, 171, 184, 197, 203, 209-10, 218-19, 229-30, 236, 266-67
Mishael (Darius's servant), 180, 201
mitzvah, xi, 24, 124, 137, 139, 154, 171, 222-23, 231, 237, 243, 247-49, 253, 255, 259-60, 267, 280, 290, 297, 307, 311-12
Mordechai (Esther's uncle), 8, 167-70, 173-74, 178-80, 182-83, 185-86, 188-91, 194, 199-200, 203, 205-12, 216
Moses (prophet), viii, x-xii, 18, 55-56, 63-67, 72-73, 85-96, 98, 102-6, 113-15, 124, 140, 195, 199, 201, 213-14, 217-20, 231, 235-36, 241, 243-44, 246, 251, 254-56, 258, 278-79, 285-87, 294, 311-12, 315-16
Muller, Lennart, viii

N

Naftali (tribe), 178-79, 197, 204
Native Americans, 37, 75
Nebuchadnezzar (king), 86, 99, 101-2, 177-78, 180, 182, 190, 201-2, 224
nefesh, 38
neshama, 37-39, 41, 43-45, 47
New Testament, 140, 268, 284, 314
Noah (ark maker), 28, 69-70, 75-78, 229
ark of, 74-75

O

offerings, 100, 266, 272-74
burnt, 89, 115, 122-23, 271-72
Old Testament, vii, 83, 225, 243, 280, 284, 316

P

Patterns of Evidence, ix, 98
Persia, 102, 166, 170, 172, 174-75, 177, 182, 189, 191, 193, 198, 203-4, 224
Pharisees, 123, 234-35, 237, 268-69, 281, 283, 291
phylacteries, 246, 249, 251-52
Pirkei Avot. See Ethics of the Fathers
priesthood, 117, 213
prophecy, 19, 45, 55, 133-34, 141, 183, 187, 197, 208, 212, 216, 229, 238, 242, 271, 275, 288-89, 297, 304
prophetesses, 66, 147, 179, 182-83, 201, 206, 208

Printed in the United States
By Bookmasters